WOMEN'S CINEMA, WORLD CINEMA

WOMEN'S CINEMA, WORLD CINEMA

Projecting Contemporary Feminisms

PATRICIA WHITE

Duke University Press   Durham and London   2015

For my students

© 2015 Duke University Press
All rights reserved
Printed in the United States of America on acid-free paper ∞
Typeset in Whitman by Copperline Book Services, Inc.

Library of Congress Cataloging-in-Publication Data
White, Patricia, 1964–
Women's cinema, world cinema : projecting
contemporary feminisms / Patricia White.
pages cm
Includes bibliographical references and index.
ISBN 978-0-8223-5791-9 (hardcover : alk. paper)
ISBN 978-0-8223-5805-3 (pbk. : alk. paper)
ISBN 978-0-8223-7601-9 (e-book)
1. Women motion picture producers and directors.
2. Feminism and motion pictures.
3. Motion pictures and women.
I. Title.
PN1995.9.w6w49 2015
791.43082—dc23   2014031330

Cover art: *Women without Men* (Shirin Neshat, 2009),
feature film still. Copyright Shirin Neshat. Courtesy
Gladstone Gallery, New York and Brussels.

Contents

Acknowledgments

This project underwent its own process of globalization as I researched its local ideas; I want to thank those whose insights and contributions shaped it, though I remain responsible for its unwieldy outlines. The temporality of the work, too, was a challenge. I set out to write about twenty-first-century women's filmmaking during its first decade, but the cyclical nature of the festival calendar is at odds with the forward progress of book writing; each annual class of films reset priorities and posed challenges to an emerging canon. This was precisely the phenomenon I wanted to write about—the generation of buzz, the inflation of value, the crash, the rebalancing—as it intersected with the politics of gender and location. But it took cycles of revision to put this in perspective. I hope the book's retakes and open-endedness reflect something of the process of discovery that changes the whole picture.

A project that encompasses so much bears the traces of many encounters. I thank my colleagues for invitations to try out some of these ideas: Jane Gaines, Duke University; Homay King, Bryn Mawr College; Jules Pidduck and the research group at Concordia University; Suzanne Gauch, Temple University; Mara Fortes, the Morelia Film Festival and Women in Film and Television, Mexico City; Nicola Gentili, the University of Pennsylvania; Kathleen McHugh and the Center for the Study of Women at UCLA; Domietta Torlasco, Northwestern; Amelie Hastie and Shelley Stamp, University of California, Santa Cruz; Anu Koivunen, University of Stockholm; Kristen Fallica, University of Pittsburgh; Elena Gorfinkel, Tami Williams, and Patrice Petro, University of Wisconsin, Milwaukee; and Karl Schoonover and Rosalind Gault, University of Sussex. And thanks to Cynthia Chris and David Gerstner, who solicited part of chapter 3 for *Media Authorship*.

Perhaps most exciting was the opportunity to participate in a growing network of feminist film scholars and activists working on these questions, and I am truly grateful to the organizers who facilitated these events. For its tenth anniversary, the International Women's Film Festival in Seoul hosted a conference titled "Global Cartographies of Cine-Feminism," where I met scholars, filmmakers, and curators, among them Sophie Shu-Yi Lin. Then programmer for Women Make Waves in Taiwan, she has shared her invaluable knowledge with me since. Ayako Saito has seen the process through: she invited me among a stellar cast to Mejii Gakuin University as I first started thinking about this book and joined me, at the kind invitation of Yuka Kanno, at Hokkaido University to discuss "The Critical Force of Women's Film" after its completion. Monash University hosted a highly productive workshop on contemporary female filmmakers, "Between Worlds," from whose contributors' work convenors Belinda Smaill, Therese Davis, and I edited a special issue of *Camera Obscura*. In Rome, E. Ann Kaplan and Veronica Pravadelli brought together an inspiring international group of scholars for "Contemporary Women's Cinema: Global Scenarios and Transnational Contexts," which has become an ongoing scholarly initiative.

From these travels, and from panels at meetings of the Society of Cinema and Media Studies and elsewhere, I benefited especially from the comments of Karen Beckman, Nick Davis, David Eng, Lucy Fischer, Terri Geller, Gayatri Gopinath, Priya Jaikumar, Olivia Khoo, Song Hwee Lim, Neepa Majumdar, Kasia Marciniak, Ivonne Margulies, Rosanna Maule, Akiko Mizoguchi, Srimati Mukerjee, Laura Mulvey, Hamid Naficy, Diane Negra, Katarzyna Paszkiewicz, Claire Perkins, Hilary Radner, Roya Rastegar, Jackie Stacey, and Yvonne Tasker. Friends, mentors, and longtime interlocutors whose ideas and/or ways of working and being in the world motivate me include Kate Bernstein, Rachel Buurma, Lisa Cohen, Ann Cvetkovich, Manishita Dass, Teresa de Lauretis, Richard Dyer, Patricia Gherovici, Sangita Gopal, Lalitha Gopalan, Chris Holmlund, Jack Halberstam, Todd Haynes, Lisa Henderson, Alex Juhasz, Tom Kalin, Homay King, Alisa Lebow, Tamsin Lorraine, Heather Love, Louis Massiah, Judith Mayne, Kathleen McHugh, Mara Mills, Gretchen Phillips, Gus Stadler, David Suisman, Tess Takahasi, Jennifer Terry, Fatimah Tobing Rony, Karen Tongson, Sharon Ullman, Joy Van Fuqua, and Amy Villarejo.

I especially thank those dear friends to whom I entrusted chapters for their wise direction: Nora Johnson, Helen Lee, Bakirathi Mani, and Meta Mazaj, whose ideas and enthusiasm for the project brought it over the finish line. Thanks to Sarah Schulman, who encouraged me when others hesitated to ask how the book was going. For various forms of sustenance over the years it took to complete this project, thanks to Tina DiFeliciantonio and Jane C. Wagner, the Ferguson-Corrigans, the Lipson-Noonans, Moira McCarty, Craig Paull and Tom Kalin, Bethany Schneider and Kate Thomas, the Schreiber-Meisels, and above all my supportive parents, Donna J. and George L. White.

A book that looks for creativity in institutions owes a debt to those as well. Swarthmore College has given me an extraordinarily rich intellectual and work life and leave to work on the project. I am in awe of my students— there are too many to name, so I extend a special thanks to those in Feminist Film and Media Studies at Swarthmore College and in Women's Cinema: Politics, Aesthetics, and Institutions at the University of Pennsylvania for working out these ideas with me. Thanks to the board and staff of Women Make Movies, who put the ideas explored here into practice, and especially to Debra Zimmerman for sustaining her intensity of vision and effort so brilliantly. My affiliation with *Camera Obscura* has been an intellectual and personal lifeline, and I thank the editorial staff and the collective, especially Amelie Hastie, Lynne Joyrich, and Sharon Willis. Cameron Bailey at the Toronto International Film Festival helped open a world to me, and Lisa Kennedy, Debra Zimmerman, and B. Ruby Rich were there to share and interpret it. Lisa's encouragement and shared love for cinema are sustaining. The enormously helpful and generous comments I received from an external reader could only have been written by Ruby; since she has owned up to this, I thank her sincerely here.

Ken Wissoker has encouraged me as an author for years, and I am proud finally to have a book with Duke University Press. Thanks to my editor, Elizabeth Ault, production editor, Liz Smith, and the design and production team who made it happen. My colleagues at Swarthmore in the Department of Film and Media Studies—Erica Cho, Bob Rehak, and Sunka Simon—weave brilliant ideas into the everyday, so that even when work demands and writing seem at odds, there's always something percolating. The Cinema Studies faculty and staff at the University of Pennsylvania have extended similar generosity; thanks especially to Tim Corrigan, who fits in just about every category I have come up with here. Finally, to Cynthia Schneider and Max Schneider-White I owe the greatest debt: thank you for your inspiration and your company through travels, travails, and lots of subtitles.

INTRODUCTION

When she read Kathryn Bigelow's name on the card as Best Director at the Academy Awards ceremony in 2010, Barbra Streisand declared, "The time has come!" She was expressing liberal feminist outrage at the academy's previous exclusion of women from the prestige category. The remark was also something of a star turn, as Streisand's own snubs in the category are well publicized.[1] Bigelow, while gracious in her acceptance, made only fleeting reference to gains made for women's equality, and then only implicitly, in her dedication "to the brave women and men of the [U.S.] military who risk their lives daily in Iraq and Afghanistan and around the world." Film industry sexism was set aside, and what Arjun Appadurai calls "the multiple worlds that are constituted by the historically situated imaginations of persons and groups spread around the globe"—among them the estimated half billion viewers tuned into the annual Oscar broadcast—were consolidated under America's watchful eye.[2]

During the buildup to the awards show, statistics about the paucity of women directors were widely reported, ruffling a longtime journalistic indifference to the glaring gender inequities in Hollywood that was increasingly challenged in the aftermath of Bigelow's win. Martha M. Lauzen's annual study of the number of women employed in key creative behind-the-scenes roles on the top-grossing domestic (U.S.) films put the proportion of female directors at 9 percent in 2008, the same percentage she had measured ten years earlier.[3] Bigelow's win was widely heralded and debated in terms of industry imbalances, in populist as well as cinephilic and feminist venues, with various theories proffered about why she was the one to break through what Lauzen calls "the celluloid ceiling" and why it was with this film.[4] Given the content of Bigelow's combat film, the moment seemed to represent the convergence of American exceptionalism with the director's own. This book challenges such appearances by looking beyond the exception, at a range of women directors, working not in the penumbra of Hollywood but in a variety of contexts worldwide.

"Top-grossing" is not the most meaningful control group for the present study of global women directors. Even Bigelow's film failed to rank among the top one hundred U.S. releases in 2009, and in box-office terms none of the films I discuss has a profile as high as hers. Nevertheless, this breakthrough moment in the U.S. culture industry offers the opportunity to explore further the pronouncement that "the time has come" for women filmmakers—to attend to factors that by the first decade of the twenty-first century determined the specific articulation of gender, geopolitics, and cinema that this book examines. These factors include the media fallout of the global war on terror, even when U.S. military action and ideological campaigns are not addressed explicitly in the works under consideration. Alternative cinema circuits took on new responsibilities in providing images of the world that countered the assaults of mainstream news media and the fragmented flows of Internet communication. Other factors include shifts in film education and national media industries that affected women's career pathways; intensified transnational financing and new online distribution opportunities; and feminist activism both within and outside media fields.

Besides analyzing and bringing into common orbit a number of exciting films and promising women filmmakers—some overlooked, some, perhaps, overhyped—this book looks at the cultural work the concepts and institutions of women's cinema and world cinema perform and project, in academic discourses and beyond, at this time. I suggest that *The Hurt Locker* and its reception index transformations in these political, theoretical, and commercial categories.

Bigelow presents a strong example of the female auteur, a concept that is centrally interrogated in this study. Authorship has been of critical importance to feminist film studies, in large part because women's access to the means of production has been historically restricted.[5] The exclusion of women's perspectives has made its imprint on films, audiences, and the cultural imaginary, and feminists have explored the work that has been made by women as an act of historical retrieval, a theoretical project of decoding biography and experience within film form and address, a site of identification and libidinal investment, and a practical matter of equity.[6]

But if Bigelow belongs to women's cinema when the term is used to refer to who makes a film, she challenges that belonging if the term is invoked in reference to genre. Bigelow is a fascinating figure from an auteurist perspective in part because she, like the Hollywood directors initially lauded by the *Cahiers du cinéma* critics who promulgated such criticism, makes her signature visible in commercial films, genre products.[7] Some critics see Bigelow's interest in masculinity and her work in "male" genres like the action film as part of a feminist exploration of gender and power. Others argue that it is these preoccupations that, in a sexist hierarchy, unfairly elevate her standing over that of women directors who make films about women.[8] The debate signals the ongoing lack of consensus on the concept of women's cinema. While some might find the term dated to the analog era of second-wave feminism, the discursive terrain referenced by women's cinema is still very much at stake.

As for the light Bigelow's win sheds on concepts of world cinema, several connections can be teased out. First the Oscars may represent a glitzy and imperialist conjunction of cinema and world, but it is also a commonsense, even populist one. My focus in this book is on independent and so-called foreign films, which, while far from defining or being defined by the Academy Awards, do have an overcrowded niche within the contest.[9] The Oscar race is a prime example of the filters, material and ideological, through which North American critics, viewers, and scholars like me access films from the rest of the world. Other such mechanisms include prizes, festivals, top-ten lists, and other English-language media coverage.

At the same time, I borrow the spotlight the Oscars shed to suggest that the publicity the event represents—red carpet reportage as a highly visible sign of the very publicness of cinema—remains crucial for feminism to tap and to incorporate. Miriam Hansen argues in *Babel and Babylon* that in the early twentieth century, the U.S. silent cinema as alternative public sphere projected a horizon of collective experience for heterogeneous groups of women coming into modernity.[10] In the early twenty-first century, world cinema has the potential to renew that public emphasis amid the privatization of global mass media and the screens on which we encounter it. Women have a crucial role as producers of this public social vision, not only as media consumers and representational supports.

In addition, as a film about the U.S. occupation of Iraq, *The Hurt Locker* is about the world—it has topical relevance purportedly lacking in most women's films,[11] too often stereotyped as aimed at audiences who are domestic in both senses. This book draws on Lúcia Nagib's work to argue that women's cinema should always be seen as world cinema. In "Towards a Positive Definition of World Cinema," Nagib urges us to give up thinking of world cinema oppositionally, as "other" to Hollywood, and instead to see it as "simply the cinema of the world." This approach pulls notions of core and periphery out of orbit and pushes U.S. directors and critics into contact and contest with their peers from other countries, a key dynamic in assessing U.S. independent film.[12] In this case, the distance from U.S. cultural imperialism taken by many of the films I analyze throws Bigelow's films' visceral take on the war (film) into ideological relief, while the economic means at her disposal, even as an independent director, call for attention to American cinema's looming, hegemonic status in world cinema even within Nagib's decentering model.

Women's Cinema, World Cinema: Projecting Contemporary Feminisms addresses all of these issues: the increasing importance and shifting valence of the public persona and image of the woman director; the value accorded women's versus men's genres; the sphere of art cinema as culture in only apparent opposition to commerce; the terms of public debate about who controls images of the world; and the way views from outside the United States are framed for consumption within it. Women directors' decisive participation in the changing formations of world cinema was well under way by 2010 when Bigelow made global news. The time has come, to echo Streisand, to turn to this work.

Global Women Directors

Though still drastically underrepresented, women directors are increasingly coming into view within the current circulation of world cinema—understood, for the purposes of this book, as the aggregate of feature films made everywhere at least in part for festival and what is called specialty exhibition elsewhere.[13] As they help to define the twenty-first-century art house aesthetic, members of a new generation of women filmmakers are also transforming film politics. Despite a perceived postfeminist cultural climate in which women's cinema is mainly associated with industry-produced chick flicks, and feminist activism is relegated to the past or projected onto the developing world, women filmmakers from all over are navigating institutional politics and making films that have a chance to travel and be seen. Though inevitably shaped and constrained by economic and ideological forces both local and global, in its publicity and circulation this work projects a transnational feminist social vision. This book looks at a number of these films and filmmakers and at the conditions that enable as well as limit their production and recognition. What are the continuities with and departures from earlier models of women's cinema? How are these works challenging assumptions about and approaches to world cinema? What do these films and filmmakers mean for the future of feminist critique and of cinema itself?

The women's films that have captured international attention have come from a variety of locations. In 2003 Hana Makhmalbaf's (b. 1988) *Lezate divanegi / Joy of Madness*, a documentary about her sister Samira making the first film in Afghanistan after the fall of the Taliban, was presented at the Venice Film Festival; as a fourteen year old, Hana needed special permission to attend the event.[14] Lucía Puenzo's (b. 1973) intersex coming-of-age film, xxy (2007), heralded her as a filmmaking talent both indebted to and independent from her famous Argentine filmmaker father, Luis Puenzo (*La historia oficial / The Official Story*, 1988). As a chapter in her ongoing, quirky exploration of globalization in China, undertaken across novels, documentaries, and feature films, Guo Xiaolu (b. 1973) adapted her own novel UFO *in Her Eyes* (2011) for the screen. Haifaa Al Mansour (b. 1974) garnered considerable publicity and acclaim for her film about a young girl's quest for a bicycle, *Wadjda* (2012), the first feature film by a Saudi Arabian woman and the first feature to be shot entirely in that country.

These younger directors' successes did not come out of nowhere, although eager international coverage tended to eclipse the contribution of their female predecessors. Tunisian director Moufida Tlatli (b. 1947), who served on the Dubai film festival jury that acknowledged *Wadjda*, directed the groundbreaking *Samt el qusur / Silences of the Palace* (1994) and two subsequent features and served as minister of culture in the interim government following the Tunisian revolution of 2011. In France, Yamina Benguigui (b. 1957), known for *Inch' Allah Dimanche* (2001) and documentaries on Algerian immigrant life, is minister for *la francophonie* (the French-speaking world). Malaysia's Yasmin Amad (1958–2009), Marilou Diaz-Abaya (1955–2012) of the Philippines, and Lebanese director Randa Chalal Sabag (1953–2008)—who each had profound national and transnational influence—all died prematurely during this period. While these women too showcased their work in international film festivals, the opportunities provided by that network and the financing and marketing arrangements attending it have expanded considerably for the current generation.

The first decade of the twenty-first century showed the contours of women's cinema being redrawn by shifts in global production, circulation, and evaluation of films as well as by changing perceptions and practices of feminism. As Hollywood franchises continue to dominate global film consumption and new technologies alter distribution and viewing experiences, world cinema presents itself as a category that preserves film art and national identity. Women directors, whether working in popular or art cinema or emerging from film schools or reconfigured national cinemas, are ambivalently recruited to this corrective project. Sometimes women active within new trends and waves in filmmaking take a back seat to male auteurs. For example, Danish filmmaker Susanne Bier (b. 1960) was overshadowed by the notoriety accorded the Dogme 95 "brothers" when their movement broke through. Although she went on to be the first of the group to win an Oscar (for *Haevnen / In a Better World* in 2010), many critics remained dismissive of her achievement.[15] While strong central female characters are signature features of the films of fifth-generation Chinese film directors and recent sub-Saharan African cinema, women directors working in these movements are much less well known internationally and receive less support at home.[16] Sometimes women come to the forefront of a national cinema, as in the case of directors Jasmila Žbanić (b. 1974) and Aida Begić (b. 1976), whose work achieved prominence in the aftermath of the Bosnian war. Yet while remappings of world cinema in the current phase of globalization are the object of growing attention in film studies, questions of gender have yet to structure such inquiry significantly.[17]

Of course, feminist media activists and organizations and film critics and scholars have fostered and advocated for women's filmmaking since the early 1970s, and such work now reaches far beyond the Anglophone contexts in which it principally originated.[18] This history of "cinefeminism" inevitably informs the twenty-first-century presence of women feature filmmakers in a range of national film industries and transnational contexts in which categories of cinematic value are adjudicated and distinction conferred. Cultural globalization, in turn, puts pressure on the concept, content, and address of women's cinema. How are women filmmakers shaping new, transnational formations of film culture? Tracing how women's work since 2000 emerges and circulates within the international film festival circuit and linked practices of distribution, exhibition, and evaluation in the

United States, this book attempts to map multiple flows of cross-cultural consumption, shifting politics of prestige and patronage, and competing definitions of feminism and postfeminism.

Where in the world are women making movies, and for whom, and who is seeing and writing about them?[19] Addressing different sites and itineraries of women's film practice, this book includes filmmakers from Argentina, Bosnia and Herzegovina, Canada, France, India, Indonesia, Iran, Lebanon, Pakistan, Peru, South Korea, and Taiwan who are making fiction feature films responsive to both national audiences and transnational concerns—economic, aesthetic, and political. It makes no effort to be inclusive but rather explores selected cases in depth. My examples come from varied media production contexts—major film-producing nations, both large and small, emergent industries, and international coproduction arrangements. The rising number of film festivals, DVD labels, film blogs, and Internet streaming sites is facilitating international exposure for these films even when they do not obtain theatrical distribution in North America. Yet dominant conceptualizations of cinema organized around national movements, waves, and auteurs often minimize or misrecognize the significance of women filmmakers' participation and the questions of representation—both aesthetic and political—that it raises. The stakes of this study lie not only in understanding the commodification and compromise that take place in the transnational circulation of women's feature films, but also in grasping their imaginative possibilities through a feminist lens.

While making connections with the feminist film culture that emerged in the 1970s and extended through the 1980s and 1990s, especially in my discussions of such established filmmakers as Jane Campion and Deepa Mehta, this book's primary focus is on directors who made their first features after 2000, when feminist cultural politics offered a less stable frame through which to view women's work. Some, like Samira Makhmalbaf (b. 1980) and Lucrecia Martel (b. 1965), have attracted significant critical attention at international film festivals both as auteurs and as key figures in hot national film movements—new Iranian and Argentine cinema respectively. A body of scholarship has already emerged on their work. Others have been written about in a multilingual array of film criticism, both print and online. Ultimately, the works of these filmmakers were selected not only for their aesthetic and cultural significance but also for the ways they reveal the institutional shapes of film culture—the politics of funding and programming, protocols of reviewing and the anointing of celebrities, and various political agendas. Indeed the very fact that I have access to these works comes under the scope of analysis. Although the films I treat are diverse and enabled by divergent meanings of feminism and different industrial formations in their countries of origin, most of them circulate through the same festival and art house networks. Their access to these networks is in turn determined by material questions like format and language as well as ideological judgments of value.

The fiction feature films by women in global circulation that this book considers are by no means the only, or even the most obvious, sites in which women's cinema and feminist film culture thrive today. With the advent of digital filmmaking, women's work in documentary is more vital, varied, and widespread than ever; short film, web-based media, gallery-based fine art, television, and popular cinema all represent significant areas of women's production within multiple national and global media fields. I do not want to ratify a hierarchy that privileges fiction features and marginalizes formats that might be more democratic, politicized, or up-to-date. But feature films in international circulation are uniquely important vectors of transnational feminist imagination and publicity—in the dual sense of press attention and publicness.

In what follows, I contextualize the concept of women's cinema historically as both an explicitly feminist countercinema by and for women and as a critical discourse in academia. Feminist media culture has always been multisited, and its joint focus on production and critique means that the histories of women's filmmaking and of feminist politics and scholarship are intertwined. However, as a transnational formation, contemporary women's cinema draws on many other histories—those of art cinema; national media industries; and a range of aesthetic, intellectual, and political movements, including feminisms, outside the Anglo-American context in which feminist film studies arose. Thus, I turn next to the burgeoning field of world and transnational cinema studies to evaluate how the axes of gender and sexuality can remap its concerns. Finally, I outline the book's chapters and their guiding questions.

The Worlding of Women's Cinema

The concept of women's cinema has animated three decades of feminist film scholarship even as, or quite likely because, its parameters remain open to debate. Is it a category of "authorship" (itself a contested term in cinema) as in films by women; or content, as in films about them? Is it defined by prefeminist "essence" (the cinema that reflects women's sensibilities), feminist activism (the cinema women make by and for themselves), or postfeminist consumption (the market for chick flicks)?[20] In *Notes on Women's Cinema* (1974), one of the founding documents of feminist film studies, the category is treated as an emergent one, to be illuminated and shaped by critical and curatorial as much as by artistic/activist practice. The approach of the contributors was multipronged: contemporary continental theories of ideology and representation blended with the deconstruction of the prevalent iconography of femininity in mainstream film and a modified auteurist approach to the work of women directors. Claire Johnston's contribution, the now-canonized essay "Women's Cinema as Counter Cinema," announced an oppositional position, and she was opposed to a lot. "In rejecting a sociological analysis of woman in the cinema we reject any view in terms of realism" she wrote, using the "we" of the 1970s politico.[21] She was also impatient with art cinema and its reliance on myths of women: "There is no doubt that the films of Agnès Varda are reactionary!" she proclaimed (216). Johnston embraced a countercinema that worked on the language of cinema, encompassing within this notion the internal critique of patriarchal ideology found in the films of women directors in studio-era Hollywood, Dorothy Arzner and Ida Lupino.

Johnston's early positions had significant consequences for feminist film studies. Work on the contradictions displayed by classical Hollywood cinema fueled the field for decades. At the extreme, the documentary mode was relegated to a naive belief in the transparency of the camera, and female auteurs working in art cinema to a kind of false consciousness. But Johnston's powerful rhetoric still has dialectical momentum. For Johnston, women's cinema itself was a projection: "In order to counter our objectification in the cinema, our collective fantasies must be released: women's cinema must embody the working through of desire: such an objective demands the use of the entertainment film. Ideas derived from the entertainment film, then, should inform the political film, and political ideas should inform the entertainment cinema: a two way process" (33–34). Anticipating a current climate that is much less suspicious of pleasure than was the cultural feminism of the early 1970s, Johnston's prescription tends to teach well in contrast to Laura Mulvey's contemporaneous embrace of "the destruction of pleasure as a radical weapon" for feminist filmmakers.[22] Yet in the postfeminist climate of the 2000s, we do well to recall both Johnston's insistence that politics accompany pleasure and Mulvey's emphasis on a feminist art practice. Today many more women in many more contexts have access to the tools of the fiction feature, the format of entertainment film; I want to illuminate through the analyses in this book the political ideas that inform the best of them.

By the early 1980s, feminist film theory had become one of the most vital strains in Anglo-American film teaching and research, and it shaped adjacent fields such as literature, performance studies, and art history as well. Mary Ann Doane's crucial work on the woman's film of 1940s Hollywood highlighted the ambiguity in the genre label by foregrounding the questions of "possession and address" implicit within it.[23] Are films that are addressed to female audiences somehow the property of women? This productive ambiguity was applied to films made by women in the direct interrogations of the less generically defined term "women's cinema" in two important works: Teresa de Lauretis's 1985 essay "Rethinking Women's Cinema: Aesthetics and Feminist Theory" and Judith Mayne's *The Woman at the Keyhole: Feminism and Women's Cinema*. Mayne's book, published in 1990, linked the term "women's cinema" with feminist epistemology. She looked at a broad historical span of examples of films by women that challenge key concepts in film studies: spectacle, authorship, and the concept of the primitive.

For her part, Teresa de Lauretis reframed debates around women's cinema that held aesthetics and political immediacy in opposition. These tensions, in her view, echoed a larger contradiction constitutive of contemporary feminism itself. As she memorably states in "The Technology of Gender," "the critical negativity of its theory, and the affirmative positivity of its politics . . . is both feminism's historical condition of existence and its theoretical condition of possibility."[24] She pushed beyond an apparent impasse between advocates of formally inventive film and those of activist media to define the "effort and challenge" of "the project of women's cinema" thus: "to effect a new vision: to construct other subjects and objects of vision and to formulate the conditions of visibility of another social subject."[25] This subject of feminism is constructed not only in the content or formal codes of women's cinema, but also through its address to a spectator in whom divisions of race, class, and sexuality (and implicitly national identity) as well as gender are subjectively inscribed, and rewritten, through social experience, including that of cinema-going. In de Lauretis's reading, formal features of works by such feminist filmmakers of the 1970s and 1980s as Chantal Akerman, Helke Sander, and Lizzie Borden figure gender as a "subjective limit and discursive boundary" that is recognized in the space of viewing, the social space projected by feminism. De Lauretis calls this an aesthetics of reception and argues that "emphasis must be shifted from the artist behind the camera, the gaze, or the text as origin and determination of meaning, toward the wider public sphere of cinema as a social technology" (134). It is such an approach that guides this study of global women's cinema.

But by the mid-1980s the artist behind the camera was barely in the picture. The near-symbiotic relationship between feminist film theory and women's film practice that characterized, for example, the early issues of *Camera Obscura* and books like Annette Kuhn's *Women's Picture* or E. Ann Kaplan's *Women and Film: Both Sides of the Camera*, as well as the work of Mayne and de Lauretis, was no longer sustainable. The interdependence of (a certain kind of) theory and practice had been challenged by feminist media scholars' turning their attention to classical Hollywood film (then television, silent cinema, and documentary, all potent areas of feminist inquiry with their own research groups, conferences, and publications);[26] by critiques of hegemonic definitions of both "women" and "cinema" that catalyzed gender and sexuality studies and opened up new directions in media studies; and above all by the sheer diversity and expansiveness of contemporary women's filmmaking practice. Not coincidentally, women of color and transnational feminist theory exploded the neat narratives and taxonomies of Western histories of feminism and film. Full accounting for this realm of cultural production became impossible and probably inadvisable. Was "women's cinema" still a meaningful term?

Certainly the millennial landscape looks much different than the cinefeminism of the 1970s. Grassroots organizations have folded, ceding ground to more professional associations like Women in Film and Television, which has multiple branches in and outside the United States. Stalwart festivals like Chicago's Women in the Director's Chair are shuttered after two decades, although in Europe, Films de femmes in Creteil, France, has operated continuously since 1979.[27] And there is evidence in the strength of new production, festival, and scholarly networks that women's cinema remains a dynamic force, linking sites around the globe. Women Make Waves in Taiwan (established 1993), the Women's International Film Festival in Seoul (1997), Flying Broom in Ankara (1998), and Birds Eye View in London (2007) have established strong identities, to mention a few examples. New York–based Women Make Movies, founded in 1972 as a production collective that quickly responded to the need for a distributor of films by and about women, has survived by looking outward. Its collection includes more and more work from outside the United States, and it facilitates the organization of festivals and other women's film initiatives globally. For example, the first Sierra Leone International Film Festival (2012) included a women's program and panel, and the FEMCINE festival established in 2010 in Chile takes the measure of vibrant women's film production in Latin America.[28] Today, women's cinema encompasses a world of difference.

Scholarship and teaching in this expansive field thus require flexible, comparative methods. Multicultural, postcolonial, and transnational feminist theories that foreground questions of power, relationality, and intersectionality have altered feminist film studies through the films and writings of Ella Shohat, Trinh T. Minh-ha, and others.[29] In addition, numerous studies of women's contributions to national and regional cinemas emerged within language and literature and area studies, bringing needed attention to cultural and linguistic specificity and national and regional media industries.[30] As Lingzhen Wang writes in her introduction to *Chinese Women's Cinema: Transnational Perspectives*, "Feminist film studies must step outside the restrictive framework of the nation-state and critically resituate gender and cinema in a transnational feminist configuration that enables examination of relations of power and knowledge among and within cultures."[31] While diversification and specialization are essential, so is an account of gendered narratives of media globalization from within feminist film studies.

Shohat has developed a transnational, relational perspective in her own books and essays and in collaborations with Robert Stam like *Unthinking Eurocentrism*. In "Post Third Worldist Culture," Shohat draws on multicultural and postcolonial studies to address the burgeoning work of women of color and non-Western filmmakers in the 1990s, challenging the canon of feminist film studies as well as debates in Third Cinema. As Shohat notes in "Gendered Cartographies of Knowledge," however, the methodological problems such commitments raise are daunting: "Given that there is no single feminism, the question is: How do we orchestrate these conflictual perspectives in order to rearticulate the feminist terrains of struggle within this densely woven web?"[32]

Alison Butler's *Women's Cinema: The Contested Screen* addresses the problem of method by adapting Deleuze and Guattari's concept of the minor, asserting, "the plurality of forms, concerns and constituencies in contemporary women's cinema now exceeds even the most flexible definition of counter-cinema. Women's cinema now seems 'minor' rather than oppositional."[33] She explains her reasoning: "Women's cinema is not 'at home' in any of the host of cinematic or national discourses it inhabits, but . . . is always an inflected mode, incorporating, reworking and contesting the conventions of established traditions. . . . The distinctiveness of women's film-making is therefore not based on an essentialist understanding of gendered subjectivity, but on the position—or positions—of women in contemporary culture . . . : neither included within nor excluded from cultural traditions, lacking a cohesive collective identity but yet not absolutely differentiated from each other" (22). This eloquent formulation conveys my own sense of the antiessentialist and essential project of connecting up all kinds of women's interventions in the medium of cinema with each other. In addition, Butler concludes her book by emphasizing resonances between the idea of women's cinema as minor cinema and women's cinema as transnational.[34]

While I embrace Butler's account of the plurality and irreducibility of transnational women's cinema, in this project I adopt neither counter-cinema nor minor cinema as a connective rubric.[35] Minor cinema captures the crucial deterritorializing work of women's cinema, its resistance to totalizing narratives of the world system—the category of gender cuts through every whole, if unpredictably.[36] But I also take as a pressing research question the way that women's work is reterritorialized through contemporary film culture—for example, as the persona of the female director is allied with a notion of art cinema that transcends politics. The category of Woman is a powerful representation to decenter, and the idea of the minor risks minimizing the way diverse women's visions can be recuperated within it. Finally, I wish to claim a major role for transnational feminist histories and practices in current media culture.

Surveying the status of women's cinema in the early twenty-first century persuades me that the categories we have used—authorship, aesthetics, and address—remain vital, yet they are insufficient at this juncture. They must be supplemented by consideration and theorization of institutional questions—of production, distribution, exhibition, and reception. Hence I draw heavily on scholarship in national and world cinema studies to anchor each of my readings of films and filmmakers. I also analyze discourses of reviewing and other frames that position cross-cultural viewing of women's films. The field of film festival studies helps illuminate the global network that regulates cinema's economic and cultural value. Finally, theorizing the place of theatrical exhibition in a new media world brings scrutiny to the term "cinema" itself. How and why are women in so many different places still working within the feature film format?

Decades of activism and theorizing by U.S. women of color and feminists outside the Euro-American traditions demand that we ask which women are included under the rubric "women's cinema." There are simply too many films by women in the world, all over the world, for female author-ship alone to have any predictable effects. De Lauretis's generative proposal that we "rethink the problem of a specificity of women's cinema and aes-thetic forms . . . in terms of address—who is making films for whom, who is looking and speaking, how, where and to whom" (135) remains timely. However, "the wider public sphere of cinema as social technology" must now be understood in terms of the whole wide world. Twenty-first-century cinema incorporates new technologies, new forms, new spaces, new sub-jects. Caren Kaplan and Inderpal Grewal define transnational feminism as "critical practices linking our understanding of postmodernity, global eco-nomic structures, problematics of nationalism, issues of race and imperial-ism, critiques of global feminism, and emergent patriarchies."[37] Addressing these critical practices to world cinema opens up Claire Johnston's "we" to interrogate fantasies of collectivity as well as collective fantasies.

The Gendering of World Cinema

As the proliferation of film festivals, blogs, online journals, book series, and anthologies attests, the contemporary mediascape is characterized by new formations of transnational cinema, even as older national models persist. Nuanced and often competing definitions of world cinema are arising to ac-count for these formations: there are those that track flows from dominant economies (the West to the rest) and those that track contraflows (regional, resistant, diasporic, generational). Third Cinema has been rethought, and "small nations cinema," "minor cinema," and "cinema of the periphery" have been proposed to challenge hegemonic understandings.[38] Indeed, fig-uring out adequate language and methods to address these shifts is one of the most exciting challenges in the field. As Nataša Ďurovičová asks in her preface to World Cinemas / Transnational Perspectives, coedited with Kath-leen Newman, "How should the geopolitical imaginary of the discipline of film studies be upgraded to a transnational perspective, broadly conceived as above the level of the national but below the level of the global?"[39] In this book I seek to explore how feminism, a discourse that has been profoundly reshaped by transnational perspectives and realities in recent decades, can inform this geopolitical reimagination. Feminist models of affiliation and connectivity are as useful to our understanding of world cinema as are systems theory and other prevalent paradigms. Yet, with few exceptions, women's cinema as a concept seems to have fallen off the map, even as the field of film studies has taken on the world.

Dudley Andrew's work is exemplary of current debates in this area. In the lead essay of *Remapping World Cinema*, one of the books that have reconfigured the geography of contemporary film studies, Andrew opens with a story about world cinema: "Film festivals long ago came up with a basic map as they sought top products to be put in competition each year as in a Miss Universe context. For a long while the cognoscenti did little more than push colored pins onto a map to locate the national origin of masterpieces."[40] This gentleman's approach, Andrew argues, is outmoded. The old notion of world cinema as a sophisticated alternative to Hollywood centered on the European art cinema has waned. But are the models that have arisen to displace it less gendered? In "An Atlas of World Cinema" Andrew proposes a collection of maps—political, demographic, linguistic, orientation, topographical—to guide the contemporary scholar's travels in world cinema.

While Andrew's atlas makes no explicit provision for charting questions of gender, his definition of "orientation maps," which argues for the importance of specific texts and questions of perspective—how the world looks from here, and how that view is textually inscribed—is particularly useful.[41] A feminist orientation positions women's films in relation to discourses of agency (authorship) as well as aesthetics (representation), in terms of the politics of location as well as place of origin. The term "politics of location," introduced by Adrienne Rich in a discussion of unthinking white feminist racism, has been carefully developed by Caren Kaplan in terms of transnational feminist cultural practice. She writes: "As a practice of affiliation, a politics of location identifies the ground for historically specific differences and similarities between women in diverse and asymmetrical relations."[42] In studies of world cinema, this entails locating and historicizing filmmaker, critic, text, and reception practices.

In a related move, Andrew replaces the connoisseur of old with a new metaphor of transnational cultivation: "This appreciation of cut flowers adorned film study in its first years but . . . today's impulse . . . would track a process of cross-pollination that bypasses national directives" (19). Andrew's recommendation that the scholar sample the "political and cultural soil" brings into play the very etymology of the word "culture," but maintains that scholar's objective perspective. Both the "cut flowers" and the "Miss Universe" metaphors are marshaled to dismiss the implicitly masculine connoisseurship that the field of cinema studies is congratulated for having moved beyond. But when display is (rightly) displaced, how can gender be brought into the new set of questions driving the study of world cinema? Does the commodification of gender as an emblem of national culture exchanged between male-headed institutions (a model the pageant metaphor's myths of equivalence, representativeness, and universal participation support) open onto the study of women filmmakers as national representatives in turn—or to new understandings of sexuality and gender in the world of cinema? It is such "gendered cartographies of knowledge," to use Shohat's term, that have yet to emerge in the field's remapping.

I bring feminist theory to bear on authorial, industrial, textual, and comparative dimensions of my case studies, practicing the relational, "polycentric" approach to world cinema recommended by Shohat and Stam and developed by Lúcia Nagib.[43] In "Post-Third Worldist Culture," Shohat argues that the filmmaking of Third World women and women of color effectively challenges "national directives" in liberationist cinema as well as neocolonial strains of feminism, citing works that "break away from earlier macronarratives of national liberation" and "call attention to the diversity experienced within and across nations."[44] But gender is not only a deterritorializing force in discourses of the nation, as Shohat's work on colonial narratives shows. "Woman" is as frequently associated with national ideologies in film as in other forms of politics, and feminist approaches must tease apart competing representations and self-representations.[45]

To give an example of femininity as emblematic of the nation: the inclusion of Marjane Satrapi and Vincent Perronaud's *Persepolis* in competition at the Cannes film festival was protested by the Iranian Farabi Cinema Foundation, which objected to the film's representation of the Islamic Revolution and its government.[46] The foundation, through its collaborations with Cannes and other international festivals, has been crucial to Iranian cinema's unprecedented international acclaim since the 1980s. For Iranian officials, this exilic woman filmmaker was not a proper representative of the nation—though of course condemning her film made her just that. In Cannes's defense of the film, Satrapi's attempt to negotiate questions of national identity and self-representation in *Persepolis* was in turn appropriated as a statement of the progressiveness of French culture. A secular Muslim woman living and working in France lends her credibility to that of a venerable French export, subtitled cinema. (*Persepolis* is discussed in more detail in chapter 2.)

Reading such a moment in international film politics underscores questions not only of representation but also of circulation and positionality. The present study seeks to illuminate the factors that determine a film's production as well as to underscore, not universalize, the perspective of cross-cultural consumption. In other words, I mark my own location as a scholar in the flows of transnational women's cinema. I encounter films at festivals, art houses, and other forums within English-language publicity frames and interpreted through English subtitles. As Shohat and Stam write of their comparative method, "The global nature of the colonizing process, and the global reach of the contemporary media, virtually oblige the cultural critic to move beyond the restrictive frameworks of monoculture and the individual nation-state."[47] My own training in film and feminist theory is brought to readings of film texts and their discursive placement in U.S.-dominated markets, communities, and critical frameworks.

This involves more than picking out women's names from festival programs and funding rosters, although those activities have become compulsive. I also question how current institutions and cultures of world cinema position women directors' work—and different women's work differently—and speculate how feminist politics has affected these shifts.[48] Underlying this inquiry is the assumption that feminism offers meaningful critiques of cultural globalization and that thinking through relations of alliance and exchange among women (rather than assuming their sameness) is crucial to both the future of feminism and any picture of the world.

In her inventive essay "The World and Soup: Historicizing Media Feminisms in Transnational Contexts," Kathleen McHugh elaborates on two of Virginia Woolf's evocative figures of speech—one concerning women's positionality and citizenship (the world), and one naming the resources required to nurture women's creativity (the soup).[49] McHugh's topic is the historiographical challenge of writing feminism into film history, and she argues for attention to transnational dynamics and institutional conditions. As she notes, "feminisms' historical role in industrial, national, and transnational independent / art cinemas has generally been registered by displacement, in literal and/or qualitative rubrics no longer recognized as historical (auteurism). Its impact is personalized (and dehistoricized) in the contributions of individual female directors. . . . Typically these contributions are catalogued . . . in books that distinguish their topics by country . . . or by region" (115). McHugh historicizes her own inquiry by focusing on a transnational cohort of women directors, born between the end of World War II and 1960, whose work was shaped by feminism both ideologically and materially. Her perspective seeks to redress the fact that "the specificities that might register feminisms' transnational effects on cinema in the latter part of the twentieth century not only exceed the primary national frameworks of film studies but also the rubrics by which the feminist movement and its waves have been understood and historicized" (118–119). Periodizing into second and third waves (or feminism and postfeminism) limits what she calls "transnational generation." In other words, she contends that a transnational feminist approach challenges both spatial and temporal assumptions about feminist film culture. She also emphasizes "the *generative* character of film feminisms and the works produced, distributed, and received under its auspices" (119, emphasis in original).

Women's Cinema, World Cinema builds on McHugh's historical argument, looking at the generation of women who came into voice in the twenty-first century. Born, with a few significant exceptions, after 1960, these filmmakers could be seen to be reaping the benefits of transnational feminist influence and activism without necessarily identifying themselves with its politics. The book explicitly takes up "the problem of the world," which McHugh identifies as twofold: feminist film history has been missed by an optic that is too narrowly national; uneven histories and exchanges and asymmetrical power relations, resources, and priorities among women have been missed by hegemonic models of film feminism. I suggest that the nature of twenty-first-century media flows makes the problem of the world even more pressing.

Consistent with a growing emphasis within film studies, I attend in this project to film festivals' function as public sphere alongside their role as capitalist culture market. Mainstream festivals may commodify national cinemas and serve as cultural gatekeepers, but they are also ludic spaces that put other voices and visions into circulation. The LGBT, women's, and Asian/American festivals that I discuss are more clearly sites that generate counterpublics. Programming and publicity, as well as advocacy around distribution, exhibition, and outreach, are central feminist concerns in all these cases. Festivals and the auteurist discourses that sustain them are the modus operandi of the circulation of world cinema today, and this book engages them in their discursive complexity.

From the exciting range of work presented at North American film festivals like Toronto, Sundance, or Tribeca (all of which have touted increasing numbers of women directors in recent years) emerges a picture of contemporary film art and commerce in which "female director" is figured sometimes as puzzle, sometimes as brand, and increasingly as promise. Perhaps now more than ever, it is impossible to know in advance what to make of the fact that the director of a particular film is a woman. Catherine Grant usefully reconsiders the function of auteurism in contemporary film culture: "The image and interventions of authors . . . help to organize the fantasies, activities and pleasures of those who consume cultural products, and in turn to construct or 'authorize' these consumers as subjects."[50] Such authorization is at stake in the feminist spectator's keen investment in women's filmmaking. My method builds on Grant's insight, using the figure—or more accurately, figures, in a rhetorical sense—of the woman director as a way to index questions central to contemporary feminism such as visibility, agency, labor, desire, and power. I attempt to carry over the public dimension of film exhibition into my critical framework, where women's works are encountered in relation to each other, to their competing histories and discursive surrounds, and to their various, expansive constituencies. Yet the differential lenses that are needed to view disparate work from widely varying cultural and production contexts are not passed out like 3-D glasses. It is in part the aim of this study to construct the terms of visibility for individual films and filmmakers as well as for their transformative encounters in a global context.

In "Towards a Positive Definition of World Cinema," Nagib cautions that defining world cinema against Hollywood privileges the latter, even when the gesture is intended as a corrective one. In her alternative definition, "world cinema . . . is circulation." The circulation of women's filmmaking on North American festival and art house screens, through DVD outlets, websites, and other public and specialized discourses provides a common horizon onto which new aesthetic and social visions are projected. From this perspective, film scholars can attend to gender both as a material dimension of the flows and hierarchies of world cinema and as a key to its imaginary. Nagib continues, "World cinema is . . . a method, a way of cutting across film history according to waves of relevant films and movements, thus creating flexible geographies" (35).

In the course of my research for this book, and my experience as a spectator and teacher of women's cinema, I have followed different paths across this ever-morphing space. My work on the board of Women Make Movies has predisposed me to organize my feminist film classes around the work of women filmmakers. I make no presumption about the significance of female authorship in this decision, one motivated by the desire for exposure to and for these films, and orienting the syllabus to work by women hardly constrains the topics I can address: silent cinema, documentary, experimental, genre, world cinema. While my teaching has been oriented to a diversity of nonnarrative and/or noncommercial work by women across formats, I began to be intrigued by the way successes in the feature-length auteurist film mode both made feminist film politics more visible across time and space and threatened to contain them in familiar forms.

Attending the Toronto International Film Festival and other venues, I jumped at the chance to see new works by filmmakers crucial to my aesthetic and intellectual formation—Chantal Akerman, Jane Campion, Agnès Varda, Margarethe von Trotta, María Novarro, Ulrike Ottinger, and Sally Potter. At the same time I eagerly explored work by women directors swept along by the touted new waves of Argentina (Lucrecia Martel, Lucía Puenzo, Julia Solomonoff), Denmark (Susanne Bier, Paprika Steen, Lone Scherfig), China (Guo Xiaolu, Li Yu, Liu Jiayin, Ning Ying), and Iran (Samira and Hana Makhmalbaf, Tahimeh Milani, Marizeh Meshkini). It became clear that women's opportunities, and more importantly their modes of expression, were shifting with the reorganization of national and regional media industries and transnational funding and exhibition networks. It was imperative that these directors' emergence and the reception of their films be linked up, both with each other and with the wider film culture, to make these feminist forces visible to their publics. At the same time, it was important to understand how gender and sexuality could be deployed in the colonizing of world cinema. Were the cinematic visions of women in the Global South being coopted by European financing and the commodity forms of art house distribution? To pursue this question, and because my task threatened to become encyclopedic, I decided to exclude most filmmakers from the United States and Europe from sustained attention in this project. Some of these directors and their work, along with fuller consideration of postfeminism and neocolonialism in world cinema, are taken up in other contexts.

Reading *Women's Cinema, World Cinema*

In keeping with its theoretical and methodological emphasis on the circulation of films, *Women's Cinema, World Cinema* is not restricted to an organization by director or region. Rather, each of five chapters analyzes a discourse that has enabled the emergence of young women directors in recent years or that allows commonalities in their work and assessment of its impact to come into view. These discourses, in broad strokes, are elite auteurism, cultural authenticity, women's genres, regional networks, and women's human rights. Each of these is elaborated in the chapter summaries below.

In the chapter introductions, I demonstrate how these discourses structure the production and reception of women's filmmaking within broader frames and explore methodological and theoretical questions. Case studies of filmmakers or films then follow. The case studies are marked by the return of the author: the personae of women directors are read as closely as their films. The table of contents includes these readings to highlight this approach and to facilitate their use individually.

The case studies illuminate the claims of the chapter introductions, but sometimes in surprising ways. Textual analyses follow a film's images and sounds, tropes and patterns into interpretations that are contingent upon but not dictated by the frames through which they are seen. These may be biographical, political, figural, or generic. The national does not disappear in the transnational, either in considerations of production cultures and policies or in reception contexts. Often the analysis will ask what gets lost between address to a domestic and an international audience, and how gender might direct these processes. Along with showing how a particular discourse is deployed by a text and in its wider framing, the case studies explore the ways that contemporary women directors take advantage of the space they are ceded.

The pursuit of multiple agendas and emphases may be even more apparent in the book's commitment to comparative frameworks. The structure addresses the "problem of the world" by considering two or more works under the same rubric in each chapter. The relationships thus demonstrated are more motivated than, say, the way one might encounter a film from Lebanon after one from Korea in a film festival. But in another way the film festival image is apt—it is the system in which the films circulate that bestows value and establishes relationality among them. Certainly the organization could differ: auteurism is operative across the chapters but given a specific inflection in the first; *Water* (Deepa Mehta, 2005) could be analyzed in the chapter addressing women's human rights, but appears in the chapter on cultural authenticity. Together the case studies are designed to give meaning to the discursive construction I am illuminating in that chapter—they yield insights that cannot be derived from study of one work or one culture alone. And in the ways that the detail of the readings inevitably sets the cases apart, the method enacts a theoretical insistence on specificity. The contours of women's cinema are projected from these details.

Chapter 1, "'To Each Her Own Cinema': World Cinema and the Woman Cineaste," looks at the articulation of aesthetics and gender that has made the woman director a singular figure in the world of the major European film festivals. Cannes, Venice, and Berlin are now, and have historically been, organized around prestige and glamour, and women represent the latter; they are most visible on screen and on the red carpet. What does it take for a woman to be recognized as a cineaste instead? Cannes's sixtieth anniversary omnibus film *To Each His Own Cinema* lives up to its (English) title in its inclusion, among its thirty-six contributors, of a single woman director, Jane Campion, who is also the sole woman to have won the festival's top prize, the Palme d'Or. In the past few decades Campion and such contemporaries as Catherine Breillat and Claire Denis have followed the success of predecessors including Agnès Varda and Lina Wertmüller in gaining entry to this elite world. Now members of a younger generation, including Andrea Arnold, Sofia Coppola, and Naomi Kawase, are receiving prizes in competition at A-list festivals, garnering enough cultural capital to be admitted to the *cinéma d'auteurs*. The chapter looks at the reputation-making function of international festivals, with a focus on Cannes, analyzing the gendering of the *politique des auteurs* through readings of both film texts and reception and programming discourses.

How do the few women directors promoted by the prestige festivals intersect with women's cinema more broadly and with feminist film studies' understandings of authorship? How has the increasing embrace in these venues of films from outside Europe in the past decades impacted both cinephile circles and feminist cultural politics? I argue that the few women directors who have risen to the top ranks of elite auteurs have cannily negotiated discourses of female exceptionality both in their personae and in their films. Opening with a consideration of Campion's contribution to the Cannes omnibus film in the context of her avowed feminism, I map the politics of globalization and gender in the awards, cofinancing, and other acknowledgments increasingly conferred on films by younger women filmmakers by these festivals.

"Lucrecia Martel's Vertiginous Authorship" looks at the place of *La mujer sin cabeza / The Headless Woman* (2008) within the national cinema of Argentina, the director's oeuvre, and the festival circuit. The film's dissection of the unintended consequences of a middle-class provincial Argentine woman's self-absorption works on another level as an interrogation of the position of women in art cinema. "Samira Makhmalbaf's Sororal Cinema" focuses on Cannes Jury Prize–winning *Panj é asr / At Five in the Afternoon* (2003), the first film shot in Afghanistan after the fall of the Taliban. Following an uneducated young woman who wants to become the president of her country, the film reflects on Makhmalbaf's own exceptional status. Martel and Makhmalbaf, who are among the younger women cineastes with the most prominent worldwide reputations, directly engage questions of national identity and historical accountability through the problematic identities of their female protagonists. The chapter includes a consideration of Hana Makhmalbaf's "making of" documentary, extrapolating from its example of a literal sororal point of view on the persona of the woman cineaste to a critical model that connects the singular woman director's work to other dimensions of solidarity in women's cinema. The remappings of world cinema represented by these works illustrate the constraints and possibilities of a cosmopolitan women's film culture as it mediates between networks that confer aesthetic value and those that imagine women's solidarity.

Chapter 2, "Framing Feminisms: Women's Cinema as Art Cinema," looks at the positioning of women's films as art in North American exhibition according to rather different taste criteria. My title echoes Claire Johnston's "Women's Cinema as Counter Cinema" and takes up a strain of her argument about the mystifications of art cinema in a contemporary context, describing the institutional and epistemological frameworks that have made the politics of countercinema difficult to sustain in the twenty-first century. I show how festival films by and about women become appropriated by humanist discourses of art cinema and by the social organization of art house exhibition as a middlebrow and arguably feminized taste culture. I take as primary examples prominent women directors whose diasporic visions of home solicit viewers' nostalgia, identification, or projection. While some aspects of these films and their ancillary discourses play into these reception patterns, others insist on transnational positionalities that resist such models of consumption.

"Deepa Mehta's Elemental Feminism" focuses on the vicissitudes of Mehta's film *Water* (2005). The original shoot was shut down after protests by Hindu fundamentalists, fired up by objections to her earlier film *Fire* (1996), which featured a lesbian romance between Hindu sisters-in-law. In positioning *Water*, I draw on the considerable scholarship on *Fire*'s transnational reception that considers Mehta's work in relation to feminist and queer South Asian diasporic critiques of nationalism and to questions of feminist and gay neocolonial representation. I track the changes in politics and media culture that shaped *Water*'s eventual form and made Mehta's feminist humanism palatable to audiences in both North America and India.

"Iranian Diasporan Women Directors and Cultural Capital" looks at related questions of cultural travel with regard to Marjane Satrapi and Vincent

Parranaud's *Persepolis* (2007) and Shirin Neshat's *Zanan-e bedun-e mardan /
Women without Men* (2010). Examples of what Hamid Naficy calls exilic
cinema, both works mark their physical distance from Iran aesthetically—
Persepolis in its use of animation, *Women without Men* in its extreme stylization. I read these artists' embrace of cinema as a medium in conjunction with their status as Iranian cultural celebrities and with their public
responses to the contested 2009 Iranian presidential elections. Through
the authorial personae of these directors, this chapter considers the role of
diasporan women filmmakers in facilitating the definition and circulation
of art cinema in the United States and in defining contemporary women's
cinema in multicultural terms.

While the first two chapters address the frameworks art house exhibition imposes on filmmakers' vision, chapter 3, "Feminist Film in the Age
of the Chick Flick: Global Flows of Women's Cinema," turns to how pleasures, meanings, and alliances circulate along with transnational women's
films into those exhibition spaces. It interrogates how women directors
participate in changing national cinema cultures by tapping into generic
formulas of the chick flick, at the same time accessing international circuits
in which these formulas are universalized. Feminist film studies has approached commercial women's genres as protofeminist social vehicles for
expressing (and managing) women's discontent, and such work has often
been posed as a populist antidote to avant-garde feminist aesthetics. But
in the context of postfeminist ideology, contemporary updates of women's
genres can appear as consumerist retreats from more politicized filmmaking. I challenge assumptions about the geopolitics of postfeminist culture
with studies of films from South Korea and Lebanon.

In "Engendering New Korean Cinema in Jeong Jae-eun's *Take Care of
My Cat*," this 2001 film is discussed as part of an emergent feminist cinema
in South Korea, one measure of which is the success of the International
Women's Film Festival in Seoul, founded in 1998. This public culture is
overshadowed at home and abroad by the identification of the country's
booming cinema with more prominent male directors. *Take Care of My Cat*
opens up gendered discourses of nation, genre, and auteurism through its
inventive style and themes of female friendship and coming of age.

"Nadine Labaki's Celebrity" explores how the extremely successful Lebanese director similarly articulates social issues and questions of women's
self-realization within the female ensemble-cast formula of the beauty parlor film *Caramel* (2007) and the musical comedy *Where Do We Go Now?*
(2011). I analyze the mediation of politics through genre as well as Labaki's

literal visibility—as an actress in her own and others' films as well as a much-photographed celebrity director—at the forefront of a resurgent Lebanese and Middle Eastern film culture that is notably inclusive of women's visions. These women directors counter their relative marginalization in national cinemas for export to infuse the transnational flows of world cinema with feminist promise.

The book's next chapter turns to a more familiar approach to world cinema, a regional one. Chapter 4, "Network Narratives: Asian Women Directors," looks at how films by young women engage and circulate feminist and queer politics regionally. Festival, scholarly, professional, and audience networks of women's cinema within Asia and its diasporas are not yet fully recognized within the economic and cultural approaches to Asian cinema that have energized the field of cinema studies in recent decades.

"Two-Timing the System in Nia Dinata's *Love for Share*" positions the prolific Indonesian filmmaker between feminist and mainstream, national and regional cinema. Dinata's work as a producer, especially of other women's films, and the multiprotagonist structure of her own film about polygamy reveal new shapes of feminism and media industries in the region.

"Zero Chou and the Spaces of Chinese Lesbian Film" looks at the travels of this Taiwan director's lesbian feature films *Spider Lilies* (2007) and *Drifting Flowers* (2008) through Chinese-language lesbian communities and global LGBT festivals as well as their success on domestic screens in Taiwan. While the international LGBT festival circuit has helped consolidate a global gay identity, the festivals are also important sites of local and regional articulations of sexuality and even encourage film production. The commercial success of *Spider Lilies* brings together national ideologies of progress, regional celebrity culture, local LGBT activism, and queer reception circuits beyond Taiwan—such as counterpublics of lesbian fans in the PRC, Hong Kong, and the Chinese diaspora. By tapping into these "queerscapes," a concept elaborated by Helen Hok-Sze Leung, the films make visible new sexual identities and forms of sociality. At the same time, they engage the power of melodrama and romance to connect with wider audiences and redefine national cinema.

The concluding chapter maps another distinctive relationship between the woman director, the national, and the global. Too often women's stories are deployed for international audiences as evidence of a nation's trauma. Women directors resist being privileged as witnesses to this trauma and/or as agents of cultural rebirth. "Is the Whole World Watching? Fictions of Women's Human Rights," looks at films by young women directors that mediate contemporary human rights issues through idioms and institutions of world cinema while countering pervasive visual tropes of victimhood. These films are at once postnational—both in financing and in their understanding of rights beyond those dictated by the state—and national insofar as they participate in an emerging or restructuring film industry.

Like most of the directors discussed in this book, the filmmakers featured in chapter 5 address national audiences through casting and topical themes while also attempting to negotiate transnational circuits of financing, exhibition, and acclaim. They take advantage of coproduction opportunities designed to revive precarious film industries or to implement cultural policies that redress former colonial relations. "Sabiha Sumar's Democratic Cinema" discusses how the filmmaker's work across fiction and documentary informs her representation of the revelation of a Pakistani mother's traumatic past through her son's growing attraction to Islamic fundamentalism in *Khamosh Pani / Silent Waters* (2003).

"Jasmila Žbanić's *Grbavica* and Balkan Cinema's Incommensurable Gazes" considers how films made within contested national cinema formations use individual protagonists to engage questions of collectivity, including accountability, testimony, and generational legacies. *Grbavica: The Land of My Dreams* (2006) explores the legacy of the siege of Sarajevo through the story of a woman whose young daughter was conceived by rape. Women directors draw upon their cultural authority, turning melodrama, orientalism, and gendered national allegory to new ends in encounters with difference.

Finally, "Claudia Llosa's Trans/national Address" looks at a filmmaker whose career in many ways exemplifies the new opportunities open to global women directors. Both positioned as a spokesperson for her nation and acknowledged as a member of the cultural elite, Peruvian filmmaker Claudia Llosa has taken a quintessential ethnographic subject—Andean peasant women—as the subject of her highly stylized intervention in world cinema. Llosa's work, supported by both North American and European funding and festival cultures, also accesses sub- and transnational connections in Latin America. Llosa's collaboration with her star Magaly Solier is a powerful performance of female alliance, yet one that is directed by Llosa's own positionality and vision as author. The book thus concludes with a case study that embraces both the promise of and the problems with the deployment of female authority in contemporary world cinema.

Looking at women's filmmaking as a current phenomenon has provided much of the excitement and the challenge of this book project, as many of the filmmakers continue to release new work. How does one evaluate a young director's oeuvre in progress? As this project has unfolded, film commentary, too, expanded. Feminist critics like Amy Taubin, Manohla Dargis, and B. Ruby Rich were joined by bloggers and online journalists, and the topic of women's filmmaking gained more traction in mainstream news. Such venues offer quicker turnaround than the book format; my aim is to provide theoretical, historical, and comparative frameworks that can establish gender and sexuality more firmly as analytics in contemporary world film culture while tracing its feminist genealogy.

Women making films today, whatever their avowed relationship to feminism, are displacing Eurocentrism and Hollywood hegemony, envisioning new relationships among gender, politics, place, and the future. Of course feature films are not scholarly analyses, news reports, autobiographical memoirs, or even necessarily art. As cultural commodities, they don't present a univocal message or stand apart from their institutional frameworks and cultural contexts. Their politics hinge on dialogic, multiple encounters between their images, sounds, and stories, and audiences' fantasies and experiences, including of feminism and other films.

I have suggested that the concept of women's cinema, advocated and contested within feminist film culture of the past four decades, is too often written out of the context of world cinema, trivializing, marginalizing, or dehistoricizing women directors' achievements and the histories and cultures that sustain them. Refiguring the imaginative public space that might belong to women (women's cinema) and what can be seen in and of the world (world cinema) engages the medium as a referential, narrative, social, and audiovisual experience. It also taps into the medium's characteristic mode: projection. Projection can of course imply cross-cultural insensitivities ("their" lives, their feminism, must look like "ours") but it is also a vision of futurity, based on knowledge, partial as it must be, that is currently available. Women's access to these influential forms of social vision—cinema and feminism—has already transformed the future.

1. TO EACH HER OWN CINEMA
World Cinema and the Woman Cineaste

The international film festival circuit has taken on unprecedented significance within world cinema in recent decades, updating the traditional concepts of art and auteur while playing an important geopolitical and economic role within contemporary audiovisual culture.[1] This network, Thomas Elsaesser writes, "has globalized itself, and in the process has created not only a self-sustaining, highly self-referential world for art cinema, the independent cinema and the documentary film, but [also] a sort of 'alternative' to the Hollywood studio system in its post-Fordist phase."[2] Women directors are better represented within this world than in the U.S. commercial sector, and which women are participating has changed over this period, with contributions by women from the Global South increasing notably in the 2000s. Within this circuit, the elite European film festivals established around World War II still confer the most prestige, even as the network has meaningfully diversified. Although inclusion of women directors in competition at Cannes, Venice, and Berlin is still deficient, these events have played an important role in the emergence of women's voices from outside Europe in the present-day sector that Rosalind Gault and Karl Schoonover refer to as global art cinema.[3]

As Marijke de Valck reminds us in her book-length study of film festivals, "dominant labels such as 'art' and 'auteur' should . . . not be regarded as intrinsic qualities of European film culture, but, instead, treated as part of the strategic discourse of the international film festival as such." This chapter looks at redefinitions of these labels along lines of gender and nation.[4] An analysis of Jane Campion's career involvement with Cannes reveals the contradictory positioning of the figure of the woman cineaste within art cinema and its hierarchies. Whether celebrated or marginalized, Campion has been confined by a discourse of uniqueness.

In Campion's wake, directors Lucrecia Martel and Samira Makhmalbaf have risen to fame through exposure at Cannes and other A-list film festivals. I argue that these talented directors reflect on their own position by problematizing the figure of the exceptional woman in their work. Representing the once considered peripheral but currently deemed prestigious national film cultures of Argentina and Iran, these two women elaborate, in their personae and in the films I analyze, a critique of the Eurocentric construction of Woman that subtends art cinema traditions. But neither director simply replaces this construction with a national or subaltern female subject. Martel deconstructs the aestheticized figure of Woman while insisting on questions of ethics and authorial desire, and Makhmalbaf creates a heroine who is a cipher for ideas of democratic agency and aesthetic autonomy. This reflexivity is not an end in itself; it thematizes geopolitical distributions of power and status that are further illuminated through attention to the films' production and reception contexts. Campion, Martel, and Makhmalbaf: these artists illustrate how women's cinema and world cinema intersect and define each other over two generations within the traveling, taste-making, flexible mediascape constituted by the film festival circuit and consecrated by Cannes.

Jane Campion's Cannes Connections

In 2007 the Cannes Film Festival celebrated its sixtieth anniversary with an omnibus film produced by festival president Gilles Jacob.[5] Jacob, affectionately known as Citizen Cannes, organized the festival tribute by inviting thirty-five filmmakers to make three-minute films around a common theme, officially phrased and rendered in slightly off English on the website as "their current state of mind as inspired by the motion picture theater."[6] The contributions to *Chacun son cinéma: Ce petit coup au coeur quand la lumière s'éteint et que le film commence / To Each His Own Cinema* are interpellated by this project title as auteurist and cinephilic (fig. 1.1).[7] Asked to bridge the position of filmmaker and audience member, closing a gap while preserving an auratic distance, each participant pays tribute to the festival in the persona of the cineaste, a French term for both "a devotee of cinema"

FIGURE 1.1 The Cannes anniversary project *Chacun son cinéma/ To Each His Own Cinema* reified the name of the author in its poster and DVD cover design; Jane Campion's was the only woman's name included.

and "a person involved in filmmaking." *To Each His Own Cinema* also lives up to its (English) title in its gender politics; the omnibus film includes just one woman director—Jane Campion, whose privileged relation to the festival is signified by her status as the only woman to have won its top prize, the Palme d'Or, for *The Piano* in 1993.

This gross imbalance in gender representation among the tribute film's participants did not escape press attention. Kira Cochrane, writing online for the U.K. *Guardian*, reports, "A spokeswoman for the film confirmed that the line-up had depended on who had the time to contribute, but couldn't say which other women, if any, had actually been approached."[8] While it would be nice to think that women directors are that busy, it is difficult to believe that the final selection was the result of a significant number of them having declined the invitation. Even Campion's agreement to participate, as we shall see, was a somewhat qualified one.

For those who attend to the statistics on films by women directors selected for prestigious competitive festivals like Cannes, Venice, and Berlin, it is not particularly surprising that this high-profile lineup features just one woman.[9] In the main competition at Cannes the same year (2007), three out of twenty-one features (14 percent) had a woman director or codirector, a relatively good showing.[10] But closing out the decade, 2010, the year of Kathryn Bigelow's Oscar for Best Director, was a shutout for women directors in the main competition at Cannes. Just as the failure of the anticipated "Bigelow bump" to materialize angered feminists in the U.S. context, so too did the Cannes shutout fuel advocacy for women directors in the elite festival sector.[11] Not always acknowledged in these campaigns, but key to the momentum of the movement, is the fact that more and younger women from more places outside the United States and Europe are directing feature films for festival consideration. The backward-looking sixtieth anniversary project thus brings into sharp focus not only the issue of equity, but also the discursive, historical, and material construction of the auteur. Film genius, of the kind that a Cannes anniversary calls forth, is presumptively male.

Who Counts as a Woman Cineaste?

Variety's review of *Chacun son cinéma* invokes the festival's ongoing role in defining auteur cinema in this way: "A mourning for the passing of the classical Euro-style art cinema of the 60s—of the sort very much represented by films commonly shown in Cannes—filters strongly through the proceedings, no doubt in great measure because they were made by men who belong to that tradition or grew up on it. (Jane Campion, still the only woman to have won the Palme d'Or, is the sole femme in the group here)."[12] Enjoying such distinction (the trade paper's clinging to its dismissive argot "femme" represents two steps back from its one step forward in noting the gender disparity), Campion evidently met the anniversary project's rather daunting criteria of being "universally famous" even if she didn't, couldn't, fully "belong to . . . tradition." Campion is made to embody Woman, the sole femme—not one woman (director) among many.[13] In fact, the New Zealand–born director's fame at the time of the commission had become rather burdensome; her minor-by-design contribution, *The Lady Bug*, was among the few short films Campion made between 2003 (*In the Cut*) and her return to features (and to Cannes competition) in 2009.

The republican sentiment that could be construed from the phrase "to each his or her own" does not exclude women's individual participation in the cinema. France values in the concept of republicanism a citizen's individual accountability, which arguably puts a check on collective identity politics and may account for some French women filmmakers' reluctance

to identify with their gender. At the same time it is among the few countries consistently promoting gender equity among film directors.[14] Due in
part to a tradition of protectionist film policy and the high cultural status
enjoyed by the cinema, and in part to feminist activism of the 1970s, there
is no shortage of French *réalisatrices* who could have been included in the
Cannes project.[15] Yet in the end no female participants were found even
within the national cinema that gives us the very word "auteur."

The fact that the omnibus film was so very imbalanced might well have
been due to curatorial idiosyncrasy or ossification, or to circumstance, as
the spokeswoman alluded. But perhaps it is the insistently individualist
nature of the demand—that the maker reflect one's own cinema—that presents an uncomfortable fit with women directors' habits and with women's
cinema as a collectively imagined formation. From this perspective, even
the inclusion of more than one female director would not have mitigated
the tokenism.[16] An updated, cosmopolitan edition of what Andrew Sarris
notoriously called the "ladies auxiliary" to his pantheon of great directors
could be considered fundamentally at odds with feminist work on authorship.[17] In *Women's Cinema: The Contested Screen*, Alison Butler develops
the generative models "self-inscription" and "the politics of location" for
thinking about women's cinema. These understandings of authorship—
addressing nontheatrical, experimental, documentary, and collaborative
work, or allied with national popular cinemas, genre-oriented or transnational projects in Butler's text—do not line up easily within traditional
auteurist discourses of genius and ownership. And in her ground-clearing
review of feminist theories of film authorship, Catherine Grant encourages
work that moves beyond the limits of textual accounts of authorship but
does not stop short of theorizing the forms of agency at work in women's
cultural production.[18]

Yet an interrogation of auteurist discourse is essential to any study of how
cinematic value is constructed. Historically and currently, certain women
directors do get called up and are materially and artistically enabled by the
aesthetic concepts of world cinema and cineaste, as they circulate within
and are shaped by the cultural politics of festival networks. Increasingly,
this burgeoning group of auteurs comes from nations considered peripheral to global cultural flows and thus challenges the asymmetrical exchange
of the representations, identifications, and affects carried by film culture.
Does the value-adding process of festival recognition work differently for
women, especially, perhaps, for those from the Global South? Reading
backward from Campion's contribution to the Cannes project, I look at how

elite definitions of art cinema and auteurism attempt to brand the careers of particular women directors. These rare cineastes in turn deploy their privileged status to bring to light connections and affinities that dominant discourses of auteurism would overlook, such as the relationship between artist and female image or between the female body and the nation.

Alone of All Her Sex

If I were to pick one woman filmmaker to stand for the lot, I would much rather it be Jane Campion, whose work speaks to feminist concerns and incites my passion, than, say, Leni Riefenstahl. I mention Hitler's favorite filmmaker, who is still one of the first names mentioned in the category "woman filmmaker," because she explicitly deployed the association between femininity and the aesthetic to emphasize her singular value and to extricate herself from politics—in her case from prosecution as a Nazi war criminal.[19] Less egregious and much more common is female directors' discomfort with the label "woman filmmaker" or disavowal of feminism in the name of art (and in practical realization of the bottom line). But, as Jacob found, Campion isn't one of this type. She doesn't have a problem with speaking as a woman—to the press or in her films. The translation of *Chacun son cinéma* as "To Each His Own Cinema" makes its sexism more audible; Campion cannot be fully defined by European art cinema traditions.

Campion, a New Zealander educated and residing in Australia, has been a direct beneficiary of cultural policy that has promoted women's filmmaking since the early 1970s, and while she is sometimes cagey about the use of the word "feminist" to describe herself, she certainly acknowledges feminist themes in her work and the centrality of women's desire to it.[20] At the press conference with the other directors who participated in the omnibus film, she commented, "It's strange to be with a great big football team like this." By comparing the showing at Cannes with what U.S. Americans call soccer, she's slyly calling out the way festivals resemble the World Cup, that other nationalist and U.S. hegemony-defying international competition, one whose masculine posturing is much more overt.

Acting as the fly in the ointment is the very topic of Campion's contribution, *The Lady Bug*, an odd little disquisition on relations between the sexes, dedicated to "the two gentlemen of Cannes, Gilles Jacob and Pierre Rissient." The film opens with a green-tinted film countdown. The image track then depicts the janitor of what looks like a community center or school auditorium trying to flush out from the loudspeaker an insect that is ostensibly both eavesdropping and filtering sound. By turning on the projector and drawing the shades, the janitor manages to draw the bug out of hiding; a female dancer in a padded green bug costume takes the stage, appearing larger than life in the projector beam.[21] The asynchronous audio track consists of jazz music and a goofy conversation between two women and a man with tony British accents on what styles of masculinity might complement a woman's desire to discover "who I am." (It comes down to a question of Jeremy Irons versus Clint Eastwood.) At the end of the short, as the conversation turns heated and the gender trenches are drawn, the audio parallels our visual: "Don't you know you are playing with a killing machine?!" the man's voice cries. Just as we hear his voice-off say, "You silly fool, I'll squash you!" the janitor stomps on the bug. Bluntly satirical about women's chances in a world where "men are in control of everything," *The Lady Bug* shows Campion being what, mixing metaphors, the *Hollywood Reporter* calls her "squirrelly self."[22] Other reviewers, like Michael Sicinski in his blog The Academic Hack, were less gentle: "Frivolous in the extreme, the film also fails to connect as any sort of indictment, since its blend of cheap mummery and doggerel would appear to justify any marginalization Campion feels post-*Piano*."[23] Certainly other auteurs who contributed to the anniversary film are lacerated for self-parody, laziness, and "shtick," by this blogger and by other critics, but as far as I know none is blamed for his own career's marginalization.

Campion's film, which she describes both as "an homage to her favorite filmmaker, Buñuel," and "a sort of feminist thing" should be taken not as a blanket indictment of industry sexism or metatextual commentary on her career course but rather as an "occasional piece." The language of "ladies and gentlemen" befits the ritualistic context of Cannes. The dedication to the two gentlemen of Cannes suggests we read the film within the festival's economy of patronage—besides her prize for *The Piano*, Campion won the Palme d'Or for her short film *Peel* in 1986 at the very beginning of her career. That same year, two of her other film-school shorts, and her first TV feature *Two Friends*, were screened in the Cannes program Un Certain Regard. This remarkable showing was the result of her discovery by Pierre Rissient when he was scouting for talent in Australia.

The question of patronage registers uncomfortably in the film. Clint Eastwood, another Rissient favorite, is referred to by the ladies on the soundtrack as a "pussy pinup." Rissient himself was the subject of a tribute documentary titled *Man of the Cinema*, by *Variety*'s Todd McCarthy, also presented at the 2007 festival, in which Campion (again the only woman director interviewed among a dozen male luminaries, including Eastwood) describes Rissient as "an ambassador, a consigliere." Within the performative act framed by her film's dedication to Jacob and Rissient, theatrical English accents poke fun, perhaps, at the solemn Francophilia that constrains everyone's cinema in the project within a certain traditional vision.

If she isn't exactly biting the hand that feeds her with this film, Campion's answer to the call to make her own cinema—whether we deem it a misfire or a targeted missile—recalls Virginia Woolf's contradictory conclusion in *A Room of One's Own* that "it is fatal for anyone who writes to think of their sex."[24] Woolf gives an example earlier in the text when her contemplation of "the great women of literature" prompts her to compare the calm of Austen's prose with an agitated speech of discontent with her lot as a woman uttered by Charlotte Brontë's heroine Jane Eyre. Of Brontë, Woolf writes, "She left her story, to which her entire devotion was due, to attend to some personal grievance" (76). Campion's film shows a woman seemingly hardwired for cinema literally crushed underfoot by a man who looks not unlike the director's countryman, superstar director Peter Jackson. Woolf goes on in her critique of Brontë: "Her imagination swerved from indignation and we feel it swerve" (76). For me, and one suspects even for Woolf, it is often the authorial swerve that is most thrilling. Read Kathleen McHugh's monograph on the director to appreciate Campion's immoderate passion, which her heroines share.[25] Rather than a timeless work of art for Cannes's sixtieth anniversary, Campion makes the angry, "silly" *The Lady Bug*, saying, like Jane Eyre, "Anyone may blame me who likes" (quoted in Woolf, 74) for airing a grievance. From this perspective, the film could hardly bear its particular burden of representation more gracefully. Implying here that material circumstances affect one's ability to aspire to a Romantic notion of authorship ("to each his own cinema"), Campion goes on in her next major work, *Bright Star* (2009)—which premiered in competition at Cannes)—to unsettle the canon by examining the collaborative nature of the creativity of an actual Romantic poet.

Cannes and/as World Cinema

In contrast to the gender-blind presumption of its charge, *Chacun son cinéma* was explicit about nationality, asking its filmmakers to "represent both their countries and a proud conception of cinema," and it is the intersection of this geographical representational politics with the disavowal of gender bias that I would like to explore. The dual focus on national cinema and film art represented in the language describing the omnibus is quite consistent with Cannes's philosophy, as well as its history. Vanessa Schwartz argues that, true to the festival's founding in the shadow of World War II as an alternative to the Mussolini-sanctioned competition in Venice, Cannes "showcased the importance of film to the project of the postwar globalization of culture."[26] It succeeded by drawing on "the association of France and the Riviera with cultural cosmopolitanism"; in other words, art cinema was marked as simultaneously international and ineffably French. The "world" of world cinema was centered in a European perspective. In the immediate postwar decades, Cannes presented a formidable alternative to Hollywood dominance (undertaken with Hollywood's full collaboration, as Schwartz shows). Organized around national cinemas' self-representation, the festival introduced neorealism and the French New Wave and honored masterpieces from India, Mexico, and Eastern Europe.

And, in keeping with the definition of film as art rather than big business, Cannes also included those women directors (*réalisatrices*) who excelled in the cosmopolitan art. Agnès Varda, Lina Wertmüller, Liliana Cavani, and Mai Zetterling—among the few women to compete in the postwar heyday of European art cinema—were joined in the 1980s by Márta Mészáros and Agnieska Holland (women from socialist countries whose governments supported both nominal gender equality and film art), and by a few filmmakers who explicitly engaged with feminist aesthetics in the 1970s and 1980s: while films by Marguerite Duras and Margarethe Von Trotta were in the invited competition, Chantal Akerman's *Jeanne Dielman* showed in the unofficial parallel section. Objections that these names are all European are precisely on point.

After the protests of 1968 led to the suspension of that year's edition of Cannes, the festival reorganized and opened up the competition to new definitions of world cinema, adding the independently programmed Directors' Fortnight and changing its selection criteria. Until 1971, films in the festival had been selected by, and represented, participating countries.[27] The installation of the figure of the festival director at Cannes and the other festivals allowed for a selection policy of discovery over diplomacy. But the taste-making function, and the growing power of Cannes as a film market, helped the festival retain and even extend its world dominance of this cultural field. By the last decades of the twentieth and the beginning of the twenty-first century, Cannes was a crucial node in a burgeoning global network of festivals, lending its imprimatur to a new kind of cosmopolitan world cinema. James F. English characterizes the rise of cultural capital in this period as "a general expansion of the field on which cultural value in all its forms is produced, driven by a society's greater and greater reliance on the maintenance and manipulation of what are at bottom arbitrary distinctions of symbolic rank or prestige."[28]

In "Film Festival Networks: The New Topographies of Cinema in Europe," Elsaesser incisively describes how contemporary film festivals confer cultural value and rework discourses of authorship and nation in the context of global cultural flows and Hollywood's continued dominance. Historically, "the gold standard of the European festival under the rule of Cannes became the auteur director," he writes. This proud figure might hail from any nation; even as world cinema currency shifted decisively from Europe to Asia in the 1990s, "throughout the decades Cannes remained the kingmaker of the festival circuit."[29] Hailing the discovery of national cinemas and directors gave the impression that distinctions conferred by men like Jacob and Rissient, rather than other, more cataclysmic economic and social changes, were responsible for shifts in cultural value.[30]

The Cannes sixtieth anniversary project's strategic commitment to a new definition of "world" that encompassed emerging national and regional cinema movements is evident in the project's willingness to advertise another set of numbers, more flattering and inclusive than that of one in thirty-five, or 3 percent, women directors: *To Each His Own Cinema* represents twenty-five countries and five continents, its publicity touts. A look at the participants shows five Chinese auteurs (from the PRC, Hong Kong, and Taiwan), Alejandro González Iñárritu and Walter Salles from Latin America, Elia Suleiman and Amos Gitai from Palestine and Israel respectively, and U.S. cinephile favorites including the Coen brothers, Michael Cimino, and David Lynch. Notably absent are Indian filmmakers, and the continent of Africa is represented only by Egyptian director Youssef Chahine. The publicizing of the numbers of countries and continents positions the "worlding" of cineculture as evident grounds for self-congratulation—see Nicolas de Villiers's cleverly titled review in *Senses of Cinema*: "We Are the World Cinema"[31]—while begging the question of representativeness. The exercise in diversity remains an additive one, with auteurs rhetorically transcending their place in the world (to each his own cinema).[32]

If, as Elsaesser claims, "the festival circuits hold the keys to all forms of cinema not bound into the global Hollywood network," then where is women's cinema lodged between the discourses of auteurism and (expanded) national representativeness?[33] In festival studies, gender has hitherto been addressed primarily as a thematic programming concern.[34] Near the conclusion of "Film Festival Networks," Elsaesser concedes, "while public discourses and prize-giving speeches may continue to reflect a commitment to art for art's sake, there are other voices and issues. . . . Film festivals have since the 1970s been extremely successful in becoming the platform for other causes, for minorities and pressure groups, for women's cinema, receptive to gay and queer cinema agendas, to ecological movements, to underwriting political protest, thematizing cinema and drugs, or paying tribute to anti-imperialist struggles and partisan politics" (100). Elsaesser invokes women's cinema in relation to the contestatory nature of festivals—his very use of the term "women's cinema" references debates within the field of film studies originating in the 1970s. Yet at the same time, his comment marginalizes gender in a list of incommensurable "other causes . . . voices and issues." For women's cinema is not congruent with the thematizing of drugs or ecological issues but rather cuts across both the political and the aesthetic meanings of representation and the organization, content, and address of festivals.[35] Elsaesser's distinction between an unsatisfactory "art for art's sake" model that doesn't broach the question of female authorship, and an "issues and agendas" model that can only pose it on a list of other pressures, leaves aside an important dimension of the new topography of cinema he's tracing.

As Elsaesser points out, the discourse of auteurism need not be apolitical; it can itself help formulate issues of agency in mappings of world cinema. He makes a crucial point in his observation about the multiple functioning of festivals: he quotes Daniel Dayan's study of Sundance, "Behind every auteur is a constituency" (99), and continues, "The author as the nominal currency of the film festival economy has proven a very useful shield behind which both the festival and its audiences have been able to negotiate different priorities and values. Film festivals thus have in effect created one of the most interesting public spheres available in the cultural field today" (101). Understanding women's cinema not as a cause but as a crucial part of this public sphere (or counterpublic sphere) helps us link the figure of the woman cineaste to a far-flung constituency.

The Emergence of a New Generation of Women Directors

How do women directors fit within Cannes's arguably neocolonialist "king-making" project? Are "ladies" courted for diversity of perspective or simply encompassed in cosmopolitan cinema's global reach? Despite its own lamentable statistics, *Chacun son cinéma* was made at a moment of change and promise at the intersection of world cinema and women's cinema, and in this context it may be something of a reaction formation. Increasingly it is not only female stars (who themselves wield power at film festivals not only through the attention of the paparazzi but also through their prominent role on juries), but also emerging women directors who "proudly" symbolize world cinema. This may even be the case at Cannes.

Obviously, the low number of women directors in competition at Cannes is disheartening, even outrageous—only 17 of 212 films screened in the main competition between 2000 and 2010 were directed or codirected by women.[36] However, the increase in the number of awards bestowed on women's films during the same decade complicates this pattern. A number of women directors have received significant career boosts and press exposure as artists through the festival: despite the boos that greeted *Marie Antoinette* in 2006, Sofia Coppola is among the best-known contemporary women directors, and U.K. director Andrea Arnold's reputation has been established by her films' awards at Cannes. Both directors have also been tapped for the festival's jury. *Wendy and Lucy*'s presentation in the Un Certain Regard official section launched U.S. director Kelly Reichardt to prominence; that section, and the parallel Directors' Fortnight and Critics' Week, which can be more critically respected than the competition, offer slots to promising women directors each year. Indeed, it makes sense that the numbers of women are greater in the sections that highlight less established directors. Within the Cinéfondation program, which is dedicated to fostering new talent, including the selection of works from film schools for exhibition, the Cannes Residence program in Paris for screenwriters, and the Atelier, which helps secure financing and distribution at the market, gender representation is more equitable. The question of how women directors are recruited to both make their own cinema and represent their countries in these venues entails a closer look at shifts in the institutions and cultures of world cinema.[37]

With Cannes at the pinnacle of the festival network, an invitation generates significant cultural capital for a filmmaker and her country, and a prize even more. Iranian Samira Makhmalbaf became the first woman in the festival's history to win the Jury Prize, third in prestige after the Palme d'Or and the Grand Prix. She received the prize for her second feature *Takhté siah / Blackboards* in 2000, and went on to win it again in 2003 for her third, *Panj é asr / At Five in the Afternoon*. To date, this prize, awarded to films selected in the main competition has been bestowed on women directors four more times. In 2006 it went to Arnold's debut *Red Road*; in 2008 Marjane Satrapi and Vincent Paronnaud's debut *Persepolis* won the Jury Prize; Arnold received it again in 2009 for *Fish Tank*; and French director Maïwenn won for *Polisse* in 2011.[38]

Cannes-cultivated Japanese director Naomi Kawase's *Mogari no mori / The Mourning Forest* took home the Grand Prix in 2007; the festival's second prize had been awarded only once before to a woman, to Márta Mészáros for *Napló gyermekeimnek / Diary for My Children* in 1984.[39] The Camera d'Or for best first feature, the category in which women have achieved their best representation (eleven wins since 1978 when it was instated), was conferred on three women's films during the decade, including Miranda July's *Me and You and Everyone We Know* (2005). Thus the aughts were a time in which the barriers to women's inclusion among the ranks of elite cineastes exhibited cracks, and a few women had designs on the pantheon—even if they missed the omnibus.

What do these changes owe to feminism or, more particularly, to women's cinema, which ostensibly has different goals than awards and rankings? Within the context of the "ever more direct convertibility of cultural with political capital," English writes, "prizes have played an enormous role in the emergence of minoritarian and oppositional cultures into positions of visibility and esteem."[40] This is why the debates about the Palme d'Or matter, though from another perspective the mounting pile of third prizes makes second-sex/class citizenship look good. Celebrity feminists like Meryl Streep and Helen Mirren command respect when they speak out about the sexism of the movie industry and the festival circuit: Mirren told Karlovy Vary's director she expected to see 50 percent women in competition the next time she returned to the venerable Czech Republic festival.[41] With a little more theater, French writer and director Virginie Despentes and director Coline Serreau were among those who joined the French feminist action group La Barbe in castigating Cannes's hypocrisy in a 2012 manifesto published in *Le Monde*: "Men are fond of depth in women, but only in their cleavage."[42]

In "The World and the Soup: Historicizing Media Feminisms in Transnational Contexts," Kathleen McHugh critiques the prevalent models of scholarship on women directors, the static compiling of lists of names according to qualitative judgment or geography, demanding, "How can we move beyond paradigms that marginalize women's film production as reference material, as specialized national or regional genre, or as exceptional anomaly (the female auteur) and instead articulate a more historical sense of women's and feminisms' productive relations to the cinema?" (115). Too close a focus on elite festivals' statistics amounts merely to a tally of "exceptional anomalies." But attending to the discourses that support the visibility of women filmmakers at Cannes, and dismantling their exceptional and anomalous status through close reading, helps reveal an incipient redistribution of image-making power.

As we have seen, McHugh also advocates a historical approach; she shows how Campion and later Tracey Moffatt (b. 1960) were afforded opportunities and exposed to ideas that figured in their work by feminist and antiracist activism and cultural policy in Australia. Such political-turned-institutional supports are harder to trace for the emergent generation of women filmmakers, and many of them may not themselves avow feminism as an influence. Initiatives of the 1970s like Australia's Women's Film Fund, the National Film Board of Canada's Studio D, and the Dutch women's film distributor Cinemien have been dissolved or redefined, their original goals ostensibly achieved. But feminist legacies persist: in the influence of mentors, in criticism and theory, in transformations of media industries and policies. I suggest that a kind of "conversion of political to cultural capital" with regard to feminism is signified by the newly emergent female auteurs. For example, Argentina's new film schools and democratized funding mechanisms, and even the professional respectability guaranteed by hijab in Iran, have facilitated increasing access by women to careers in directing in these two countries.[43] Whether guided by a concerted effort to bring about cultural change, youthful iconoclasm, or coproduction directives, these women and the film movements in which they participate are having a political impact on world cinema.

World Cinema and the Woman Cineaste

In the two analyses that follow, I look at directors of festival films for whom exposure at Cannes has been crucial, women whose access to world cinema differs from Campion's not only because they come from the Global South but also because they belong to different generations of women artists with different relationships to feminism and publicity. Lucrecia Martel and Samira Makhmalbaf have emerged as auteurs with considerable attention from the international film press, online networks of cinephiles, and scholars; they are positioned internationally in relation to cinema as art form rather than to cinema as heritage or entertainment or to the public spheres of politics or celebrity (although these boundaries are shifting ones, as I argue in chapter 2). Immediately hailed for their debuts, both women are writer-directors who have been able to sustain the personal quality of their filmmaking in production arrangements suited to expressive filmmaking. Their sophomore and subsequent works have circulated and received commentary under the brand of their directorial signature. While neither has been able to maintain a prolific output, interruptions to their productivity make their works even more precious. Aspects of their biographies and personalities (and even of their sartorial styles) mark them as newsworthy and unique beyond their films. Above all, the modernist difficulty of their aesthetic strategies, which defer to authorial personality or style to decide ambiguities, qualify them as what I am calling cineastes.

Selection for and success within the Cannes main competition of their arty, though not apolitical, feature films has confirmed these directors as world-class female auteurs, still a rare enough commodity. Yet as I have indicated, auteurist discourses of exceptional individual achievement and/or national representativeness should also be indexed to a wider increase in women directors' representation in world cinema more generally and in Argentina and Iran more particularly. Without diminishing the significance of the breakthrough their accolades in cinephile circles represent, I hope to show that Martel and Makhmalbaf are as significant for challenging authorial or female exemplariness as they are for their undeniably unique talents. While Martel uses her shy and reflective persona to identify aesthetic ambiguities with political contradictions, Makhmalbaf puts herself on the line in the context of her filmmaking family, differentiating herself from her father's reputation while sharing his dissident position. Moreover, by treating together directors easily worthy of individual study (indeed of monographs), I underscore my comparative approach: no single woman filmmaker is characteristic of current film culture, and singularity should be displaced as a mainstay of authorial ideology.

My methodology is primarily textual, and I hope to show that the geopolitical and material determinants of production are readable even in the traveling aesthetics of the festival film. Through their modernist strategies, Martel and Makhmalbaf resist representing their countries as geopolitical trouble zones by disrupting a familiar recourse to realism and national allegory. The two women are participants in wider national movements or waves of independent directors that, however divergent the Argentine and Iranian contexts may be, have international coproduction support, visibility, and modest market prospects. Both the Argentine and Iranian new cinemas are sustained in countries with significant popular film traditions, though Iran's industry is notably culturally closed and subject to government censorship. Questions of film policy are directly relevant to these directors' output, even to their coming to the profession of filmmaking. Thus production circumstances influence how auteurism is deconstructed and reconstructed in these works, and my discussion gives attention to these factors.

Significantly younger than the transnational cohort of women filmmakers (born before 1960) identified in McHugh's account of feminism's impact on film history, Lucrecia Martel and Samira Makhmalbaf do not produce work that is immediately intelligible in terms of the narratives of second-wave feminism. Absent from their work are equivalents of Campion's spunky heroines, as is the built-in address to women audiences of the generic conventions of the romance and costume drama, which Campion borrows from and transforms. On the contrary, Martel's films enmesh their female characters as much as their male ones in existential murk. And while two of Makhmalbaf's four features are overtly feminist, the other two are about men and male communities. However, feminist legacies—material, political, and aesthetic—are apparent in their work. Campion may have been more blunt with *The Lady Bug*, but Martel and Makhmalbaf each answer a call to participate in and change the landscape of world cinema by making "a cinema of her own." Martel creates an immersive world of ambiguous signs where national amnesia is indistinguishable from personal nightmare, allocating the viewer an uncomfortable place within her tale of accountability. Makhmalbaf uses her characters as figures in a high-stakes drama of autonomy and recognition. As I detail in my readings of their films and the contexts of their production and circulation, their authorial personae come to signal an ethical feminist practice.

These directors work in a cultural moment characterized by changes in film financing, policy, technology, and access in the context of neoliberalism and globalization. While their films are shaped by personal, national, and regional forces, they are marked in both production and exhibition contexts by the reinvigorated international cinephile circuit. Thus they renew questions about singularity (the stock in trade of auteurism) and collectivity, national cinema and transnational reception in the context of feminist genealogies.

Lucrecia Martel's Vertiginous Authorship

Lucrecia Martel's success with her first feature, *La Ciénaga*—prizes at the Berlin, Sundance, Toulouse, and Havana Film Festivals in 2001, ten-best lists, laudatory reviews—marked what might be the most auspicious debut of a woman cineaste so far this century. Martel was born in 1966 in Argentina's northwestern province of Salta, the setting of her three features to date. Her work helped define New Argentine Cinema as a movement and thus put women's voices at the center of its novelty. Starting in the mid-1990s, against a backdrop of neoliberalism and economic crisis, young Argentine filmmakers began making fresh and immediate films that connected with both domestic audiences and international critics. Legislative and financing changes resulted in a resurgence of film culture in the country. Established producer Lita Stantic, well known for her work with internationally recognized director María Luisa Bemberg, became a key figure in the careers of the new generation, serving as producer of *La Ciénaga*. The film is a portrait of a provincial bourgeoisie in decline, in which lethargy combines with erotic intimacy and other bodily forces in a mesmerizing, subjective swamp of feeling. While its ensemble cast and creepy tone might not fit rigid definitions of women's cinema, *La Ciénaga* is nevertheless concerned with the quotidian, with desire and the family, and female characters' perspectives direct the drifting narration. The result is a kind of deconstructed, oneiric melodrama.

Martel's reputation as an irreducibly singular talent—an auteur—was confirmed by the selection of both of her subsequent features (produced by the Almódovar brothers' company El Deseo), *La Niña Santa / The Holy Girl* (2004) and *La mujer sin cabeza / The Headless Woman* (2008), for the main competition at Cannes. Few women have enjoyed such a favored relation with the festival, which also awarded Martel a residency to develop *La Niña Santa* in 2002 and a spot on the jury in 2006. The consistency of Martel's oeuvre to date also contributes to her standing as a true cineaste; her films all share a similar layered and moody audiovisual style, inconclusive endings, and common tropes—extended, quasi-incestuous middle-class provincial families; swimming pools; a covert queer politics. Finally, she has a distinct persona. Intellectual, serious and publicity-shy, she wears sunglasses to protect her eyes, combining a stereotypically male-coded virtuosity and a female-coded mystery and inaccessibility in a queer kind of reticence (fig. 1.2).

The Headless Woman was the only film in competition by a solo woman director in the 2008 edition of the Cannes festival, and the slow-moving and narratively underdetermined film about a woman's behavior after striking something with her car was notoriously greeted with boos. Yet the reception in some ways confirms rather than belies Martel's insider status at the festival. Objections seemed to center on the slightness of the plot and the overall obscurity of the film; Andrew O'Hehir suggested in *Salon* that the film's

FIGURE 1.2 Lucrecia Martel. Courtesy Strand Releasing.

deconstruction of class privilege was opaque to audiences blind to their own status.[44] At its New York Film Festival appearance, followed by a limited late summer 2009 U.S. release by the art house distributor Strand (known for its gay-themed as well as Asian, French, and other boutique releases), the film found astute critical champions and, despite some detractors, landed on many top-ten lists.[45] None of the film's reviewers tied Martel to other women filmmakers; almost all invoked auteurist discourses of unique style and sensibility. Peter Brunette's language in the *Hollywood Reporter* is characteristic: "Argentinian director Lucrecia Martel is nothing if not subtle. She is also a master of visual and aural technique, which is on full and splendid display in *La Mujer Sin Cabeza* (*The Headless Woman*)."[46]

But Martel's mastery is not transcendent; it arises from a particular personal and political history, within a national movement and wider Latin American and feminist contexts. In her history of Argentine film, Tamara Falicov traces the shift in Argentine film from the bourgeois cinema of quality during redemocratization after the military dictatorship of 1976–1983—exemplified by Luis Puenzo's Oscar-winning *La historia oficial / The Official*

Story (1985) about the "dirty wars" (state-sponsored violence against the left during dictatorial rule)—to edgier, more localized fare—like Lucía Puenzo's *XXY* (2005), a family drama about an intersex teenager set on the coast near Uruguay.[47] The politics of gender and sexuality, youth, region, and indigeneity engaged by the films of the New Argentine Cinema displace the allegorical universalism of the 1980s (and the militancy of the 1960s and 1970s Third Cinema / Tercer Cine).

Falicov's history focuses on policy and describes how changes instituted in 1995 used taxes on cinemas and TV to foster both commercially successful films on domestic screens and the smaller-budgeted and internationally acclaimed films of the independent New Argentine Cinema. Martel first achieved success with the short film *Rey Muerto / Dead King* (1995), part of a funded compilation of shorts by young directors. Founded in 1997, the Ibermedia fund, with significant resources contributed from Spain and participation from countries across Latin America and the Caribbean, has added to regional cinema's rejuvenation by supporting coproductions throughout Latin America. Still, many of the films produced in Argentina have difficulty finding domestic distribution and audiences. International audiences, acclaim, and financing remain crucial to sustaining the industry.[48]

This national and regional cinema history intersects with another, feminist narrative. The generation of Latin American women filmmakers who came to international prominence in the 1980s were influenced by second-wave feminism in their revisions of national narratives and forms. For example, Bemberg's *Camila* (1984), one of the most prominent international successes from Argentina in the 1980s and widely read as a clear indictment of the military dictatorship, tells the true story of a nineteenth-century aristocratic woman who faces the firing squad with her lover, a priest, at her side. Mexican director María Novaro's hit *Danzón* (1991) depicts the liberation of a single mother enamored of the national dance form, combining an affirmative narrative of self-discovery with enjoyable music and dance. Like internationally successful Latin American women writers of the period, these directors might be described as deploying what Jean Franco characterizes as the "art romance" to connect with popular audiences.[49]

Martel works in a different idiom. Like many other women filmmakers who made their feature film debuts in the 2000s, she explores the micropolitics of gender, sexuality, and location rather than national narratives of oppression and collective liberation. Yet I hope to show that in its embrace of a partial, inconclusive point of view, *The Headless Woman* shows consciousness of its positioning in these multiple histories. It is certainly plausible to read the protagonist's amnesia as a national allegory about the legacy of the dictatorship, but the film doesn't directly thematize such events. Instead it explores the ethical failure to acknowledge culpability as a major theme and does so in gendered terms. For example, at one point we suspect the heroine has forgotten she has children, an almost humorous twist on the iconic status of Las Madres de la Plaza de Mayo, whose protests brought worldwide visibility to the plight of the disappeared population of Argentina (the eponymous subject of the classic 1985 feminist documentary by Lourdes Portillo and Susana Blaustein Muñoz). As we shall see, Martel's protagonist is not permitted a relation to her own act; through this staging of the question of accountability, the director claims a responsibility for her own art, while acknowledging the frames and forces that position it in the world.

Martel brings a global reputation to bear on *The Headless Woman*'s very local tale about race, entitlement, and the politics of location. Aware of an international gaze, Martel disrupts easy articulations of femininity, the national, and the individual—whether in terms of authorship or liberation. The problem of female individualism and representativeness is on one level the subject of Martel's film, and on another level it inflects the discourse that circulates around it as an auteur film. Hence the politics of her art lie not only in critiques of authoritarianism, quiescence, racism, and patriarchy, but also in how the director positions herself and is positioned in this circuit of distinction.

Unthinking Heroines

The Headless Woman is a subtle drama of consciousness and conscience, turning on its middle-class provincial heroine's accountability for a death that may or may not have occurred. Themes of political amnesia and complicity regarding the years of dictatorship are overlaid with racialized and place-based class and gender hierarchies. The film opens in medias res, first showing three indigenous boys playing with their dog near a lonely stretch of highway and then cutting to a gathering of middle-class women, kids in tow, just as it is breaking up. In both distinct spaces, movement is chaotic, relationships unclear, and identities unknown. We follow one of the women as she drives away, radio tuned to an upbeat pop song. This arbitrary assignment of our consciousness to hers is consequential; we never return to a parallel montage that would give the others' perspective on events.

Reaching for her cell phone, Vero (played by tall, blonde Maria Onetto, cast in part for those physical qualities) strikes something on the road. The

FIGURE 1.3 Framing emulates the dangerously limited perspective of the main character. Maria Onetto in *The Headless Woman*. Courtesy Strand Releasing.

wide-screen, lateral framing remains tight as she hits her head on the steering wheel, momentarily losing her sunglasses (fig. 1.3). She doesn't know what she's hit, whether it's an object, an animal, or a person she's run over; she doesn't look back. Instead, she replaces her glasses and drives on, as a 1970s pop song continues on the car radio and the camera continues to stare. Eventually, Vero pulls over, gets out, and stands at the side of her car, framed from the neck down, as it begins to rain. The film title comes up. Her "headlessness" signifies our separation from a purposeful consciousness early in the film's unfolding and offers a visible body as supplement to what- (or whom)ever is left behind on that stretch of road.[50]

In the aftermath of the accident, it is unclear what Vero knows or feels; she lets herself be carried through her days by others' instructions, just as the film's narration is driven by instinctive movements and half-formed intentions rather than plot. As Vero transitions from a concussed haze to some semblance of her ordinary life (not so very different, it seems), evidence comes to light that a young boy from a nearby village has died during the recent storm. The men in Vero's extended family, to whom she has confided her doubts about what might have happened that night, act to cover up her involvement and protect their class interests. The film's final image, shot through glass doors, shows Vero greeting guests at a party, as another dated pop song blares. Ending a beat too soon for us to be sure of what we're looking at, the film catches Vero flanked by her husband, brother, and cousin / sometime lover as if they have closed ranks around her. The film explores the conundrum of middle-class female "headlessness," a severing from intellect, self-awareness, and ethical subjectivity imposed by the mind/body split and a restrictive social order. The film goes further to show that that position is secured at the expense of others. Our lack of access to that other scene is a source of the film's horror-film undertow.[51]

While an exploration of female subjectivity and sexuality is at the center of her films, Martel does not represent feminism as a recognizably collective concern. Her heroines are privatized in a familial setting. Indeed they could be classified as hysterics who somaticize their predicaments (holy girl, headless woman). Though arguably *The Headless Woman* represents her most sustained critique of the restrictions on women's lives, it is far from presenting an individualist solution, whether liberal feminist emancipation, postfeminist consumerism, or another therapeutic discourse. Consciousness-raising, for Vero, would be a contradiction. Instead, the film deconstructs female individualism, and arguably Eurocentrism, through its attention to the heroine's place in aesthetic and social hierarchies.

The Headless Woman recasts the European art film heroine, "Othered," from Bergman, Buñuel, and Antonioni on down through art house history, as beautiful ciphers, muses, and clichés, by presenting female interiority as a question. Eschewing naturalistic characterization through style and the heroine's dissociated state, Martel blocks readings in terms of psychological motivation. But the film also prevents what Claire Johnston, in her Barthesian critique of the European art film, called the "invasion" of art film's perfect female forms by the myth of the feminine.[52] For Johnston, the stereotypes of femininity that prevailed in Hollywood films more easily facilitated the critic's "detaching" of myth from "nature."

Martel extends Johnston's insight by locating stereotype within the art film tradition itself and then detaching it from its moorings. Unlike the Antonioni heroines she references, her dyed-blonde protagonist does not invite, or cannot sustain, comparisons to the eternal feminine. This distance is achieved in part by keeping Vero vacant, almost comically so. The day after the car accident, Vero arrives at a dental clinic, summoned and relayed there by the female staff who populate her office and home, and sits down in the waiting room; it is only the amusement of the patients awaiting her attention that clues us in that she herself is the dentist. The scene gently satirizes her privileged stature, literally signified in her height compared to the darker-skinned workers and servants nearby.

Yet the film is genuinely concerned with female subjectivity. Amy Taubin concludes her astute review of *The Headless Woman*, "The film becomes . . . the description of a condition of consciousness. We are all, to one degree or another, headless women," provocatively universalizing the female subject, however culpable or clueless she/we might be.[53] How can a feminist critic

FIGURE 1.4 The protagonist's hairstyle evokes those of *L'Avventura* and *Vertigo.* Maria Onetto in *The Headless Woman.* Courtesy Strand Releasing.

not be intrigued by the film's title? Vero represents the problem outlined by Simone de Beauvoir in *The Second Sex*: "the myth of the woman, of the Other," "[un]able to accomplish herself in projects and aims," trapped in "the immanence of her person."[54] Nevertheless, Vero is not let off the hook. Her bottle-blonde hair insistently marks the place where her head should be, and also marks this myth of Woman as one of European origin. Admired by other characters—though she concurs when her sister comments that damage by dye and chlorine has rendered it "disgusting"—Vero's hair conjures Monica Vitti and Kim Novak in their signature roles as unknowable women in films by Antonioni and Hitchcock, art film auteur and Hollywood master, respectively.

The film's *Vertigo* (1958) intertext is signaled by frequent shots of Vero in profile or with her head turned, and its citation of *L'Avventura* (1960) by the disheveled coiffure (fig. 1.4). However, Martel bypasses the male subject who would focalize the question of femininity as his existential conundrum.[55] When near the end of *The Headless Woman* Vero dyes her hair dark, it is to cover not gray but the "crime" (fig. 1.5); it's a blanket of anonymity she pulls over her appearance just as the men keep up appearances, making sinister offscreen arrangements to shield Vero from suspicion. And yet, this hair color, like Judy's in *Vertigo*, is also a giveaway, a sign of her desire. Is it perhaps a shade too dark for a *blanca*?[56] If Vero's loyalties are finally unclear,

FIGURE 1.5 The protagonist's dyed hair functions as a disguise and an emblem of desire. Maria Onetto in *The Headless Woman*. Courtesy Strand Releasing.

it is not due to female capriciousness; the film has raised real questions about white women's power and responsibility.

Martel's cinephilic references reflexively cite her own film's place in the male-dominated art house and in the lineage of auteur cinema. But they also raise the question of her relation to the heroine. Vero isn't simply stand-in or muse; at the same time, she's a little bit of both. While I have spoken so far about Vero's impasse as female subject, I believe that the film also transforms, while retaining, her position as object of desire—including female authorial and erotic desire. The film brings together two signature tropes of sexuality in Martel's work: incest and lesbianism. Desire is always a current of familial dynamics and a significant source of energy in Martel's films. In her affair with her cousin / brother-in-law, Vero both transgresses the law and submits to it (he has an in with the police force that he uses to help her). Even more infused with authorial significance is the convergence of these tropes in the persona of Vero's randy, hepatitis-infected lesbian niece, Candita. Candita's desire, so palpable and seemingly random, is a vector of contagion that collapses boundaries—of gender, bloodline, and generation (fig. 1.6).[57] Left intact, these boundaries might support an allegorical reading of the film; instead their corruption returns us to real bodies, messy places, and mixed legacies.[58]

In his classic 1979 essay "Art Film as a Mode of Film Practice," David Bordwell explains that art cinema differentiates itself from classical Hollywood modes of narration by eschewing linear, cause-and-effect narration and privileging both realism and authorial expressivity. The apparent contradiction between these impulses is resolved with "ambiguity as the dominant principle of intelligibility. . . . Life lacks the neatness of art and

FIGURE 1.6 Lesbianism and incest, threaded throughout Martel's work, come together in the portrayal of the protagonist's niece. Maria Onetto and Inés Efron in *The Headless Woman*. Courtesy Strand Releasing.

this art knows it" (156). Woman—as Other and as filmmaker's canvas—plays a key role in this operation, though Bordwell's poetics doesn't emphasize this point. *The Headless Woman* certainly privileges ambiguity; the very plot hinges, like that of Antonioni's classic art film *Blow-Up* (1966, based on a story by Argentine writer Julio Cortázar), on evidence of a death that is under erasure. As Brunette goes on to complain in his review: "[Martel's] narratives can be maddeningly slight, causing the viewer to struggle to comprehend even basic character relationships or motivations. It's difficult to invest much emotion if you have little idea who's who."[59] But it is perhaps the film's point that Vero can't distinguish between the boy who has died and the one who washes her car—or that we can't without difficulty distinguish her husband from her cousin/lover and brother. What this film seems to "know" is that differences matter. Refusing the universal—whether authorial transcendence or myth of Woman—Martel goes beyond ambiguity to material contradiction.[60]

Racial and class hierarchies specific to Argentina and to Salta in particular structure *The Headless Woman*. Martel's meticulous control of framing, storytelling, and focus, both narrational and optical (through shallow depth of field), reveals these fault lines without spelling them out for her audience. Here the author and (art house) spectator are implicated with middle-class white culpability, as Vero treats the women and boys who serve her as interchangeable and expendable. Yet however tempting (and accurate, in part) it might be to read *The Headless Woman*'s central theme as a metaphor for collaboration during the military dictatorship and amnesia in its aftermath, the fact that there are no references to the state, the past, or even the capital suggests that private dramas are as significant as, and deeply imbricated with, public ones.

In one haunting scene, the senile Aunt Lala, watching home movie footage of a family wedding, mistakes her relatives for local government dignitaries. The social forces the film evokes are all in the family. Martel frequently states that her work draws inspiration from eavesdropping on and filming her family as a child, and here she shows the home movie grown into an art film, to be watched with the same self-consciousness. A sort of failed exogamy is attested to not only in the wedding footage but also in the many scenes in which servants and workers occupy prominent places within the frame. Watching home movie footage with Aunt Lala becomes a tutorial on film viewership, posing the question of how one connects the characters on the screen, the real lives they are meant to represent, and the unrepresented others. In this film, the question of blame you can't quite put your finger on seeps into the scene of spectatorship. Like Aunt Lala, we begin to see the dead.

These ghosted images give the viewer, perhaps especially the cross-cultural one, the impression that there is something more we are supposed to know. The undecidability of certain images is answered by what would seem to be an opposed practice: the location shooting in Salta. Yet the intimate mise-en-scène that grounds the movie in place also presents the viewer with a startling strangeness (similarly, the film's interiors and fashions seem lived in and curiously undatable). Art cinema's necessary address to foreign audiences to recoup its investment often entails the erasure of the specifics of history and culture by design. Cofinancing deals may demand such deterritorialization, even as they capitalize on local color. In *The Headless Woman* a stretch of barren road is marked and remarked with differing significance by the characters who traverse it. It is a space of adventure for the boys who play with their dog in the precredits sequence, and one contaminated by the odor of the blocked-up canal when Vero's family members drive by just as the body is being recovered. Even the white characters know this terrain better than their habits of attention suggest; for example, they are able to find the site of the accident even at night.[61] Depicting a social ecosystem from the perspective of the willfully blind middle-class, the film refuses the spectator a clear image of the exotic. Indeed Martel seems to play with such expectations; the indexicality of the location shooting invites the foreign audience's gaze, to verify Martel's authenticity as a regional artist and to indulge tourism, but no secrets or sights are revealed.

In *The Headless Woman* aesthetic articulations of national identity and femininity are shaped by transnational film culture and art film history rather than by an imagined authentic national culture or clear-cut narrative. As in Campion's more explicitly framed short film *The Lady Bug*, a feminist critique of patriarchal complicity emerges despite and within the structures of international financing, discourses of authorial celebrity, and aesthetic styles that are codified by a cinephile culture with Cannes recognition at its apex. At once privileged and provincial, Martel engages a world where damage done to neighbors consequentially marks personal as well as political histories.

Martel's heroine iconically invokes European art cinema posturing, only to ask how that genre's existential dramas apply to her as a subject. This question—of agency, of history, of location—is one I have been suggesting that the female author from outside the European tradition herself poses. In *The Headless Woman* both an ethical position and a desiring one are marked by Martel's aesthetic signatures: indeterminate point of view, tense wide-screen composition, enveloping and disquieting sound, lack of narrative exposition, queer erotic energy. My reading suggests that her film deconstructs the cinematic production of an ineffable femininity (pace Antonioni and Hitchcock); by thematizing Vero's accountability, Martel associates her own aesthetic choices with a female subject rather than making of her heroine an aesthetic object. Placing her reflection on these matters in contemporary, provincial Argentina, but blurring the markers of space and even time (through 1970s pop and decor) as deliberately as she does the question of blame, she both alludes to a national trauma and implies that historical and geopolitical ignorance haunt the consumption of world cinema like a nightmare.[62] The mixed reception of Martel's film seems to extend the problematic of collusion and cover-up that is at stake in it.[63]

Samira Makhmalbaf employs a related set of strategies in *At Five in the Afternoon*, her well-received bid to put Iranian and Afghan women's stories on the world cinema map: ambiguous art film language and elliptical narration, seemingly allegorical locations that are in fact all too real and indexical, a nonpsychological use of actors.[64] Because of the inevitable othering she encounters in art cinema venues as a Muslim woman director wearing hijab, the contemporary political positioning of Iran, and the fact that she shares a house style with the four other image makers who constitute her family, Samira Makhmalbaf's directorial persona is also a very visible site of negotiation of the meanings of female exceptionalism and aesthetic agency. In contrast to Martel's mystique of provincial, self-taught, and cerebral writer-director who navigates a competitive national industrial context, Makhmalbaf is almost melodramatically positioned as a voice that echoes the agonistic relationship of her father with the Iranian theocracy. The different ways that the two directors both invoke and complicate the abstractions of genius auteur and Woman as icon, taken together, help map the terrain of female authorship in global art cinema at the start of the twenty-first century.

As Jonathan Romney states in the *Independent*, "Samira carries a responsibility that few film-makers have to contend with, . . . partly by virtue of being the only young female director from an Islamic country to achieve international fame."[65] Makhmalbaf resoundingly answers the A-list film festival call to auteurist singularity, figuring the conundrum of the woman cineaste against a stark geopolitical background. Like Martel, she is alternately seen on the festival circuit as standing in for and transcending the nation. I hope to show that in a manner similar to Martel's ethical refusal of both these positions, Makhmalbaf's work in Afghanistan troubles her exceptional status.

Samira Makhmalbaf's Sororal Cinema

Samira Makhmalbaf (b. 1980) became the youngest director selected for the main competition at Cannes with her extraordinary directorial debut, *Sib / The Apple* (1999). She remarked of her reception, "One critic asked: 'What kind of a country is Iran? Is it a place where twelve-year-old girls are incarcerated or where eighteen-year-old girls make movies?'"[66] She shows that it is both—even a place where young women make movies about such girls. *The Apple* depicts twin sisters, whose overprotective father and blind, mentally ill mother had kept them inside their whole lives, in their first weeks of contact with the outside world. Arriving on the scene with camera and 35mm film stock (allocated to her father for another project) shortly after social services intervened and the story broke, Makhmalbaf makes her first contact with the outside world as a director through the story she crafts with her father's script and the participation of the girls and their father.[67] Gender, youth, questions of public and private and familial and cultural identity—crucial discourses constructing Makhmalbaf's persona—are all featured in this first film, as are ethical issues of consent and the border between documentary and fiction. After this debut, Samira continued to use the international film festival circuit to access a public forum.

For cinephiles, Samira Makhmalbaf's path to Cannes is not uncharted. The selection of *The Apple* can be seen as part of a juggernaut of Iranian films competing and winning prizes in international festivals since the late 1980s, led by Abbas Kiarostami, whose *T'am e guilass / Taste of Cherry* won the Palme d'Or in 1997.[68] If Makhmalbaf's youth renews Kiarostami's national legacy on the international film circuit, generational succession is even more notable in relation to her father, Mohsen Makhmalbaf, whose films and political involvement have kept him before the public eye—in Iran and internationally—to a much greater degree than most cineastes. Active in the 1979 Islamic Revolution and jailed under the shah, Makhmalbaf emerged as a leading humanist voice in the 1980s and 1990s when Mohammed Khatami served as minister of culture before assuming the presidency in 1997. Soon Mohsen's daughters Samira and Hana (b. 1988) and his wife, Marzieh Meshkini (b. 1969)—who, along with his son Maysam, were homeschooled in cinema—established individual reputations as filmmakers with significant track records at major international festivals. The first of the family's films to be shot in Afghanistan, Mohsen's *Kandahar*, screened in competition at Cannes in 2001.[69] When the Khatami regime ended in 2005 with the election of Mahmoud Ahmadinejad and Mohsen's exile, European financing sustained the family's work.

Working in a theocracy with strict censorship, the Makhmalbafs shared with Kiarostami and other prominent Iranian filmmakers an adaptive aesthetic combining formal beauty and restraint with documentary-like realism, nonurban settings, and simple stories. Detractors accuse these art film directors of adopting a generic style that ignores urban reality and appeals primarily to foreign viewers, pointing to the large number of international awards for Iranian films since the late 1980s.[70] In fact, despite the country's tense political relations with the United States and European Union, Iran could be seen as a strategic ally on the international festival circuit. As a form of cultural diplomacy, Iranian cinema's participation in film festivals humanized the country's image and reminded the world of a rich Persian artistic lineage, while at the same time allowing for filmmakers to challenge official culture indirectly.

An aestheticized film language whose surface conforms to the censors and that courts international success brings to mind the 1980s work of fifth-generation Chinese directors. Rey Chow argues in *Primitive Passions* that these filmmakers coded their critiques of contemporary Chinese society by constructing a "primitive" image of China identified with tradition, the rural, and femininity. Yet Iranian cinema for export could not rely on such explicitly gendered encodings of the national because of Islamic restrictions on the depiction of women and relations between the sexes enforced by government film policy and censorship as well as social norms of modesty. Women shown on screen are appearing in public, no matter the setting or fiction they inhabit, and thus actors must wear head covering. Filmmakers often avoided showing women in domestic situations or even altogether—accounting for the high number of films with outdoor settings or child protagonists. But gender and feminism became increasingly foregrounded in the New Iranian Cinema, in the work of dissenting male and female auteurs and in the incisive scholarly literature.[71] Given the close ties of the Makhmalbafs with the film festival network as Samira and her siblings were growing up, her festival debut can be seen as part of the political deployment of images of Iranian women between West and East, on screen and off.

This reading is not to downplay the number of successful Iranian women directors who preceded Samira but rather to suggest that she, like them, uses this double inscription to her advantage. Rakhshan Bani-Etemad and Tahmineh Milani are among the country's most prominent filmmakers, and they have both made numerous outspoken films about women and women's issues. Bani-Etemad works in both documentary and fiction and Milani explores women's oppression in highly successful melodramas.[72] But these directors are best known to Iranian audiences. Samira Makhmalbaf has stepped confidently into an international public role—that of unique auteur historically characteristic of the prestige festivals.

Coming from a country vilified for its Islamic extremism presents her as an "exceptional anomaly," even though the situation in Iran, or even in her family, belies this unique status. Excessive press attention to appearance, a familiar trope with women directors—ranging from comments on Riefenstahl's or Bigelow's beauty to Sofia Coppola's designer clothes—undergoes a twist in her case. Not only does she employ the built-in iconic value of the woman director, but she also wears hijab. Amply illustrated press accounts portray her as dressed characteristically in black, a black scarf draped loosely over her head, a style particularly striking when juxtaposed with equipment or the trappings of film festival glamour (fig. 1.7). Her appearances at press conferences for The Apple made Makhmalbaf, with her striking youth, slight build, and physical and verbal expressiveness, a cinephile's celebrity. Samira began a close association with the Cannes Film Festival—with three of her four features officially selected, two Jury Prizes, an invited address on the subject of the digital revolution in 2000, and a stint on the short film jury.[73]

FIGURE 1.7 Samira Makhmalbaf.

One might argue that this prestige means that Makhmalbaf has been reterritorialized as a national film director. Or that—like Coppola or Asia Argento—as the daughter of a famous filmmaker, her authorship is a sign of Mohsen Makhmalbaf's authority. Interestingly, the paternal question and the national question converge in a single entity—the production company Makhmalbaf Film House—that can't be reduced to either discourse. A contradictory formation, the production company is domestic and artisanal rather than industrial or state sanctioned, headed by the father and identified with the family name, yet home to more women than men. The family moved to Afghanistan in 2006 and finally left for the West after the contested reelection of Ahmadinejad in 2009; the house is in exile.

Clearly the Makhmalbafs, famous and politically outspoken in Iran, have a complex relationship to the nation. Their interest in sub- and transnational filmmaking—making films about ethnic minorities and filming in and across borders with the help of coproduction funds—arose as much to evade official censorship as for humanitarian reasons. Hamid Dabashi argues that Afghanistan served as both simulacrum of Iran and terra incognita for the Makhmalbafs. He quotes Samira on making her films in Afghanistan rather than Iran: "My father says I belong to the cinema now, but I still feel like I belong to my homeland."[74] Her authorial persona is an especially salient example of how gender shapes the conflict between being a cineaste and representing the nation that is highlighted in festival programming.

In 2004, Jonathan Romney described the family thus: "While Mohsen Makhmalbaf has long been something of a popular hero in Iran, Samira is now by far the most prominent family member abroad." By the end of the decade Mohsen was back in the global news media. After Ahmadinejad claimed the reelection victory, many of the nation's most prominent directors joined the wide protests in alliance with challenger Mir-Hossein Mousavi. In France at the time, Mohsen Makhmalbaf came forward as Mousavi's spokesman outside the country, delivering documentation of Mousavi's victory and the suppression of this result to the European Parliament. (He was accompanied on this occasion by another high-profile Iranian-born resident of France, Marjane Satrapi; see chapter 2.) Hana premiered her film *Green Days*, shot on the streets of Tehran during the protests, at the Venice Film Festival in September 2009, and the family soon left Iran.[75] Samira appeared on film festival juries after that time, but otherwise remained out of the spotlight. Not least because of the complexity of the family's positioning, Samira's role within the morphing entity of Makhmalbaf Film House defies the apolitical, singular auteurist script.

In her essay "Cinema without Frontiers," Asuman Suner discusses Samira's second feature, *Blackboards*, set in the Kurdish borderlands between Iran and Iraq, as exemplary of transnational feminist cinema in its critique of nationalism and ethnic oppression and in the way it "frustrate[s] Western desire to reveal the 'truth' of the Middle-Eastern Muslim woman, lifting her veil and liberating her."[76] Although *Blackboards* is set among an almost exclusively male community of nomadic teachers, the film maps patriarchal power through questions of politics and sovereignty. Samira's third feature, *At Five in the Afternoon* (2003), is more overtly feminist. Based on her photographic work among Afghan women and adapted from a novel by Mohsen, the film addresses the plight of women in Afghanistan, women's leadership, and the prospects of reform within the border-crossing frameworks of war, migration, and filmmaking. Like *The Headless Woman*, *At Five in the Afternoon* comments on female authority and relationality and broaches geopolitics in intimate terms. In this case, the story behind the film's making complicates Makhmalbaf's authorial last word, building on the open-endedness so palpable in the film's setting.

At Five in the Afternoon features a protagonist whom I read as a director-surrogate, a disenfranchised young woman who dreams of running for president of Afghanistan. My reading of this surrogate status is facilitated by the picture that emerges from Hana's feature-length documentary, *Lezate divanegi / Joy of Madness* (2003), which follows her sister as she makes the feature film under difficult conditions in Kabul. The first film shot in Afghanistan after the fall of the Taliban, *At Five in the Afternoon*, with its slow cinema aesthetic, is an antidote to images of Afghanistan drawn exclusively from cable news feeds.[77] Rather than attempting to convey immediacy, the film shares with post–World War II Italian neorealist and German "rubble films" a profound sense of historical contingency, a kinship made evident in its aesthetic choices.

Filmed entirely on location in war-damaged Kabul in the spare, poetic realist style of *Kandahar* and Meshkini's *Roozi ke zan shodam / The Day I Became a Woman* (2000), *At Five in the Afternoon* draws its title and its existentialist accent from the refrain of Federico García Lorca's poem about the goring death of a bullfighter.[78] The film centers on Nogreh (Agheleh Rezaie), a young woman who, unbeknownst to her devout father, a cart driver, sneaks away from her religious education (which consists of reciting passages on women's subordination from the Koran) to attend a newly established secular school for girls.[79] Nogreh, her father, sister-in-law, the latter's mortally ill infant, and several chickens live with many other displaced people in the ruins of a bombed-out building, barely subsisting on what her father earns with his horse and cart. When a teacher sets up a school election, Nogreh is inspired with the desire to become president of Afghanistan. A distant impression of Benazir Bhutto, formed when Nogreh was a refugee in Pakistan, shapes her ambition, and she is helped in her campaign by a young poet who arrives in Kabul among yet another busload of homeless Afghans.

Lest this still seem like an inspirational tale, an allegory for a rebuilt, democratic Afghanistan in which women are liberated, let me make clear that Nogreh's quest is depicted as a bitterly impossible one, despite the dignity with which she's portrayed. Even Bhutto, as her rival in the school's election points out in a debate, supported the Taliban (the politician's assassination when she returned from exile for elections occurred in 2006 after the film was made). This schoolmate is later killed by a mine; word arrives that a similar fate has befallen Nogreh's brother. Soon, Nogreh's fanatical father withdraws the destitute family group from the "blasphemous" city of homelessness and chaos, and he breaks down after the baby dies in the desert. The film ends as it began, with grim ambiguity, as the two women lead the horse across the desert, Nogreh's whisper reciting Lorca's lament.

FIGURE 1.8 The protagonist poses for a portrait by a street photographer, her burka mirroring the cloth draped over his box camera. Agheleh Rezaie in *At Five in the Afternoon*. Frame capture.

Defeated in her political ambitions, Nogreh remains linked to poetry and, despite the grimness of their fate, the sister-in-law who remains at her side represents a social tie to women of her generation facing the future together.

Another bar to an emancipatory reading is erected by the film's minimal dialogue and action and nonprofessional cast, which deflect any psychological identification. Instead, Nogreh's serene but unsmiling face, framed in the folds of a lifted blue burka, and a pair of white shoes she wears when her father is not looking function as what Howard Finn and Shohini Chaudhuri call open images, ambiguous or unclaimed shots that are distinctive of the political poetics of New Iranian Cinema.[80] The film is full of such images: beautiful compositions of women with blue parasols and burkas or white headscarves that echo Samira's photos of Afghan women.[81] The film even includes a scene of image composition: Nogreh's friend the poet, acting as *metteur-en-scène*, takes her to the square to be photographed by an itinerant photographer with a box camera (fig. 1.8). Intended as campaign posters, these strong images—including one of her covered by her burqa—end up decorating the pillars of the abandoned palace that has become her itinerant family's refuge. This installation, and the poem Nogreh memorizes, attest to the power of the aesthetic, not as transcendence but as glimpses of an as yet unrepresentable future.

Makhmalbaf's authorial inscription lies both in these figures of art making and in the film's core proposition: female subject of unlikely ambition who challenges, in image and enunciation, concepts of the nation. Yet if I read Makhmalbaf's authorial imprint in the film's staging of a story of female aspiration to authority and uniqueness within a (remade) nation, it is with a consciousness of the differences between a young Iranian world-class filmmaker with a famous father and an uneducated Afghan woman refugee of roughly the same age. As we learn in *Joy of Madness*, the young teacher who portrays Nogreh represents yet another story. She was persuaded to accept the role only with great difficulty (fear of Taliban reprisal and concern about the demands on her time were weighed against the chance to alter her life circumstances). Even as Makhmalbaf acknowledges kinship, making her movie across a political border in a war-torn country, with actors with whom she can communicate in Persian, a divide is inscribed in the form of the film, in which lyrical touches of mise-en-scène and stylized dialogue compete with actual devastated locations in the gravity of the impression they make. Portraying her heroine as a surrogate and implied interlocutor, Makhmalbaf foregrounds the issue of the female director as both subject and object, creator of the image and object of the gaze. These divisions signify as what Teresa de Lauretis calls "differences among women or, perhaps more exactly, *within women*."[82] That is, Samira is divided in her own identification with her Afghan "sister."

In one scene, Nogreh dons her white shoes to walk the length of the abandoned palace corridor in a private processional. The clicking of the shoes marks the passing of real time in neorealist style. The shoes clearly symbolize her desire, white like the school's head scarf that she is too timid to wear, fearing it would alert her father to her attendance at the school. The shoes are easier to hide, and they are a different kind of symbol. They are a metonymy of consumerism: the goods that might more readily be supposed to represent Western freedoms to young women like her than the political ambitions that the film attributes to her. (The documentaries *The Beauty Academy of Kabul* [Liz Mermin, 2004] and *Afghan Star* [Havana Marking, 2009] offer fascinating pictures of young women's negotiation of consumer and popular culture post-Taliban.) The seeming divide between a populist message in the plot and the demanding aesthetics of the film could be seen as the familiar impasse of modernist elitism. Yet if, as Samira claims, the film is intended to counter—to slow down—the flood of media images of Afghanistan, then not only the film's content but also its form constitute its political message.[83] The white shoes, despite their impracticality, still take Nogreh places. As independent art cinema from the same

FIGURE 1.9 Hana Makhmalbaf.

region, the film occupies a borderland between self-representation and international media objectification, addressing the world through the film
festival, rather than a cable news, network.

The difficulty of balancing the aesthetic with the topical and affinity
with outsider status in the director's enunciative position is commented
upon further in Hana's documentary of the filming of *At Five in the Afternoon*, shot on digital video when Hana was just thirteen (fig. 1.9).[84] Depicting Samira as a driven, even manipulative, figure as she persuades reluctant residents to appear in the film, *Joy of Madness* is as rich a portrait of
the woman cineaste as any in this underpopulated genre. Since the film's
backdrop is a time and place of acute geopolitical import, the documentary foregrounds the fiction film's politics of referentiality: how does an
election cycle, say, work with the cyclical structure of the film, of life and
death as depicted in the Lorca poem and emulated in Samira's modernist
narration? Clearly news coverage and art film are distinct media. Yet any
simple opposition between documentary and fiction as authenticity versus
aestheticization falters on the footage of Samira debating politics with her
would-be cast. The making of *At Five in the Afternoon* appears as a collaborative, open-ended process, despite her high-handedness.

The complex power relationships between Samira and her actor, and
between Samira and her sister offscreen, indeed among all of the women

involved, modifies by multiplying cinematic figurations of female exceptionality. In a casting scene inside a bus, a young woman candidate who
ultimately rejects the lead role is chatted up by Samira. Mohsen can be
heard supplementing Samira's arguments from the back of the bus, but
Hana's camera is rarely distracted by his interjections. The impassive (one
might say skeptical) face of the young Afghan woman contrasts notably
with Samira's gesticulating, impassioned one. The director cajoles and lec-
tures, arguing, seemingly at cross-purposes, that appearing in the film will
not draw retaliation by the Taliban—because the movie will never come to
Afghanistan. Mohsen, on the other hand, attempts to persuade the young
woman to participate by invoking Samira's standing in world cinema: there
are books written about her, he says. These two positions condense debates on the value of global art cinema. The young woman stalls, invoking
an offscreen fiancé she needs to consult, seemingly more to have an out
than as deference to male authority. To make this triangulating politics of
gender and prestige even more complicated, Samira offers the girl's fiancé
her father's patronage: "If he's been to Iran, he knows [of] my father." The
filmmakers' fame is capital, but the young woman is promised not a big
break but the opportunity to help the women of Afghanistan (if also to
supplement her income) in return. In contrast to George W. Bush's cynical
deployment of the oppression of women under the Taliban as a justification
for war in Afghanistan, Samira offers herself as a mirror: a young, Muslim,
female director can tell your story, even make you a candidate for president.
But even as sisterly solidarity is invoked, Samira remains in charge. The
image that graces Tartan's DVD cover of Hana's film is emblematic of this
tension. In their proximity and the direction of their gaze, the two women
are allied. But Samira dominates, and with her heroine's face modestly
framed, the image carries a vampiric frisson (fig. 1.10).

Arguably the sororal model of authorship offered by this pair of films
can be taken as a complex response to the interpellation through festival
patronage that encourages the woman cineaste to make "each her own cinema." It suggests that female authorship will always open onto multiplicity
(the differences between filmmaker and heroine, the differences within
women, the address to a spectator). The Makhmalbaf sisters may not be
able to establish complete autonomy from their father's reputation, but they
deploy their association with him as cannily as they do the support of the
international film world. At the same time the dialogism of and within
their films makes a place for the Afghan women whose images are indelible
though they may not speak in their own voice.

FIGURE 1.10 Samira Makhmalbaf directs Agheleh Rezaie in Hana Makhmalbaf's documentary. Cover art for Tartan Video's release of *Joy of Madness*.

Recall that *Chacun son cinéma* included thirty-three vignettes by thirty-five filmmakers: one woman but two sets of brothers (Coen and Dardenne). The sisters of Makhmalbaf Film House help redress such statistics, working within and rewriting the prestige festivals' discourses of world cinema, with their nepotism and *fraternité*, while opening them up to new mappings of gender and transnational representation.

In this chapter I've looked at how discourses of aesthetic value and auteurism associated with Cannes, when used to advertise a new inclusiveness toward women and/from the South, may actually turn on a politically indifferent politics of taste: "To each his—or now her—own cinema." Yet films by the critically recognized women cineastes highlighted here show with their distinctive and internally divided visions that cinema is a much more expansive place. While Lucrecia Martel and Samira Makhmalbaf extend Jane Campion's unquestionably high aesthetic achievement and her interrogation of female autonomy and subjecthood into a new cinematic generation, they differ both from Campion and each other in their positioning of the world. Martel's heroine has the capacity to act but does not;

Makhmalbaf's acts without the capacity to change things. Through the aesthetic implication of author and addressee in her heroine's plight, Martel suggests we cannot see the other clearly; Makhmalbaf, perhaps inadvertently, demands attention to the way we superimpose our images on her. As feminist, formalist parables with cryptically composed women at different ends of a spectrum of political power at the center of their frames, they represent a crucial intervention in the world of art cinema.

2. FRAMING FEMINISMS
Women's Cinema as Art Cinema

While A-list international film festivals ostensibly privilege film art—and women directors' access remains governed by elusive aesthetic standards— many films by women that circulate in the wider festival network and find North American distribution deploy the concepts of art and authorship in more accessible ways, branding themselves, and consequently their producers and audiences, as tasteful, serious, or brave—"artistic" in a middlebrow understanding of the term.[1] Within this discursive construction of art cinema, women directors can be seen as attracting notice not necessarily because of their superior artistry, but by virtue of their sincerity. In the case of representations of women from the Global South, this association may derive from the victim status of a protagonist and/or the sympathies U.S. audiences are called upon to feel for their less privileged sisters elsewhere. This chapter considers how films by women directors are positioned within a humanist definition of art cinema as well as by the social organization of art house exhibition as a middlebrow and arguably feminized taste culture. More specifically, I explore how what Hamid Naficy calls "accented cinema"—films made in the West by exilic, diasporan, or "ethnic" filmmakers—converges with female authorship to accrue cultural capital in this arena. I suggest that new critical practices are needed to cultivate the potential of art cinema to serve as transnational feminist public sphere.

Both Deepa Mehta's *Water* (2005) and Marjane Satrapi and Vincent Paronnaud's *Persepolis* (2007), two of the films I discuss in detail, were recipients of the Freedom of Expression Award from the National Board of Review. Both stories of young girls, one a cartoon and the other a historical drama, the films may not immediately seem that topical. I suggest that it is their very settings in Iran and India, as well as extratextual controversies, that position the films for North American reception in terms of discourses of freedom. Such tropes are not exclusive to films directed by women—indeed, middlebrow foreign-language cinema cuts a wide swath through art house exhibition sectors—but too often women's access to directing is correlated with a perceived affinity with worthy subject matter.

"Women's cinema as art cinema" is the phrase I am proposing to diagnose the commodification of a range of women's film production in humanist terms. Instead of being received in the context of feminisms or of collective, political, or representational debates, they are recast as exemplars of expressive sensibility, risk, the human spirit, or local color. Marked with subtitles, work by or about women from the Global South is further domesticated as "foreign film." This is "art cinema" as a taste category, and its institutional correlation is what the trade press calls the specialty-market film release.

"Art cinema as institution," as Steve Neale defined it in his influential 1981 essay of that title, has become all the more ensconced in market terms in the last twenty-five years with the rise of U.S. commercial independent cinema alongside foreign-language films as a niche in theatrical release.[2] I use art house or specialty cinema as overlapping with art cinema in Neale's sense, as an economic as well as an aesthetic formation. Diasporan women directors often work at the switch point between the foreign films that are the traditional fare of art house cinemas and the independent sector that has emerged since the 1980s. I am especially interested in how categories of the foreign and the feminine shape this contemporary institutional setting.

My phrase rewrites Claire Johnston's "Women's Cinema as Counter Cinema" at a time when the political and epistemological motivations of women filmmakers in the 1970s seem to have been absorbed by market categories. I postulate that the "invasion of myth" around the feminine she saw art cinema as inviting occurs in exhibition and promotion as much as it does in textual practices, with reference to authors as well as to content.

Women directors continue to be interpellated discursively and positioned industrially in relation to gendered genre categories and market assumptions. In the sector of independent and foreign films, the phenomenon I'm diagnosing as "women's cinema as art cinema" mystifies the very differences of perspective, aesthetic means, and strategies of address that women's films may deploy. I argue throughout this book that such reductive reception frames need not diminish the complexity of these films, the viewer's experience, or the achievements of their directors. However, they do shape conditions under which the next crop of films is financed or green-lit, positioned at festivals, acquired for distribution, exhibited, and reviewed.

More particularly, as I discuss below, the commercial category "foreign film" effectively displaces debates within transnational feminism that these works may engage. Diasporan directors like Mehta and Satrapi are granted a privileged relation to cultural authenticity in their representations of India or Iran. They are asked to speak "as" or "for" their culture. The countries in which the films are produced—Canada and France, respectively—are displaced by assumptions about the countries they depict. Within their positioning as translators or relays between East and West, oppression and liberation, however, these filmmakers find ways to reinvest their cultural capital.

I adopt Pierre Bourdieu's concept of cultural capital in the sense of middle-class audiences' education into the codes of art house cinema (auteurism; absence of genre formulas, special effects, and happy endings; subtitles; historical and anthropological subject matter). I also invoke it to refer to how the filmmaker's expertise and prestige are culturally valued, to "symbolic capital."[3] I argue that these films and the liberal media coverage that accompanies them map gender and ethnicity onto cultural capital, which in this case is not just about status, being cultured, but also about being from—and having left—another culture.

The directors' public profiles draw their films into multiple spheres of politics and culture, including feminisms and diasporas as sites of production and contestation. Moreover, relating these works to each other and those of other South Asian and Iranian diasporan filmmakers recalls their dialogic nature. I begin by sketching the contemporary U.S. art house exhibition context and the place of women's films within it more broadly. Then I consider the implications for transnational feminisms of the manner in which diasporan directors bridge the female and the foreign in these reception contexts.

One evening in fall 2009, the marquee of my local art house, Philadelphia's Ritz 5, advertised these films: *Amelia* (Mira Nair), *Bright Star* (Jane Campion), *Coco before Chanel* (Anne Fontaine), and *An Education* (Lone Scherfig). As a filmgoer and scholar, I had been following the gender distribution of programming in art house cinemas like the Ritz for some time and found this a noteworthy occasion. I had never seen four films by women directors playing at the same venue: the marquee looked like a women's film festival. It was November, awards season, when "quality pictures" make their bids for critical attention—no longer was independent women's work exclusively buried in the summer as under-the-radar blockbuster counter-programming. Were women directors reaching critical mass in the specialty sector?[4] Exerting cultural influence like their novelist forebears did in the nineteenth century? Were the art house and the multiplex becoming gendered separate spheres? Certainly 2009 was touted as a strong one for women directors, culminating when Bigelow's *The Hurt Locker* brought home the first Best Director Oscar for a woman's achievement in the academy's eighty-two-year history.[5]

At the same time, the moment was marked by the shutdown of a number of studio specialty distribution wings amid economic downturn, a widespread perception of a glut of independent and foreign films, and uncertainty about the impact of new delivery platforms.[6] Was there some correlation between a critical mass of women's voices and threats to the very future of independent film?[7] A film like Lisa Cholodenko's *The Kids Are All Right*, which earned five times its budget at the domestic box office in 2010, indicates otherwise. Besides doing all right theatrically, women's films had a strong showing among top critical selections. Midway through 2010, *Indiewire* reported that in a poll of critics and bloggers' favorite films, 40 percent of the top vote getters were directed by women. Since only an estimated 7 to 10 percent of films are directed by women, the figure "suggests that while they might still not make anywhere near as many films as their male counterparts, they also make disproportionately greater films."[8]

Philadelphia is a fairly typical city in terms of art house audiences: the fifth-largest U.S. city and a market into which films expand after opening in New York and Los Angeles, it supports a single chain of three specialty cinemas totaling twelve screens. Reliably branded, the Ritz was founded in 1976 by local developer and visionary Ramon L. Posel and remained independently owned until 2007. The website in 2007 explained its programming thus: "The Ritz Theatres aim to play films which will appeal to a discriminating audience—movies which portray people and experience in ways that bear a reasonable relationship to the way life is lived, or which possess elements of artistic merit or provide an entertainment based on adult wit. Our selections therefore frequently include foreign films and independently produced ones."

As Michael Z. Newman argues, "Cinema is often a lucrative commercial enterprise, and one without the kind of cultural legitimacy accorded opera and ballet. It is only by distinguishing some kinds of films from others that the cultural logic of the arts institution can be made to apply to cinema."[9] Women directors may be ideal ambassadors of the humanist art cinema Posel favored. One might invoke an array of stereotypes in support of women's driving this taste market. In the spring and summer of 2005, the Ritz showed Susanna Bier's *Brødre / Brothers* (Denmark), Agnès Jaoui's *Comme une image / Look at Me* (France), Lucretia Martel's *La Niña Santa / The Holy Girl* (Argentina), Miranda July's *Me and You and Everyone We Know* (U.S.), Alice Wu's *Saving Face* (U.S.), and Sally Potter's *Yes* (U.K.). Women's supposed penchant for character and/or relationship-driven stories and for conversation over action are illustrated in *Look at Me*, *Brothers*, and *Saving Face*; *The Holy Girl* and *Me and You* exhibit the interest in sexuality that initially won art cinema a U.S. market as well as the focus on children and coming of age that women reputedly excel at (combining sex and children is what makes these particular films the subversive works that they are); and women as guarantors of good taste couldn't be better illustrated than by a film written in iambic pentameter (*Yes*).

Philadelphia's art house films traditionally found their audiences through lively and smart alternative weeklies, radio, and nationally syndicated reviewers like Carrie Rickey, a strong feminist voice as daily critic at the *Inquirer* from 1986 to 2011.[10] When Landmark, the United States' largest chain of art house theaters, purchased the Ritz venues shortly after Posel's death, it counted on the area's large number of universities, art schools, and affluent suburbanites to keep audiences robust. To speak in generalities (Landmark did not provide breakdowns) the audiences for art house fare are older, wealthier, better educated, whiter, and more evenly distributed according to gender than those for multiplex films.[11]

Landmark shows films in its theaters that have already been vetted. After premieres at festivals like Sundance and Toronto, they have received enough buzz to be acquired for distribution by studio classics divisions or smaller independent distributors. Although Landmark's website claims the chain's theaters show "many avant-garde films," the most challenging auteurs do not necessarily make it to their screens. That same fall of 2009, for example, I waited in vain for *The Headless Woman* to receive a theatrical release in Philadelphia; but I was able to send students to the theater to see *The Beaches of Agnès* (Agnès Varda), *35 Shots of Rum* (Claire Denis), and *Amreeka* (Cherien Dabis) after their festival dates. Unlike the first postwar generation of art houses in America, which featured predominantly foreign films, indieplexes like the Ritz are sustained by American independents, including documentaries, among which women are comparatively well represented as directors.

As the Internet nurtures new forms of cinephilia, and thus of distinction, there are no hard and fast correlations between aesthetic quality and economic viability. Are the films that get shown in art houses art? Are they good? According to whose taste? Must they be in good taste? One way to approach the middlebrow market is to consider debates around the Oscar nominees for Best Foreign Language Film. Each country or territory chooses one film to put forward, a process fraught with nationalist politics. While long-standing patronage systems may bias these choices against women on the one hand, allegorical associations between women and nation seem to play to their advantage on the other. That there is behind-the-scenes jockeying is indicated by the fact that, as the annual journalism cycle details, the films that get short-listed, and especially those that win, are often not those that snag the top prizes at the elite European festivals. This ongoing embarrassment led to a 2009 change in the category's selection criteria that provided for such critically acclaimed titles to be reintroduced by committee.[12] Without this influx of connoisseurship, the academy's tastes run to the edifying, serious, and important. The nominees' very foreignness implies that audiences who get (let alone get to see) them are "cultured." I use the term with at least two of the meanings excavated in Raymond Williams's *Keywords*: culture as a "way of life" that foregrounds culture as "arts and letters"—and now specialty films.

Let's consider some examples of art cinema as culture, with feminine connotations. Of the four marquee titles at the moment of convergence mentioned above, *Coco before Chanel* is definitively foreign, with French being at once the most distinguished and domesticated of art house languages. *An Education* is well positioned to give us just that; after French, British accents could be the sector's linga franca. While three of the films were well reviewed, the exception of Mira Nair's *Amelia* (21 percent favorable on RottenTomatoes.com, thus indisputably rotten)[13] reminds us that not all films that receive U.S. distribution and get November release dates—even those with director name recognition—are equally acclaimed. Yet these are all undoubtedly "quality films" in the generic sense that Charlotte Brunsdon and other theorists of "quality television" have tracked in the tastemaking function of that term. *An Education* was even nominated for Best Picture (the category was expanded that year to include ten nominees and thus give smaller films—and more popular, read "female," ones like *The Blind Side*—a chance). In *Screen Tastes*, Brunsdon describes her attempt to open up the term "quality," to distinguish between the adjectival and the generic uses, to determine "whether 'quality' was redeemable from the strong sense of class, gender and ethnic privilege that had traditionally informed the making of legitimate aesthetic judgment."[14] While the genre of "quality film" is not as driven by broadcasting policy and ad revenue as is the parallel genre in television, where the term "quality" is used explicitly, art house programming does present itself as worthy fare.[15]

A closer look reveals generic affinities among the four films that support this understanding of "quality" as appealing to good, even refined taste. Ranging in setting from the 1810s to the 1960s, they are all based on actual women—biopics of Amelia Earhart and Coco Chanel, a historical drama redeeming Keats's beloved Fanny Brawne, and an adaptation of contemporary British writer Lynn Barber's memoir of early 1960s London. All are costume dramas, a genre associated with female audiences. Feminist scholars argue that one function of costume drama is to put women at the center of histories from which they are too often erased. By associating their costumed characters' creativity with the making of clothing, *Bright Star* and *Coco before Chanel* might be seen as extending that allegory of agency to focus on things women produce, thus pointing to female authorship itself (in dialogue perhaps with the deconstruction begun by Sofia Coppola's clotheshorse Marie Antoinette).

If the films are about taste (including taste in men, marking a generic grounding in romance, a point on which feminist critiques of these films touched), the personae of their filmmakers are guarantors of that taste. All four directors were born before 1960 and are accomplished, even veteran, independents with commercial track records. In chapter 1 we looked at Campion's historical centrality and her crucial position as a woman director who boasts both critical accolades and positive reception by female audiences. Mira Nair is one of the most respected woman directors working today, her cultural capital invested across several categories: literary adaptations, cosmopolitanism, and liberal politics. Anne Fontaine (*Coco before Chanel*) and Lone Scherfig (*An Education*) have worked within industries (French and Danish respectively) with strong cultural-commercial identities and relatively good gender balance among directors, and both have received considerable international festival and critical recognition, including in the United States.

All four films would appear to address audiences of a certain education level—those interested in Romantic poetry, literary writing, couture, and American history as much as in film aesthetics. In terms of gender and age, they target the middle-aged female demographic that forms a significant part of the art house audience, stereotypes of the cinephile as unwashed young man notwithstanding. In short they represent cinema as cultural programming for cultured audiences.

However, the culture shared by the four films I mentioned is notably Euro-American, though Mira Nair's Indian American identity might be seen as bringing a touch of multiculturalism to perennial woman-power postcard icon Amelia Earhart. Yet if a certain liberal feminism might be said to characterize the women's cinema of the contemporary art house, so does an interest in the world. Audiences' receptivity to women's films from outside the United States has been shaped by multiculturalism, identity politics, and cultural globalization over the past several decades, from the most trenchant transnational feminist theory to the selections in Oprah's Book Club.

As I have shown, the art house today is the purveyor of a more expansively defined world cinema. Women have a crucial role in mediating how other cultures are served up in this space, not least as a demographic in this market. Rama Burshtein's *Lemale et ha'halal / Fill the Void*, the first film by an Orthodox Jewish woman made for a secular audience, is an example of how women's films often play to an interest in culture as custom, with subtitles adding value as they preserve linguistic specificity. Like *Fill the Void*, Karin Albou's *Le chant des mariées / Wedding Song* (2009), about the friendship between a Muslim and a Jewish girl as the Nazis occupy Tunisia, uses the trope of the wedding to show courtship rituals and marriage rites, dress and cuisine—and women's role in preparing it—as markers of cultural difference.

In their edited collection *Going Global: The Transnational Reception of Third World Women Writers*, Amal Amireh and Lisa Suhair Majaj seek to "highlight the role of both accountability and the reception process in fostering a transnational feminist practice able to avoid the pitfalls of global feminism as well as of a limited politics of location."[16] These pitfalls include in the first case the homogenization of Third World women as victims "under Western eyes," to use Chandra Mohanty's phrase. In the second, a "politics of location" can lead to a "de-politicized relativism," if invoked simply to situate the scholar and not to historicize her assumptions. By establishing the middlebrow, proto-feminist context of art house exhibition before turning to my case studies, I have attempted to highlight the reception process.

Water is a costume drama, set in a colonial moment on the brink of change, introduced from a child's point of view. Its subject—the treatment of widows in 1930s India—appeals (and appalls) on one level through an anthropological definition of culture. But the film also positions culture didactically—the teaching of Gandhi and spiritual knowledge are seen as redemptive to its characters—signaling the filmmaker's own educational agenda. *Persepolis*'s mark of distinction is the wide acclaim received by its literary source, Satrapi's graphic novels recounting her Iranian girlhood. I contrast the film's success with the more avant-garde *Zanan-e bedun-e mardan / Women without Men*, by artist Shirin Neshat (in collaboration with Shoja Azari). The film is an adaptation of Shahrnush Parsipur's novel of the same title, written in the 1970s and published in 1990 in Iran and then banned there; neither woman's reputation leveraged a national release for the film in the United States. Both texts reverse stereotypes of Iran but arguably still "other" the current regime through the exilic perspective. The consumption of diasporan films brings together the independent and foreign film sectors, and puts Western feminist tropes into play in shaping art house cinema.

Deepa Mehta's Elemental Feminism

It was in anticipation of the 2006 release of Deepa Mehta's *Water* that the design of this book took shape. The film is the much-delayed final film of a trilogy, so my curiosity ran high. Ten years earlier, Mehta's *Fire* (1996) made inroads into the North American art house market as a woman-of-color outlier to the mostly white male successes of the New Queer Cinema. When it was later released in India, then under the leadership of the Hindu nationalist Bharatiya Janata Party (BJP), *Fire* provoked political controversy. Having taught the film many times, along with the scholarship about its controversial reception, I wondered about the different political and cinematic context of the middle of the first decade of the 2000s. Was the new film designed to address the multiple constituencies that made *Fire*'s reception so explosive and instructively dialogic?

Mehta's generation of filmmakers—which includes Nair, Campion, Potter, Marleen Gorris, María Luisa Bemberg, María Novaro, and many others—can be credited with shaping the worlds younger women directors now inhabit.[17] How does their ongoing work, and the vision of feminism it projects, fare in today's globalized specialty market? Again a film festival will help tell this story: when the Toronto International Film Festival (TIFF) opened with *Water* in 2005, I could be sure the film was safely on its way to an art house near me.

Foreign Films from Toronto

Between the continuing influence of elite film festivals as seeming bastions of pure cinematic art, and the leveling effect of art house exhibition, the festival sector broadly speaking has been dynamically shaped by feminist, multicultural, queer, and radical politics over the past several decades. Festivals established and programmed around identity and community—women's, Asian American, Latino, African diasporan, LGBT, and others—showcase works that might not otherwise be seen and that provoke dialogue and critique, shape taste and challenge viewers, and bring audiences together. Yet these events rarely function as launches for feature film releases and do not confer prestige or attract distributors and press attention in the way that the economics of feature film distribution and artists' livelihoods demand; their influence lies in the culture and community, not in the film world.

Many of the works I discuss in this book had their North American premieres at TIFF. A very large festival held in early September, TIFF is attended by stars, distributors, and journalists and is widely seen as the first stop in the Oscar campaign. Despite this commercial dimension, the festival is a noncompetitive event that caters to devoted audiences. It is informed by the context of North American identity politics and shaped by the tastes and politics of individuals, institutional histories, locality, and its place in the overall film circuit. From 1987 to 1993, TIFF was headed by a woman, Helga Stephenson. Programmer and feminist film scholar Kay Armatage was charged with seeking films by women directors. Current artistic director Cameron Bailey originated the festival's Planet Africa section.[18] Festival coverage by critics like B. Ruby Rich, the online journal *Indiewire*, and numerous bloggers brings forward questions of representation and the implications of programming choices amid the din of commercial promotion that characterizes much film reviewing. At best, the festival's progressive programming is reflected in the many exhibition sites that are fed by it.

Precisely because festival films tend to be skewed to the midrange budgets, emerging talent, and subsidized national cinemas in which women have a better chance of attaining the privileged position of director, festivals like Toronto and, increasingly, Sundance open the floodgates for global women's filmmaking even as they function as gatekeepers for the art house market.[19] Without giving in fully to a reading of the utopian or festive space of the event, I want to keep these dimensions in play against the politics of the bottom line, the festivals' market function of determining what is seen on North American art house screens.

Water arrived at TIFF with considerable publicity. Its original production in the Indian holy city of Varanasi had been shut down in 2000 by Hindu fundamentalists, and the film was eventually shot in Sri Lanka under another title. The attack stemmed from protests directed at Mehta for the allegedly anti-Hindu lesbian content of *Fire*. But *Water* wasn't programmed as the 2005 opening night film at TIFF simply because of buzz, subject matter, quality, or director reputation. *Water*'s headline status at Toronto was due in part to another kind of nationalist politics: the opening night film at TIFF is traditionally a Canadian feature.[20] Highlighting Canadian films is a key function of the festival, too often overlooked in the red carpet coverage of the event as ushering in the fall lineup of studio releases.[21] Showcasing the film was good for the festival, as Mehta has not always had an easy relationship with the designation "Canadian filmmaker."[22] The well-publicized (and opportunely revived) controversy around *Water*'s production—Mehta was burned in effigy, we were reminded in press materials—was certainly an angle promoting the film. But it was also the festival's commitment to women directors, multiculturalism, and non-Western subjects and cinemas that gave *Water* pride of place. Indeed, all of these mandates converge, without sacrificing celebrity politics, in the person of Mehta: she's a controversial, outspoken woman of non-Western descent, and an independent filmmaker, and she has lived and worked for decades in Toronto.

Mehta was born in 1950 in Punjab and grew up in New Delhi exposed to the Indian film world through the work of her father, a distributor and exhibitor. At the University of Delhi, where she got her degree in philosophy, she met and married Canadian producer Paul Saltzman, with whom she emigrated to Canada in 1973; they later divorced. She broke through with her first feature, *Sam and Me*, in 1991, and was tapped by George Lucas for the television series *The Young Indiana Jones Chronicles*. *Fire*, the first film in her elemental trilogy, was made in India, with her second husband, David Hamilton, producing with Canadian financing.

As an auteur, Mehta is regarded in a markedly different manner than are such globalized male cineastes as Abbas Kiarostami, Wong Kar Wai, or fellow Canadians David Cronenberg and Atom Egoyan. Cultural politics, a realist and generally tasteful aesthetic, direct and forceful opinions, and a sometimes irreverent wit—rather than cosmopolitan intellectualism, badboy posturing, visceral genre bending, or hipness—shape her persona. Her visibility is also literal: photos show a woman of commanding presence, with long, straight, center-parted hair, choosing—or combining—Indian and Western dress on different occasions. All told, a significant component of Mehta's authorial persona is authority itself. Deepa Mehta presents: *Fire, Earth, Water!*

The director describes the themes of her trilogy on Indian women as the politics of sexuality, nation, and religion, respectively. *Fire* indicts arranged marriage, depicting a lesbian relationship that blossoms between the wives of two brothers distracted by faith and philandering. *Earth* (1998), based on Bapsi Sidhwa's novel *Cracking India*, portrays sectarian violence against women during the partition of the Indian subcontinent in 1947 in the context of a coming-of-age story and a tragic romance. *Water* indicts the treatment of Hindu widows. (Pakistani author Sidhwa later published *Water: A Novel Based on the Film by Deepa Mehta*.) All three films convey their humanist messages through melodramatic formulas of revelation and rescue and all feature spunky, outspoken heroines who defy custom and signify the modern. *Fire*, which is set in contemporary, middle-class, urban India, is an English-language film, and although Mehta's claim that the family at its core would speak fluent English has some plausibility, the language is a clear indicator of the film's primary address to North American art house audiences. *Earth* and *Water* were written and filmed in Hindi, but the question of national identity and address remains an interesting and contested one in her oeuvre.

After a positive reception at TIFF, *Water* continued to acquire cultural capital. Released in fall 2005 in Canada, the film received nine Genie nominations and won in several categories. It was acquired by selective specialty distributor Fox Searchlight for the U.S. market and released in April 2006 to strong critical response. Andrew Sarris declared the film "quite possibly the best picture of the year thus far [July 19], with three of the most luminous female performances I have ever seen onscreen."[23] Fox Searchlight's campaign included sponsoring the search function on the *New York Times* online edition, and press coverage was ample on NPR—both venues conferring prestige and associating the film with social issues.

The director's brother, photojournalist Dilip Mehta, who worked with her as the film's production designer, followed up with a feature-length documentary about widows in India, *The Forgotten Woman* (Canada, 2008). Her daughter, Devyani Saltzman, who participated in the shoot, published a memoir of the protests and of reconnecting with her mother during the experience.[24] These projects extend the film beyond the diegesis out into the world, but they also keep it in the family, emphasizing the personal dimension and contributing to the humanist reception of films by women.

Mehta is positioned as cultural informant as much as she is an artist practicing a craft. Amireh and Majaj explain, "Instead of being received and read as literature, and assessed on literary grounds, Third World women's literary texts have been viewed primarily as sociological treatises granting Western readers a glimpse into the 'oppression' of Third World women."[25] Mehta's identity shaped the reception of the film as a statement denouncing the oppression of widows in traditional Hindu culture, simplifying the filmmaker's transnational background and perspective. This conflation is as prevalent among feminists as among generic art house audiences—both *off our backs* and the *New York Times* published reports of the protests against the film's shooting, despite the fact that these were, in 2006, old news. This essentialist depiction of India as oppressive to widows and filmmakers alike also helps conflate the film's historical setting with the situation of women in India today.

Thus not only is this a film by a director with proven feminist credentials, but *Water* is also (liberal) feminist in subject matter. In bringing to light the suffering of a group of forgotten women, it may be most effective as a melodrama, but the art house's realist reception frames somewhat diminish this potential.[26] Set in Varanasi in 1938, against the stirrings of the independence movement (and featuring a last-act Gandhi *ex machina*), the film centers on Chuyia (Sarala), an eight-year-old child-widow who is sequestered in an ashram (fig. 2.1). The widows who live there subsist by begging—supplemented, we soon discover, by pimping and prostitution. These corrupt activities, and the hierarchies within the ashram, are presided over by Madhumati (Manorama), a corpulent, pot-smoking widow in her seventies. Nevertheless, Chuyia finds several allies, including a toothless old woman who dreams of the sweets she tasted on her wedding day, the devout yet strong-minded Shakuntala (Seema Biswas, star of *Bandit Queen*), and the radiantly beautiful young Kalyani (biracial Canadian actress Lisa Ray), whose light hair remains long, ostensibly to please her clients, while the other widows are stigmatized by their shaved heads.

The child Chuyia's irrepressible urge for freedom is represented cinematically by a moving camera that captures her running, dancing, and playing pranks, accompanied by lively music. One day while visiting the city's famous ghats (the steps lining the banks of the Ganges) with Kalyani to wash, she meets the idealistic Narayan (heartthrob John Abraham), who has returned from law school a follower of Gandhi (fig. 2.2). The romance that inevitably blooms between Kalyani and Narayan ends tragically; to

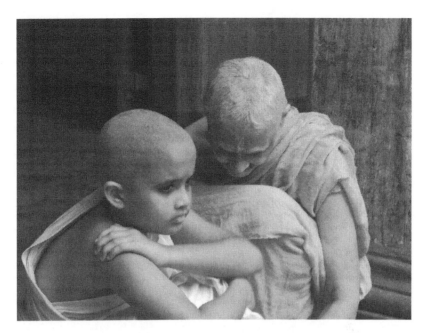

FIGURE 2.1 Child and aged widows convey a humanist message. Sarala and Dr. Vidula Javalgekar in *Water*. Photo by Devyani Saltzman. Courtesy Hamilton-Mehta Productions.

FIGURE 2.2 The idealized romantic couple Kalyani and Narayan. Lisa Ray and John Abraham in *Water*. Photo by Devyani Saltzman. Courtesy Hamilton-Mehta Productions.

avert a similar fate for young Chuyia, Shakuntala becomes her protector. In the final scene, the older woman delivers the now mute and catatonic girl into the arms of the departing Narayan, who has boarded the very train from which Gandhi has just delivered an inspirational whistlestop speech.

As the description suggests, the film has no problem being didactic. *Water* opens with Chuyia's father's question, "Do you remember getting married?" "You are a widow now," he explains, and her response, "For how long, Papa?" goes unanswered, becoming the film's own question. The symbolism is also striking, with water a site of ritual cleansing and sexual trafficking, and, in scenes at the burning ghats, death.[27] Primed for embrace by North American art house audiences as a foreign film in locale and language, *Water* communicates in the universal language of movie sentiment.

Water received an Oscar nomination for Best Foreign Language Film, highest of honors among guarantors of art house credibility. But it's unlikely that U.S. viewers were paying attention to the fact that it took a rules change to have it acknowledged in this category. Now that minority language submissions were allowed, Canada could compete in a language other than French.

I do not minimize the film's power and pleasures, nor the importance of the fact that an independent film about Third World women's rights, by a feminist South Asian director, gained such prestige and attention. But as a diasporan film, *Water* presents a particularly instructive case study for the reception of work about Third World women's oppression. Mohanty's classic essay "Under Western Eyes" analyzed the "construction of 'third world women' as a homogeneous 'powerless' group often located as implicit victims of particular socioeconomic systems" in Western feminist scholarship of the early 1980s.[28] Detecting such objectification should be a familiar critical move. Does Mehta address "Western eyes" in this movie? And if so, to what end?

The film's position as the third in a trilogy (and how many women have made trilogies? Mehta was a protégée of George Lucas, after all) and the renewed publicity around personal attacks on Mehta and the original shoot meant that *Water*'s release was eagerly awaited by North American feminist and art film audiences more widely.[29] If a leveling universalism informs anticipation of *Water* as a film about Indian women's oppression—a reading that the film allows—it fails to direct attention to its politics of enunciation. These are shaped by Mehta's insertion within discourses of Canadian state multiculturalism, the changing position of the Indian diasporan population in relation to globalizing Bollywood, and the 2004 election that removed the Hindu nationalists from power in India.

Water and the Politics of Enunciation, or, Can the Director Speak?

The plight of widows in India is a locus classicus of Western eyes judging the victimizing customs of a traditional social system. Since the 1829 British ban on sati (widows' immolation on their husbands' funeral pyre) the practice has been manipulated by nationalists and reformers alike.[30] Gayatri Spivak's "Can the Subaltern Speak?" famously traces the discursive contradictions around condemnations of sati through juridical and social texts and theories that ultimately guarantee the woman's voicelessness. *Water* is not about sati (though the practice is invoked in the trailer and there is a metonymic association with the burning funeral pyres at the ghats),[31] but rather depicts seclusion, tonsure, and strictures on widow remarriage, as well as conditions of general misery from which sati is sometimes thought to have been an escape. While the film in some ways plays into liberal feminist protectionism toward the mute Third World Woman, it also draws on the affective power of melodrama to encourage identification with these positions. Its 1930s setting positions Gandhi, rather than the British, the UN, NGOs, or the Indian women's movement, as the advocate of widows' rights. Legal reform is taken up by the person of Indian supermodel Abraham as Narayan. (The trailer isolates a particularly glaring example of this paternalism in the film's dialogue: "Who shall decide what is good?" Narayan asks. "You," Kalyani responds.) However, the film's arbiter of good and bad, the one who assigns voice to Chuyia and takes it away, is the figure who stands behind both the idealistic young man and Gandhi in this picture, Deepa Mehta herself (fig. 2.3).[32]

It was Mehta who was targeted by protestors. A discussion of the attacks against Mehta's previous work is important not only in order to understand how *Water* was positioned with the commercially advantageous epithet "controversial," but also to make visible the specific struggles smoothed over by the later film's historical setting. Given the vehemence of the protests, *Water* was anticipated as Mehta's most audacious film yet. (One Internet fan site exaggerates, "*Water* is the most controversial film ever to go into production in the history of Indian cinema.") Mehta comments that protestors who had not seen the script claimed they were objecting to a "film about lesbian widows," conflating the sensationalism of the controversy over *Fire* with *Water*'s targeting of religious strictures on Hindu women. (Although the ashram contains some of the usual stereotypes of

FIGURE 2.3 Deepa Mehta. Photo by Devyani Saltzman.
Courtesy Hamilton-Mehta Productions.

the women-behind-bars genre, lesbianism is a cliché that is absent from the
film, for better or worse.)

Fire's DVD packaging promotes the film as "banned in India" and includes as an extra an Australian TV segment titled "Firestorm," which begins with footage of the Mumbai cinema showing the film being vandalized
by members of Shiv Sena, the Hindu fundamentalist group whose leader,
Bal Thackeray, publicly denounced the director. "The controversy over *Fire*
occurred at a historical moment when Indian woman was being reconstituted as a diacritic of Hindu nationalism," Sujata Moorti explains.[33] The
attacks were widely condemned, including by Indian feminist and lesbian
groups, and the incident escalated into a parliamentary debate, a remarkable series of events that Jigna Desai relates in *Beyond Bollywood*. Claims
that lesbianism was not Indian and vilifications of Mehta as an inauthentic
Indian filmmaker because she lives in Canada both projected national purity. As Moorti continues, even "those who supported the movie appropriated the female body to narrate a trajectory of progress and modernization.
Impelled by different understandings of the global, both Mehta and the
religious right opportunistically used the representation of lesbian sexuality" (122).

Mehta's own contradictory statements about the film's lesbian content
also indexed long-standing North American feminist debates on the "lesbian continuum" and crossover filmmakers' wariness of the box-office con-

sequences of positioning a film overtly in terms of LGBT audiences. Gayatri Gopinath complicates the tradition/modernity opposition by reading the film's Western-style coming-out narrative frame as competing with a more subversive female homoerotic discourse, in which the women's sexual activity emerges within traditionally homosocial forms of relating. Gopinath traces the latter to Urdu writer Ismat Chughtai's 1941 story "The Quilt," which Mehta credits as the film's inspiration. These rich transnational feminist and queer diasporan accounts emphasize the specific contests at stake in the reception of the film and make *Fire* a touchstone in feminist film criticism.

Alison Butler even concludes *Women's Cinema: The Contested Screen* with a discussion of the film, signaling the importance of "transnational cultural politics" to the field. As Butler remarks, with Hindu objections to *Fire*, "the film becomes part of a wider public sphere within which femininity figures as a nationalist and fundamentalist cipher" (121). Arguably, the head of the women's wing of the Shiv Sena is positioned in this way in the "Firestorm" segment in which she is interviewed. In turn, I suggest that as the woman director travels outside contexts that can situate responses to her work in terms of these cultural politics, including Indian traditions of vigorous film and cultural commentary and indeed of political publicity stunts such as those that have greeted her films, she too becomes a cipher.

Positioned at the time of its release outside India as a risky, courageous endeavor on the part of a filmmaker who had been publicly denounced in her native country, *Water* was received within a binary division between Western free speech and a backward, misogynist India. Given foreknowledge of the film's controversy, viewers were encouraged to elide the religious and social oppression of women depicted in *Water* with contemporary Indian reality. (And for U.S. Americans, Canada was nowhere on the map.) However much Mehta might actually wish to indict resurgent Hindu fundamentalism by means of a story about the past, the invasion of myth enabled by the art film's deployment of the category of the universal overtakes the woman director's more strategic position and naturalizes women's suffering and endurance.

Setting aside the prodigious and varied cinematic output of the Indian subcontinent, the *Economist* praised *Water* as "the finest Indian film for a generation."[34] The review continues, "Like *La Terra Trema* and *The Battleship Potemkin*, *Water* uses great artistry to challenge orthodox views. It is in the grand humanist tradition of Satyajit Ray, Ms. Mehta's mentor." Such official assessment imposes judgments and associations—with Ray and neorealism here—to distance the film from the lively political and aesthetic debates of its production and reception contexts.

In Mehta's body of work, the turn to *Water's* historical setting helped smooth out the contours of diasporan politics, reifying "India" and its customs for middlebrow consumption.[35] I've argued that this process is facilitated by fitting the work into an art film niche. As the president of Mongrel Media, *Water's* Canadian distributor, Hussain Amarshi testifies, "To me it's a film that brings back to the fore the whole tradition of humanist cinema." Sketching in some of that tradition, Roger Ebert writes, "The film is lovely in the way Satyajit Ray's films are lovely. It sees poverty and deprivation as a condition of life, not an exception to it, and finds beauty in the souls of its characters. Their misfortune does not make them unattractive. In many Indian films it is not startling to be poor, or to be in the thrall of 2,000-year-old customs; such matters are taken for granted, and the story goes on from there."[36] The evocation of Ray (again) functions here to underscore Ebert's cultural sensitivity and his film historical expertise. Elsewhere in his review, Ebert tries to avoid orientalizing (comparing the ashram to a Western institution of female oppression that features in another 2006 release, *The Magdalene Sisters*). Yet India, "in the thrall of 2,000-year-old customs," is not granted contemporaneity—even its world-dominant commercial film industries are bracketed by a comparison to Ray's midcentury realist art cinema.

How does a historical film manage to represent India as timeless? In fact, *Water's* story is that of a film launched into one political moment and then produced and released into another. As Devyani Saltzman describes the shoot, the dramatic last scene on the train platform was finished just as reports arrived of the Congress Party coalition victory in 2004.[37] The Hindu nationalist BJP party was no longer in power, and the film, which was shot in secrecy under the title *River Moon*, would come out as *Water*.

Positioning the film transnationally also restores its historicity. The Canadian production was moved to Sri Lanka, where the nonprofessional actor playing Chuyia learned to speak her Hindi lines phonetically. There is some irony in the fact that Mehta can only speak her truth through the construction of a simulated India. Other casting choices were up to the moment, with the actors playing the lovers already popular models in India and the diaspora. There is another dimension of cultural exchange in this casting. Kalyani is played by Canadian actress Lisa Ray, who established herself as a serious actress with her starring role in Mehta's *Hollywood/Bollywood*. (She lives between England, Mumbai, and Toronto and has since worked mostly on similar independent films, including two lesbian features by U.K. director Shamim Sarif.) The film's transnationalism is marked in its production, personnel, and aesthetic, if not overtly in its story.

Mehta is among the Indian diasporan filmmakers who have incorporated Bollywood tropes like song and dance sequences in their Western-style narratives—even as the Bombay industry globalizes to address its growing nonresident Indian (NRI) audience. In contrast with a film like *Hollywood/ Bollywood*, set in the Canadian present (and winner of the Genie for best Canadian film), *Water*, set in the colonial past, is a more subtle example of diasporan aesthetics. But *Water*'s songs by Hindi film and Broadway celebrity composer A. R. Rahman inject its earnest art house humanism with Bollywood romance and affect.

Indian film culture was changing rapidly at the moment of *Water*'s production, with audience participation in fandoms, debates, and controversies facilitated by the explosion on the web of Indian film industry- and celebrity-oriented dot-coms, many of them in English.[38] This audience is by no means restricted to the subcontinent but extends to the South Asian diaspora and everywhere Indian films are exported. On the eve of the film's release, the web-based Indian news agency Rediff's headline "Mehta Vindicated?" alludes to the fierce hostility the director experienced; in the interview Mehta says that although she had not yet received further death threats, "any number of 'concerned' Indians . . . are very eager to offer friendly advice . . . like, the 'issues the film deals with are too complex for Americans or Canadians to understand.'"

Although at the height of the controversy around *Fire* she had been accused of pandering to the West, simplifying or falsifying Indian culture, generating scandal, and being a bad director, Mehta, who divides her time between New Delhi and Toronto, now seems more in step with Indian film's interest in NRI experience. As Indian cinema globalizes under the banner of Bollywood (previously a suspect term for many insiders and now considered indicative of this most recent transnational era), the vectors of migration, address, and style at work in the films of diasporan directors like Mehta multiply in meaning.

By the time it was completed and released, *Water* could be received by Indian audiences both as progressive and as a marker of Indian cinema's diversity and global reach. One woman columnist for *Calcutta Times* online describes *Water*'s Oscar nomination as a *thappad* or "slap in the face to film men," referring to the celebrity producers of the vast, Mumbai-based film industry as well as to the "hysterical mobs that stopped Deepa from filming her moving story in Varanasi." As Canada's official entry in the Oscar race, the film called attention at the same time to the absence of India's own nominee on the short list and to the worldwide influence of Indian film culture—routed, in this instance, through the Toronto International Film Festival rather than Mumbai.

If Mehta has been seen as a foreigner by some Indian commentators, it is a cinematic as well as a political designation of citizenship. Like Nair and Gurinder Chadha, she made her high-profile films independently of the country's hugely influential film industries. The fact that all three make films that could be described as feminist distinguishes this loose transnational formation of South Asian women filmmakers, as Desai discusses. "I could not have made *Water* if I was living in India," says Mehta. "It's that distance I have as an Indian-Canadian."[39] Shaped by second-wave feminism, Canadian multicultural policy, Indian secular politics, migration, and global art cinema, Mehta's career sets a precedent for the complexities of transnational women's filmmaking today.

We have seen how, within the humanist construction of the institution of art cinema as moral, edifying, or anthropological, a film like *Water*, set in the past with a victimized child heroine, can be reduced to the most elemental feminism. My reading of Mehta's work shows how the filmmaker's own extratextual image, and her standing as a creator of images, is leveraged to work against her conflation with the figure of the oppressed woman. In the remainder of this chapter I turn to Iranian diasporan women artists who tell harrowing and also humorous tales of women's lives in their country of origin. Their authorship is marked both by an outspoken presence in the public sphere and by the stylization of their texts. Like Mehta, they are enmeshed in contradictory discourses of past and present, here and there, subject and object of enunciation. But as exilic filmmakers they are unable to represent their homeland directly. To what extent does the author's image fill the frame instead? Marjane Satrapi's popularity as a graphic novelist and Shirin Neshat's prominence as an art world star become flexible forms of cultural capital.

Iranian Diasporan Women Directors and Cultural Capital

In 2007, *Persepolis* (Marjane Satrapi and Vincent Paronnaud), the film adaption of Satrapi's best-selling autobiographical graphic novels *Persepolis* and *Persepolis 2* (released in France in four volumes in 2000), won the Jury Prize at the Cannes film festival. *Persepolis* was successfully released in France that summer and premiered in an English-language version in the United States on Christmas Day, a high-profile release date for Sony Pictures Classics that served as holiday film counter-programming. Shirin Neshat's *Women without Men* was launched in prestigious festival contexts, winning the Silver Lion at Venice in 2009 and showing at TIFF and New Directors / New Films, but received no national release. These directors' worldwide reputations as Iranian exilic artists and feminists position their debut films as part of their dissident personae.

To some extent these directors share a discursive field with Mehta and other successful South Asian diasporan filmmakers. Their authenticity as women born in the countries with which their work deals is delivered with the class and cosmopolitan credentials of the woman of culture. Their accents as women artists in the public sphere are educated ones. South Asian and Iranian diasporas are linked culturally and historically; post-9/11 security culture, anti-immigrant racism, and Islamophobia have imposed threatening associations on these groups, while ties within progressive politics and multicultural, postcolonial, and feminist academic circles have mobilized to counter such threats. There are of course significant differences between (as well as within) South Asian and Iranian diasporan cultures. Many of the estimated 4–5 million Iranians now living outside their homeland have been displaced not by postcolonial migrations but by the 1979 Islamic Revolution, creating an exilic community at political odds with the homeland.

Satrapi and Neshat are among the Iranians best known outside these communities. Perceived as liberated women, they provide an antidote to Western stereotypes of fundamentalist Iranian men. Successful book tours that showed off her wit and fluent English made Satrapi accessible to U.S. audiences, as did the genres in which she works—multicultural literature as well as comics and cartoons. The fact that she lives in Paris adds glamour. As a fine artist, Neshat has a more rarefied reputation, associated with European art circles, but she too deploys what might be called a familiar exoticism.

Both films and their sources interrogate representations of women and Islam—priming their authors for insertion into the "neocolonial humanist scripts" that Bishnupriya Ghosh argues repeatedly shape Western reception of global women's texts and the construction of the figure of the artist crusader. Ghosh names several discourses governing Western reception of global women writers: "the role of 'free speech' in neocolonial humanism; the celebration and scrutiny of democratic spheres, including questions of 'human' rights under nonegalitarian political regimes; and Western feminist readings of the plight of Third World women."[40] These scripts also frame how diasporan directors and art house feminism are seen: nonegalitarian political regimes and the plight of Muslim women are treated in the content of the films; their makers' exilic status and the censorship of their work in Iran emphasize the artistic freedoms of the West.

Yet Satrapi and Neshat, to varying degrees across and within their individual art practices, resist the assimilation of representations of post–Islamic Revolution Iranian womanhood into parables of oppression and liberation, dramas of veiling and unveiling. They do this figurally in their deployment of signifiers of women and Islam. The black silhouette of the chador is foregrounded as a key inspiration for *Persepolis*'s graphic style, which uses black-and-white shapes and patterns to evoke decorative elements of Persian art. In addition, several humorous episodes turn on the signifying possibilities of the head scarf. Neshat's most widely circulating photographic work superimposes Persian script on veiled female figures; the stylization disrupts settled referentiality. Thus even as their authors are recruited for politically opportune popular discourses of multiculturalism or dissent in the West, the films' accented styles disrupt fixed meanings. Finally, as I discuss in more detail below, the contested results of the 2009 presidential election in Iran, resulting in mass protests, brought Iranian women's political engagement, as well as their cultural standing, into the media, where Satrapi and Neshat already had a forum.

Persepolis, a French-U.S. coproduction, has a higher profile than *Women without Men*, a lower-budget French/German/Moroccan coproduction (with dozens of company credits) whose U.S. distributor Indiepix is an online platform for streaming independent cinema. But both films circulate and do cultural work under the signs of authorship. That is, they are marked by the figure of the diasporan female artist as a cultural authority and as participant in a counterpublic sphere. The multiple inscription of the name of the author—*Persepolis* the movie is billed as an adaptation of a best seller (and the book is marketed with a "now a major motion picture" sticker) and *Women without Men* is an adaptation of a famous text by a censored writer—locates both films within the discourse Timothy Corrigan has called the "commerce of auteurism," albeit on the art house end of the commercial spectrum. Corrigan explains that, contrary to mystifications, auteurism is "hardly the pure reincarnation . . . of literary models of the author as sole creator of the film or of Sartrean demands for 'authenticity' in expression. Rather, from its inception, auteurism has been bound up with changes in industrial desires, technological opportunities, and marketing strategies."[41] Corrigan urges us to shift the concept of the auteur from the high grounds of expressive individualism to "wider material strategies of social agency" (98). In the industrial context of post-studio-era Hollywood filmmaking, the mark of the author was mobilized to sell films no longer guaranteed by studio capital. It is hard to imagine a woman director today deploying the figures of misunderstood artist and reckless entrepreneur with the aplomb of Francis Ford Coppola—the godfather of the commercial auteur category and Corrigan's primary example.

Instead, the diasporan woman filmmaker may be overidentified with the work itself, as in coverage of *Persepolis*'s fifteen-minute ovation at its Cannes premiere: "The crowd was paying tribute not only to a funny, sometimes dark, always affecting story of surviving the worst through a sense of humor, but to Satrapi herself—for being not only the creator of this beguiling film but for having put her own life on screen."[42] If we set aside the patronizing tone, we can recognize Satrapi's use of autobiography as a "material strategy of social agency." Her celebrity also enhances the visibility of women in the international film festival arena that confers prestige and thus market value on the name of the author. I use two key frames to analyze the commerce of auteurism surrounding Satrapi and Neshat as film directors: elite film festivals, with the circuits of awards and reviews they initiate; and the Western reception of women artists, especially those from Islamic cultures. Though both global film festivals and global feminism involve the transnational politics of the image, they bestow value in different ways—and these directors occupy that gap.

The broad outline of Satrapi's biography is known from her work. Born in 1969 to a politically active and cultured family (in her words, "caviar leftists"), Marjane Satrapi was sent to lycée in Vienna in 1983 several years after the Islamic Revolution. She later returned to Iran and attended art school; since 1994 she has lived in Paris, where she published the first of her graphic novels in 2000. Satrapi soon gained an international reputation through lecture and publicity tours accompanying the books' translation into more than a dozen languages. In 2005 she wrote a column, "An Iranian in Paris," for the *New York Times*.

After winning the Jury Prize, *Persepolis* moved to other festival dates, closing the New York Film Festival, a rare showcase for a woman's film. France and the United States are of course very different contexts for perceptions of film, feminism, and political relations with Islamic states. The Cannes premiere positioned French culture in a progressive relationship to women and Islam (while both continuing its promotion of Iranian art cinema and drawing Iranian ire over which Iranian artists were acceptable). Even the voicing of the three generations of women in Satrapi's family by French cinematic royalty—Danielle Darrieux, Catherine Deneuve, and Chiara Mastroianni—assimilated Satrapi's film to French national cinema and underscored her own status as a cultured and liberated Frenchwoman.

Sony Pictures Classics' English-language version used American voice actors including Sean Penn, Gena Rowlands, and Iggy Pop (though with the real mother-daughter team Deneuve and Mastroianni reprising their roles, now literally accented). The film followed the English version of the books into a market seeded with strong anti-Iranian media images—from the 1979–1980 hostage crisis to George W. Bush's hawkish declarations of an axis of evil—and offered something very different. Satrapi's pop culture references (Michael Jackson, Adidas, and "Eye of the Tiger") facilitated identification on the part of American readers and viewers with a female voice of culture rather than a male voice of politics. At the same time, Satrapi's exile status put her on "our" side. The film eventually grossed nearly $23 million worldwide (but earned only $4.4 million in the United States and Canada, comparable to *Water*'s $5.5 million), the biggest moneymaker of all the films discussed in this book. Like *Water*, it was nominated for an Oscar. But not for Best Foreign Language Film; although it was France's official submission, it didn't make the cut. Refreshingly, it was nominated as Best Animated Feature, temporarily reminding us that a category that was instituted in 2001 and has been dominated by large-budget Hollywood computer-animated movies (*Persepolis* lost to Pixar's *Ratatouille*) is also literally an art film category.

The reception of Satrapi's comics set the tone for the film's pedagogical, middlebrow function. As she writes in the *New York Times* of her book tour, "I had come to the U.S. to try to explain to people what Iran was really like: that not every woman in Iran looks like a black bird. That the axis of evil included people like myself." Satrapi's sharp humor and frank opinions leaven the humanist hype. But time and again in the dozens of press clips that emerge from a feature film's press junket, Satrapi speaks of the film's universality. Significantly, she cites animation as a technique in the service of this wide appeal: "With live-action, it would have turned into a story of people living in a distant land who don't look like us. At best, it would have been an exotic story, and at worst, a 'Third-World' story." In her use of "us," Satrapi identifies with her audience—a national French and transnational public outside Iran, and she disavows, even as she critiques the objectification of, the Third World. Animation universalizes because the humans on screen are not referential and the mise-en-scène has no indexicality. But this placelessness is specifically that of exile; one must draw a picture of home when one is far away from it. In *Persepolis*, animation is also a technique of estrangement, of deterritorialization or accented style—one of whose characteristics, Naficy notes, is an emphasis on textuality, writing, and inscription.[43]

In a scene from the film that illustrates this particularly poignantly, the narrator recounts the passage from childhood to adult femininity, when Marjane lived far from her parents in Vienna. Satrapi identifies this moment with cultural liminality and physical monstrosity, using animation expressively to convey these themes. Marjane lies in bed, as the first-person narration describes "a period of drastic change" when she "turned from a girl to a woman overnight." After a fade, one eye opens to face the viewer, and the narration continues: "First I grew eight inches, then my face changed. My head got longer; my right eye got bigger, and my chin followed" (fig. 2.4). Accompanied by cartoon sound effects of stretching and rebounding, the self-portrait morphs though images evoking Picasso's *Guernica*, Quasimodo, and Barbie to end up as a teenager dressed in new-wave fashion. The figure topples over when the narrator says, "my breasts inflate like balloons" and rights itself when she continues, "my butt expands, restoring my center of gravity" (fig. 2.5). Breasts and butt are thus both simply parts of the human body—like right eye and chin—and freakish external impositions on it.

The narration concludes, "last but not least, an enormous beauty mark provided the finishing touch," as a single black dot expands to fill the center of the frame (fig. 2.6). Then, as the film simulates zooming out, the mark appears on Marjane's face as she applies the last swipe of eyeliner (fig. 2.7). She stands before a full-length mirror, fully reconstituted (fig. 2.8). But while the eyeliner is removable, the beauty mark is not. Emerging at the same time as breasts and butt, the mark is a focal point for an adult female identity, one formed amid displacement. In the next scene, Marjane will meet a boy and pass as French, as if this newly accessed feminine masquerade can facilitate her ethnic assimilation or make it readable as an acceptable exoticism.

But that beauty mark is also an inscription of the author: an indexical sign of her hand, the trace of her pen point as a graphic artist and animator. The purely formal image that fills the screen—the scene's somewhat exceptional departure from the film's stylized, yet still anthropomorphic realism—gives this moment emphasis, as does the next image of a poised

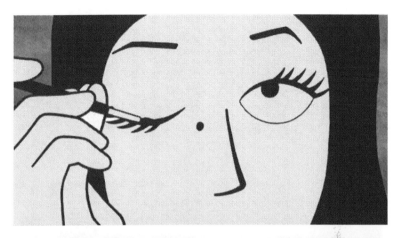

FIGURES 2.4–2.8 Marjane transforms overnight into a woman (with a pencil) in *Persepolis*. Frame captures. Sony Pictures Classics.

Marjane, (eye) pencil in hand. The beauty mark also distinguishes Satrapi's iconic authorial image. The mole is prominent in her self-portraits, part of what she sees in the mirror as uniquely resembling herself and then reflects to her readers. Finally, it is symbolic—Satrapi's graphic signature, a dark spot that in the autobiographical narrative signifies her accession to adult female and arguably also exilic identity, a racialized difference from the Austrian and later French people she lives among.

In carrying strong elements of her graphic style into the movie's animation, from artisanal self-inscription to an industrial model of collective production (the movie was hand drawn with a large team of animators), Satrapi creates a dimension of referentiality. But it is decidedly not photographic referentiality, not only because such a technique would in her view exoticize the movie, but also because access to Iran was forbidden. Animation thus functions as a dimension of accented style, which in Naficy's framework works against universalizing.[44] Finally, like the comics from which it is adapted, *Persepolis* risks alienating, through its use of a popular form, precisely the middlebrow audiences I am suggesting are most primed to consume authentic testimony from Third World women writers. The film refuses local color—except in framing scenes set in the airport in France, it's even in black and white. Although it does reach out in its storytelling to audiences who are addressed as ignorant about, even potentially hostile to, her country, it also motivates that address by positioning readers in relation to childhood and adolescent discovery. As part of Satrapi's corpus, this feature-length cartoon contributes to an authorial persona that is marked by, but not reduced to, the discursive frames of middlebrow reception I have outlined. By describing the pain of her migration and developing a style to render both here and there strange, her works disrupt easy tradition/ modernity, East/West, and high/low dichotomies.

Aesthetic correlates of exilic deterritorialization are strikingly foregrounded in the work of Shirin Neshat; but in contrast to Satrapi's embrace of animation as a potentially populist form, Neshat, a fine artist, turns the feature film format into something strange and perhaps inassimilable even to an art house palate. Born in 1957 to parents she characterizes as Western-identified under the shah, Neshat left Iran to be educated in the United States before the 1978 Islamic Revolution. After visits to Iran in the early 1990s, she began producing the body of work about women and Islam that earned her international reputation. In her acclaimed series of photographs titled *Women of Allah* (1993–1997), women in traditional Islamic dress, often posed with guns, are inscribed with Persian calligraphy.

Neshat's installation works were at the forefront of the convergence between the gallery and moving-image media. One of the two facing screens in the video installation *Rapture* (1999) features women's black-draped forms as aesthetic elements in a mysterious landscape; the other depicts men in white shirts. The viewer, caught between the genders in physical space, is simultaneously culturally displaced. In these works, Neshat's critique of patriarchal Islam is more symbolic than straightforward. In contrast to the manner in which Satrapi fills the iconic image of the chador with autobiographical (if irreverent) content, Neshat deliberately empties her highly formalized images of veiled women of concrete reference.

Neshat's move to feature filmmaking is a way to address a larger audience, to narrativize the mysterious images of her photography and installation work. Yet fittingly, Shahrnush Parsipur's novel *Women without Men*, usually described as magical realist, does not lend itself to straightforward storytelling. The text interweaves the stories and desires of five Iranian women from different walks of life—including a widow, a victim of rape, and a prostitute—who come to live together in a house within a walled garden. While preparing the theatrical feature, Neshat produced installation pieces and shorts (*Mahdokht*, 2004; *Zarin*, 2005) featuring the individual female characters, thus multiplying intertextual references to Parsipur's text. Both dissident feminist artists become implicitly included in the series of remarkable Iranian women the work portrays.

Women without Men provides a different kind of immersive presentation of the style and themes of Neshat's gallery work. The central visual and thematic trope of the garden, the orchard where the women gather, combines the open and the closed space-times (chronotopes) Naficy identifies with representations of homeland and exile respectively.[45] Sweeping camera movements open up what might seem to be a garden enclosure to a wide-screen cinematic expanse, and mystical encounters in which women merge with landscape elements function as stylistic markers of exile both physical and psychic (fig. 2.9). I do not wish to argue that the fine artist's formalism thwarts middlebrow consumption in this case; on the contrary, I want to suggest that it is Neshat's attempt to translate her work that allows us to pose the question of art house address outside familiar frames.

Women without Men opens with a remarkable sequence of images of a black-haired, black-draped young woman (her name is Munis, we soon learn, played by Shabnam Toloui) on the roof of a whitewashed building against a blue sky during the call to prayers. A point-of-view shot of the pavement below and a long shot of her nervous pacing create anxiety. A

FIGURE 2.9 Shirin Neshat's beautiful composition shows a female figure in a landscape of exile. Orsolya Tóth in *Women without Men*. Indiepix.

low-angle shot of her peering over the roof's edge is followed by a medium shot from behind from which the black shape of her head and shoulders slides and disappears in what seems like slow motion—the ends of her hair are the only trace of movement within the frame (figs. 2.10–2.11). But instead of a thud or a repetition of the point-of-view shot, a match on action follows the black head scarf puddling on the pavement (fig. 2.12). As the image cuts to a medium shot of Munis's face and bare head framed against open sky, flying like Superman, the diegetic sound cuts out abruptly (fig. 2.13). A female voiceover comes in: "Silence, now I'll have silence, and nothing." The soaring motion from right to left is picked up across several dissolves by a virtuosic crane shot that carries the film along a stream and under a natural bridge into the orchard, where, a full three minutes later, the film's title appears, in English and Persian, over an image of trees animated by fog and natural sounds.

As otherworldly as the 3-D establishing shots of Pandora in *Avatar* (2010), the introduction to the space of Neshat's film links spectatorship to a disembodiment that is female and powerful, at once culturally anchored and transcendent. Is Munis dead, or liberated? The question is deferred by the film's sounds and images, including those of other female characters in extremis. The precise syntax of these opening shots transforms continuity to conjure an impossible location.

Shot in Morocco with a predominantly Iranian diasporan cast, the film also represents literal deterritorialization. The specifications—running time, date, country, aspect ratio—on the DVD box include an asterisk. "*Women Without Men is a French/German/Moroccan Production filmed with an Iranian Crew. This film is currently banned in Iran." Cinema itself

FIGURES 2.10–2.13 Munis's jump from the rooftop in the opening scene is revisited later in the film. Shabnam Toloui in *Women without Men*. Frame captures. Indiepix.

is figured as a powerfully fantasmatic nonplace, while its manifestations are directly tied to geopolitics.

Women without Men premiered at the Venice Film Festival in August 2009 amid a spectacular display of green on the red carpet, in solidarity with Iran's Green Revolution that had erupted in June of that year. Neshat, Parsipur, and the actors wore green gowns and sashes at the premiere, as did many celebrity guests.[46] The jury, led by Ang Lee, awarded *Women without Men* the Silver Lion for Best Director, providing a preview of a possible convergence of transnational feminist cultural politics with the popular protests, successful revolutions, and violent crackdowns that would soon spread into the Arab world.

Neshat's award was also a classic sign of European cultural distinction. She had already been feted in Venice, where she received the prestigious International Award at the forty-eighth Biennale in 1999 for *Turbulent* and *Rapture*. As a Middle Eastern woman artist who makes work about the gender politics of Islam, she has been patronized as a cultural insider by art establishments in both Europe and North America. Writing for the *Huffington Post* in December 2010, critic G. Roger Denson declared Neshat Artist of the Decade, "because more than any other artist I can call to mind, the impact of her work far transcends the realms of art in reflecting the most vital and far-reaching struggle to assert human rights."[47] Although the essay offers an extensive analysis of her work, the discourse of human rights comes to the fore.

Parsipur's novel is set in 1953, during the CIA-led coup to reinstate the shah over the democratically elected leader Mohammed Mossadegh. Neshat's script brings forward the novel's historical setting, expanding Munis's political commitment (she avidly listens to the radio in the book) and having her participate in the demonstrations against the coup. At the time of the film's premiere, these scenes of street protests had uncanny topicality given the news images of men and women protesting Ahmadinejad's reelection. The muted palette and wide-screen composition of these street scenes evoke both the historical record and sumptuous dream images of protests still to come. Although the film had already been edited, Neshat was able to acknowledge this resonance by including a dedication to the protesters.

The democratic movement in Iran had become a decisive frame for perceptions of celebrity exilic Iranian women cultural producers. Neshat helped organize a hunger strike at the UN in summer 2009 in solidarity with the Green movement. Marjane Satrapi played a very public role when she appeared before the European Parliament with Mohsen Makhmalbaf on June 17, 2009. By arrangement of Daniel Cohn-Bendit of the Green Party, they presented evidence that Mir-Hossein Mousavi had indeed won the presidential election and asked the body to protest Ahmadinejad's declaration of victory. *Variety* quotes Satrapi about taking a public stand on the election: "I told myself I was through with mixing politics in my films, but this is now a question of humanity."[48] However historically fortuitous, both filmmakers' solidarity with the Green Revolution underscores the "collective mode" that Naficy argues characterizes Iranian exilic production and helps make visible the Iranian diasporan constituency overlooked in these artists' reception as unique or elite.[49]

In his work on exile culture, Naficy has shown how successive waves of Iranian emigration "favored the creation of a dynamic, advertising-driven exilic pop culture and ethnic economy, which consolidated a symbolic and discursive Iranian collective identity."[50] Avid consumption of Iranian movies and other media primes the audience for the art films, and Satrapi's crossover and Neshat's elite cultural productions affect this symbolic collective identity. A vision of collectivity is implicit in Neshat's film's multiple protagonists and energizing scenes of mass unrest and in Satrapi's embrace of popular idioms. Their work is intertextual and collaborative (marks of accented style) and it envisions a mass audience (although not always successfully)—whether all sitting in one place or linked across political borders by the web.

For feature films circulate in many and unpredictable ways. Like the Western pop music cassettes the young Marjane purchases on the Tehran streets in one of *Persepolis*'s funniest scenes, black-market DVDs of Satrapi's movie quickly appeared in Iran. Neshat reports a call from her sister in Iran saying that her pirated film was already available there in April 2010: "That's what I love about Iranians. They are already ahead of the game."[51] (Similarly, Mehta is proud to claim *Fire* was the black-market best seller in India during the controversy.) As gallery-based fine art, Neshat's previous works were difficult for any audience to access. Now her film may be viewed throughout the diaspora alongside *Persepolis* and art house films made by directors in Iran (the "award winners" category on Iranianmovies .com) as well as popular films.

Satrapi and Neshat make visible, in their works' form and content, enunciation and address, feminist Iranian identities in the transnational public sphere. These identities are constructed in relation to public statements and commentary as well as through their films, works that refuse strict referentiality while bringing history into play. Cinema, while not the exclusive medium of either artist, functions as a collective horizon—even as new media may be called for to organize the revolution on the ground. As Amireh and Majaj remind us, "reception analysis draws our attention not simply to the ways in which local responses may resist globalizing tendencies, but also to the ways in which local responses are themselves shaped by the global discourse."[52]

My analysis of South Asian and Iranian diasporan women filmmakers who have achieved celebrity in North America emphasizes the construction of unique authorial personae around two forms of cultural capital—film festival recognition and Third World feminist authenticity—that have come to represent value to a generic middlebrow Western art house audience. But does such an audience exist? For one thing, the diasporan communities included in these films' address displace easy distinctions between inside and outside, text and subtext, there and here. And whether they respond to the material because it resonates with popular genres and corresponding taste communities and affects (romance, comics, Bollywood, or Persian pop) or gratifies the identification with culture (museum-going, second-wave feminist principles) film audiences are characterized by both their publicity and their multiplicity.

Moreover, these artists can't be constructed as singular personae. For example, Mehta is identified with Indian and Canadian nationalities, feminisms, and film cultures. Satrapi's use of autobiography paradoxically calls attention to her multiple selves. The mysteriousness of Neshat's imagery refers the viewer back to the author to give coherence to the oeuvre, guaranteeing gaps in understanding. By considering these filmmakers' works (and the work they do) together, I want to accent solidarity and collaboration in the sphere of women's filmmaking.[53]

I have argued that women's cinema consumed as art cinema compresses into a humanist frame of reception the dimensions of point of view, historical consciousness, political critique, and formal vision that the strong sense of the term "women's cinema" identifies with feminism, or at least with the female collectivity it addresses. Despite their positioning for consumption as works about Third World women's oppression in the rhetoric of a problematic global feminism, the best of these films reimagine that collectivity from a transnational perspective. Audiences' desire for culture—aspirational and exotic—is solicited and rerouted by the work and persona of the diasporan woman director.

In addition, I've suggested that the very commodification of the feature film—Netflix has me pegged as a lover of "dark dramas with female leads"—

guarantees that cinema will go traveling. As important as the art house remains, films find their way into other spaces, times, and generations. The directors treated in this chapter are working within postcolonial and multicultural frameworks with hybrid forms addressing multiple constituencies: their films include songs, graphics, and antirealist interludes even as they conform to the terms of address of feature-length, fictional art cinema. Perhaps in the transnational feminist public sphere constituted around such work, the revolution will be subtitled.

3. FEMINIST FILM IN THE AGE OF THE CHICK FLICK
Global Flows of Women's Cinema

Five female friends struggle to stay in touch after graduation as the demands of adulthood impact each differently. In another film, the women who visit and work in a beauty salon support each other in the face of romantic difficulties, the demands of family, career setbacks, and social expectations. These scenarios are recognizable from the world of the woman's picture; they activate familiar dynamics of spectatorial identification through their marked, though not exclusive, address to a female audience. Will the girls stay friends? Will the salon owner find love and fulfillment? In the time-honored traditions of film melodrama, political and social conflicts are displaced onto such personal concerns and resolved (or not) emotionally rather than systemically.

But these are not Hollywood women's pictures: they come from South Korea and Lebanon, respectively, and they didn't circulate in a genre ghetto. They were favorably received in international festivals as well as highly regarded in domestic release. Jeong Jae-eun's *Goyangileul butaghae / Take Care of My Cat* (2001) is about friendships tested and affirmed amid the economic realities facing young women at the beginning of the 2000s in the environs of Seoul; Nadine Labaki's *Sukkar banat / Caramel* (2007) stars the director herself as proprietor of a Beirut beauty parlor where social divisions between Christians and Muslims barely register across close female bonds. I argue that Jeong and Labaki participate in changing national cinema cultures by tapping into generic formulas of the chick flick, while at the same time accessing international circuits in which these formulas are universalized. Engaging with coming-of-age and female friendship tropes common to popular women's genres, these films help formulate questions about gendered authorship, subject matter, and address in both national and transnational frameworks.

Tensions among definitions of women's cinema as a genre or set of genres (melodrama or romantic comedy), a niche or programming category, and a feminist project have always cut across the designation. Not only do these tensions make for productive debates within feminist film studies, but they also register actual social contradictions surrounding women's artistry, empowerment, pleasure, and connection with each other. Considering women's cinema in a global framework brings new dimensions to these questions.

While they differ in origin and visibility, *Take Care of My Cat* and *Caramel* are similarly situated in the flows of world cinema: festivals, prizes, limited art house and DVD release in U.S. and other markets, supported by a measure of English-language film journalism and online commentary as well as national and regional coverage. Their directors work within two very different national contexts, both of which, although compelled to embrace international viewers, have cannily used this visibility to revitalize domestic film cultures. In these very negotiations, the geopolitics that might seem at best indexed by the films' plots are rendered newly visible.

While *Take Care of My Cat* was mostly a succès d'estime, *Caramel*, from the moment of its Cannes premiere, was a bona fide hit, establishing its director/star as an international film world celebrity. Jeong's film was one among many Korean exports in 2001; the bigger news for Korean cinema that year was that five out of the ten top-grossing films domestically were Korean made. In contrast to Korea's booming film industry, Lebanon has virtually no cinema production infrastructure, as Labaki frequently comments, and the success of her film, made with a French producer and showcased in the Middle East, was heralded as a breakthrough. Nevertheless, both films' standing allows us to read processes of gendering of national cinemas on the world stage: recent Korean cinema has a distinctly masculine profile, and the reception of films from Lebanon has historically been filtered through the frame of war. Thus the films' feminist politics are tied to the visibility of their female subject matter as well as to that of their female directors.

While these directors may challenge the subject matter of national cinema for export, the plot scenarios I've described also indicate that the time-honored typecasting of women directors as most suitable for domestic and personal stories is not limited by cultural boundaries. One might argue that the directors' achievement behind the camera resonates with the gains envisioned for the female subjects within their diegeses—more cultural than overtly political. Yet these measures of autonomy are significant. Both films articulate problems of female subjectivity and agency with dimensions of contemporary consumer society much as do Hollywood chick flicks, if on a different scale. But the way these films mark their embeddedness in a greater world offers a critique of the culture of postfeminism that defines (if not confines) those U.S. films.

"Chick flick," is, of course, a generic term used to characterize—and dismiss—contemporary (usually Hollywood) women's pictures, romantic comedies and serious dramas that receive little critical but much fan love. In contrast to the protofeminism attributed to the classical Hollywood women's picture, the chick flick as a genre of production and a ritual of consumption is often associated with the postfeminist presumption that the collective goals of feminism have been adequately achieved, leaving the emancipated woman to address her narrowly individualized needs through heterosexual coupling and conspicuous consumption. Female friendship has an important place in this fantasy, as long as the solidarity it figures is both privatized and platonic. In *Interrogating Postfeminism*, Yvonne Tasker and Diane Negra explore such media representations in which feminism is "taken into account," in Angela McRobbie's words, but only "in order to emphasize that it is no longer needed," noting the Western, classed, and racialized nature of postfeminist discourse.[1]

When the geopolitical dimensions of this neoliberal narrative are acknowledged, it is to map the Global South onto the feminist past, at an earlier stage in women's emancipatory narrative, which sets up expectations for stories of women's oppression. Feminisms from outside the West go unrecognized in such narratives. And there is arrogance in the assumption of a cultural lag time, given that postfeminist culture exports the very ideologies of consumerist individualism that neutralize common struggles. (The cringe-worthy moment in an Abu Dhabi hotel lobby in *Sex and the City 2* [Michael Patrick King, 2010] is nevertheless telling: a group of Muslim women in abayas who have been eyed with sympathy by Carrie and friends finally return their gaze, flashing the high fashion they are wearing underneath.)

I'm arguing instead that the globalization of aspects of the chick flick taps into feminist energy through the link with popular forms.[2] Labaki's second feature, *Et maintenant on va où? / Where Do We Go Now?* (2011) makes this strategy explicit, using musical numbers and comedy to convey its female-solidarity, antiwar message. Popular romantic comedies, domestic dramas, and star biographies are enjoyed, and made, by women in Europe, Latin America, Southeast Asia, and elsewhere. Their scenarios—mother-daughter dramas, work/love conflicts, makeover plots, weddings gone awry, and so on—can hardly be considered Hollywood exports. Their themes—homosocial bonds; critiques of women's limited role in the public sphere and inequities in the domestic one; the radical implications of reformed kinds of intimacy—also inform the global chick flick.[3] The scholarship on world cinema has yet to address these multidirectional flows and the ways women filmmakers modify the process by which national cinemas cross into transnational fields.

Jeong Jae-eun's *Take Care of My Cat* represents a moment of promise in women's cinema in South Korea, a movement that participates, albeit at a disadvantage, in the momentum of that country's remarkably vigorous domestic film culture. At the same time it critiques and offers an alternative to the characterizations of contemporary Korean society in films made by more prominent male directors (and their often larger-than-life heroines). The film centers on a group of school friends from the major South Korean port city Incheon near Seoul. They have just graduated and are making their way in the world, and the film follows the rhythms of their intimacy with a rare attention. Released in 2001 in the wake of the 1997 International Monetary Fund bailout of South Korea, *Take Care of My Cat* identifies the friends' uncertain futures with globalization in the new millennium without making any great allegorical claims.

Nadine Labaki's *Caramel* similarly uses a female ensemble cast formula to articulate changing questions of national identity with the urgency of women's self-realization and the energy of their solidarity in a fractured culture. *Caramel* brackets war and politics to focus on women's everyday lives. The film was lauded in some sectors precisely for its apolitical qualities—with a plethora of reviews calling it "sweet."[4] Yet the subtext for international audiences is oversaturated media images of the civil war that wracked Lebanon from 1975 to 1990, as well as current conflict in the Middle East, especially after the 2006 Israeli-led war with Hezbollah shattered a fragile but decade-long period of peace and prosperity in the country.

Thus, in cross-cultural context, these films by women directors can be seen as carrying out a civilizing mission—not unlike the cultural ambassador role analyzed in chapter 2's discussion of diasporan filmmakers. How do women's films as a genre align with women's films as a matter of author-ship in these exchanges? This chapter explores the gendered politics of genre informing the circulation of global films by women.

Engendering New Korean Cinema
in Jeong Jae-eun's *Take Care of My Cat*

When *Take Care of My Cat* was released, Korean cinema had begun a spec-tacular rise internationally, and a new wave of domestic blockbusters was transforming the Korean box office. But as a woman director, Jeong was and remains a minority among the auteur-stars of Korean cinema, virtually unknown among Korean cinema fans in the West and relatively obscure among audiences in South Korea, for whom male directors like Park Chan-wook and Bong Joon-ho are household names.[5] Yet *Take Care of My Cat* is not an isolated example of feminist feature filmmaking in South Korea, where a number of young women made first features around the same time. Its focus on girls' culture, though in striking contrast to the stylized vio-lence that has attracted international attention to contemporary Korean cinema, is by no means out of step with other aspects of Korean and Asian popular culture more generally, from pop music to comics to television drama. But the film taps girls' culture in a realist, indie auteur mode that also conveys something of the economic and urban shifts of contemporary Korean society.

Take Care of My Cat was highly regarded critically in Korea but a com-mercial disappointment. The film closed after one week, its box-office take of only 35,000 tickets attributed to a failed wide release strategy.[6] Yet the film is referred to as a benchmark in several major studies of contempo-rary Korean cinema, and it has a loyal following and a growing reputation among younger audiences on DVD.

Internationally, *Take Care of My Cat* was selected for the Film Society of Lincoln Center / MoMA's prestigious New Directors / New Films show-case and picked up for distribution in the United States by Kino Interna-tional.[7] A nonsensational story about girls, *Take Care of My Cat* impressed critics both as an assured debut and a change of pace from other Korean exports. In *Sight and Sound*, Lesley Felperin called the film "a clear-eyed post-feminist assessment of what it's like to be young and female in con-temporary Korea."[8] Yet critical reception has obscured the women's genre affinities that I suggest contribute to the film's transnational feminist po-tential. Chi-Yun Shin suggests that Jeong's film "challenge[s] some of the gender assumptions that underpin male-dominated buddy films" like the box-office hit of the same year, Kwak Kyung-taek's *Chingoo / Friend*.[9] Amy Taubin's review suggests a related generic intertext in her characterization of the film as centering on female "adolescents who are strikingly uninterested in sex and whose fantasy of freedom involves going on the road together." But while the film's revisions of the traditionally male genres of buddy film and road movie are significant, they are grounded in the film's inhabiting of chick flick tropes.

The outward markers of this genre's identification with postfeminist culture may be missing from *Take Care of My Cat*. The consumerism celebrated in phenomena like *Sex and the City* is certainly countered by a much more measured and poignant relationship to consumer identity in Jeong's film, which was made in the uncertain aftermath of the 1997 Asian financial crisis and registers specific pressures on women in the work force. If the film is, as Felperin notes, postfeminist, it is in a temporal rather than a political sense—suggesting that the social movements and identity politics of the previous century are not sustainable in the same way in millennial, globalized culture.

My reading explores two primary and interrelated chick flick tropes: (1) the resistant potential of girlhood as a subjective and social position; and (2) the strength of affective bonds between women, including erotic ones, made possible and even structurally necessary within the ensemble-cast film. These characteristic preoccupations of the women's picture challenge postfeminist individualism and normative narratives of successful femininity.

Lesbianism is at best only implied in the film, which is notable among women's films for its indifference to romance in any form (the one male character is consistently frustrated in his appeals for his girlfriend's attention). However, I argue that this implication, within the film's coming-of-age narrative, provides a stronger critique of heteronormative social structures than do many identifiable lesbian characters deployed as accessories within other women's pictures (see my reading of *Caramel* below). The affective bonds between the friends echo the homoerotic currents running through the contemporaneous cycle of Korean horror films set in girls' schools.[10] If Jeong avoids titillation by not making these explicit, the structure of "unknowing," in Sedgwick's term, fuels erotic feeling. The film's challenges to the association of the chick flick with postfeminism are authorial, generic, affective, and thematic.

While perhaps not its most typical representative, *Take Care of My Cat* is very much a product of the contemporary Korean film renaissance. After a golden age in the 1950s, in a context of postwar social trauma, military rule, and strict government regulation, Korean cinema waned in influence both at home and abroad. But after the end of the military dictatorship in 1987, policy reform, corporate investment, and relaxation of censorship produced blockbusters like *Shiri* (1999) and *Joint Security Area* (2000) that transformed Korea into a force in film production ("the new Hong Kong" as the subtitle of one of a number of books on the topic would have it). A-list film festival recognition began in 2002 when Im Kwon-Taek jointly won the director's prize for *Chihwaseon* in the main competition at Cannes, and continued throughout the decade. The international visibility of such auteurist art films complemented the excitement around the blockbusters (many by commercial auteurs, writer-directors like Bong and Park) that dominated domestic screens, where Korean films surpassed Hollywood receipts, and were also successful export and cult fare. In the meantime the Pusan Film Festival in Korea joined the Hong Kong Film Festival as a major force in shifting the epicenter of world film culture east. So-young Kim characterizes the climate as one of "cinemania"—a proliferation of film schools, magazines, festivals, and media convergence at home. Meanwhile, the films found regional and global success as part of Hallyu (the Korean wave in Asian regional popular culture). The involvement of government and industry allowed Korean cinema's reformation into what Chris Berry calls a "full-service" cinema: one that includes commercial and auteurist successes, shorts, animation, and numerous exhibition platforms.[11]

In terms of gender politics, Kyung Hyun Kim argues in *The Remasculinization of Korean Cinema* that the New Korean Cinema of the 1980s and 1990s was characterized by a "recuperation of male subjectivity," a way "for Korea to cope with its rapid shift into a modern, industrial, urban, and global nationhood."[12] Kim's study concludes with a reading of the two blockbusters widely heralded as kick-starting the current renaissance: "If the 1980s was a period of male masochism for Korean cinema, by the end of the 1990s men freed from anxiety, fear, and trauma dominated the cinema" (231). In the new millennium, hits like the comedy *My Sassy Girl* (2001), the horror film *A Tale of Two Sisters* (2003), and the sensational successes *Sympathy for Lady Vengeance* (2005) and *Mother* (2009) complicate this narrative somewhat with their fascinating female characters. Yet Kim's reading of cinema's mediation of national identity in masculinist terms remains relevant; moreover, all of these films are directed by men.

Dominant narratives of Korean cinema's attention abroad and cinemania at home threaten to elide the creative presence of women in the industry—except on screen as stars. A film such as *Take Care of My Cat* is an important antidote to higher-profile masculinist films, both in its story of post-IMF economic challenges to young women and in its backstory of feminist film advocacy and infrastructure within Korean film culture. To rewrite the story of contemporary Korean cinema's stylistic and narrative innovations and its mediation of national and globalizing identities, women's structural participation needs to be part of wider perceptions of Korean film culture.

Although more than twenty women directors debuted with feature films in the first decade of the 2000s, with a total of twenty-seven releases from 2001 to 2007 according to Ahn Ji-ye's research, none has the exposure of her internationally lauded male counterparts. However, several women have made commercial hits, including *The Way Home* (Lee Jeong-hyang, 2002) and *Forever the Moment* (Yim Soo-rye, 2008), and Lee's film was released in the United States. *Missue Hongdangmu / Crush and Blush* (Lee Kyoung-mi, 2008) has circulated widely due to producer and codirector Park Chan-wook's following. In the context of Korean feminism, director Byun Young-Joo made her name with a trilogy of documentaries about Korean "comfort women" forced to accompany Japanese troops during World War II and has subsequently directed several successful commercial features.[13]

Emerging women directors have in the main attended the film schools that have burgeoned in the past fifteen years.[14] Jeong Jae-eun was in the first graduating class at the newly established Korean National University of the Arts.[15] After gaining attention for her short films, Jeong teamed up with *Tale of Two Sisters* producer Oh Ki-min to write and direct *Take Care of My Cat*. The relative success of women directors in negotiating Korea's commercially oriented film world at the beginning of the 2000s occurs in the context of patriarchal and authoritarian ideology that remains pervasive in the industry and in Korean society. While a considerable number of young Korean women have started on Jeong's path to film school and feature film debuts, their films are rarely released theatrically in the West. As I've suggested, none of these directors has a career scaled to that of her male peers, and only a few women producers have significant power in the industry.[16] However, South Korea's "cinemania," as Kim describes, goes beyond publicity for auteurs and stars and genre formulas to encompass film discourses within academic and political, countercultural and subcultural locations, including festivals, magazines, film schools, and media coverage. In this climate, an emphatically feminist culture of women's cinema has taken root.

The infrastructure of women's cinema is most notably grounded in the annual International Women's Film Festival in Seoul (IWFFIS), which attracts significant audiences, many of them young people, to a major cineplex in a popular commercial district. Funded by government and corporate sponsors, the festival is professionally run with a dedicated staff, appealing design and merchandising (including publications and DVDs), and it is relatively competitive for premieres of new women's films in Seoul. Under the direction of Lee Hyae-kyung, the first WFFIS ("international" was added later) was presented in 1997, at a time when the women's film showcases established in the 1970s and 1980s in the West were on the wane. The forum coincided instead both with the resurgence of Korean cinema and with feminist and LGBT theory and activism in Korea. It presented international films and a broad range of Korean women's work, both historical and contemporary. Jeong's short film *Yujin's Secret Codes* (1999) won the Grand Prize in the second edition of the festival's Asian Short Film and Video Competition. *Take Care of My Cat* was exhibited at the festival in 2002. Today the event is central to the global women's film festival circuit and one of many festive moments on the cinema calendar for the city.

The IWFFIS has ties to feminist and LGBT scholarly and activist communities in Korea and throughout Asia. Over more than a decade of programming, the festival has made the Asian shorts competition into an important showcase, featured queer and transgender threads, run workshops for migrant women and young filmmakers, invited scores of international guests, and presented international conferences. The festival's profile, and the respected feminist scholars and programmers linked with the festival, have kept women's filmmaking before the public eye and fostered a culture of "cinefeminism." The term was revived in the tenth anniversary conference, which reflected on the globalization of feminist film culture beyond the Anglophone contexts in which the term arose.

Among the first of the new generation of women's films to be released theatrically in Korea, *Take Care of My Cat* gained a following for the way it captured some of the emerging contradictions around women's symbolic successes and actual setbacks within Korean cinema and culture. Jeong was trained in a director-oriented cultural and industrial context among a group of women directors, against a background of investment in the education and career achievements of young women; however, both her film's content and her subsequent career suggest young women's economic and public standing remains precarious.

The movie begins with its five central characters in their school uniforms celebrating their graduation by the waterfront in their hometown of

Incheon, an industrial port twenty-five kilometers from Seoul. They gleefully sing a school song whose lyrics involve marching over fallen comrades toward a new future, while the busy port looming in the background fixes them in a not-too-promising present time and an in-between place. Tae-hee (Bae Doona), who will in the course of the film take on the role of mediator among the friends, waves the girls to one side and then the other to get the best background for a group photo. Far from providing a utopian image of schoolgirl innocence, both Tae-hee's framed photo and the film's opening scene already suggest complexities, both internal and external to the group, that prevent that image from ever becoming fixed. The uniforms signify not only a bond among the girls but also the uniformity in the social structure that will put very real restrictions on their futures. The uniforms are soon shed for clothing that bestows on each girl a marker of individuality—though the identical twins Biryu (Lee Eun Shil) and Onjo (Lee Eun Joo) remain difficult to distinguish. Yet even personal style is indexed less to consumer taste than economic opportunity—with Hae-ju's (Lee Yu-won) career-girl suits contrasting with the oversized red mittens Tae-hee wears when leafleting for the family-owned sauna business.

At the same time, the multiple vectors of connection within the group give the film, and this moment of transition, an exciting sense of potential. Tracking shots and shots of movement pick up the detail and flux of the locations, a sense of commerce that charges the frame with energy. As graduates the girls are emblems of social transition and economic growth; yet the uncertain economy renders them precarious subjects, sustained in the film's tender yet skeptical perspective. Images of transit—particularly of the Incheon-Seoul subway, which the girls traverse numerous times in the course of their comings and goings, meetings and snubbings, but also of buses, escalators, and finally a plane—capture the unsettledness of this time in their lives. The film's geography is one of locality intersecting with multinational capital. Hae-ju, the most ambitious of the girls, works as an assistant in a brokerage firm, and the office in Seoul has a giant, pixellated world map on the skyscaper window. In the streets and subways and glass-enclosed structures, local and transnational flows and forces seem to jostle the girls like a videogame. With its mobile style, the film intimately signifies the effects of globalization on girls, even as its narrative shows how, as girls, they are likely to get stuck.

As a city film, *Take Care of My Cat* presents a contrast to the cozy or even claustrophobic domestic spaces typical of women's films—indeed, home is a fraught space for these young women as they transition to adulthood.

Only Tae-hee comes from an intact family, and it is one she wants to leave, and with it her father's arbitrary exercise of authority. She locks her bedroom door to keep out the family members with whom she also works side by side. Her final gesture before leaving town is to cut her picture out of the family portrait on the wall. Hae-ju lives with her sister, and when their Incheon apartment building is vandalized, moves to a new one in Seoul. The living situation of Ji-young (Ok Ji-young) is the most precarious: she lives in a shantytown with her elderly grandparents. She spends the film looking for work, finally borrowing money to get their roof repaired. But the home collapses, tragically killing her remaining family and leaving her homeless. While we don't have the full story of why the twins are on their own, they do offer an image of autonomous female domesticity; the film's dramatic centerpiece is a slumber party at the apartment they share.

However, this gathering of the friends is also the occasion for a scene signaling how the girls may be shut out by the larger social structure. Visiting the roof to look at the moon, the five friends get locked out of the apartment. In the frigid night air, they dig a hole and lie covered with newspapers to keep warm until someone lets them into the building. Sleeping outside, the girls are metaphorically allied with the kitten that Ji-young rescues and that moves from friend to friend as their unstable friendships and living situations shift (a dissolve to the kitten at the end of the scene makes this association clear). Femininity on the cusp of adulthood does not line up easily with private/public or even an inside/outside dichotomy. Indeed, much of the film is shot outside—the desolation of wintry Incheon contrasted with gleaming Seoul—suggesting both an interstitial space to correspond with the transitional time between youth and adulthood and that these streets are the girls' rightful home. Yet the film stops short of imagining what a fully public female presence would be; instead it uses the pathos of its genre to signal social inequities and lack of access. Celebrating autonomy and mobility in the analogy of the cat, the title also advocates a message of social welfare—"take care"—rather than neoliberal "investment" in the capacity of girls as earners.[17]

In contrast to the rationalized links made by tracks and rapid transit systems, cats travel over roofs and through alleyways, rendering seemingly dead or uninhabitable spaces lively—the cat survives the collapse of Ji-young's grandparents' home. In this they resemble the other major network trope of the film, what Derek Elley's favorable *Variety* review refers to as "that special Korean obsession": the cell phone.[18] (Driven by corporate giant Samsung, the Korean market led in global cell phone adoption; in

2001 mobile phones and texting were still relative novelties on screen.) Keeping them connected after graduation, the girls' cell phones just as often function as vectors of disconnection and disappointment. While Stephen Holden in the *New York Times* marvels at the then-unfamiliar ringtones and emoticons, which figure centrally in the sociality of the group, he ultimately condemns the phones: "As they incessantly jingle and toot through the movie, and the characters carry on their frantic, fragmented communications on the run, the devices come to symbolize a junky environment in which nothing, not even friendship, is made to last."[19]

Holden's dismissal of cell phones recalls a long-standing cultural devaluing of girls' subcultures and forms of sociality, which were organized around telephones long before the introduction of wireless technology. While the tenuousness of a friendship may indeed be correlated to a variable cell phone signal, the correlation goes deeper than the metaphor of planned obsolescence. Jinhee Choi points out, "The conflict among five protagonists in *Take Care of My Cat* partially resides in the contradictions embedded in social institutions—there are so few options available for the underprivileged after graduating from a vocational school."[20] When these graduates are "underprivileged" *girls*, narratives of success beyond the individual are even scanter. While Holden doesn't implicate the film itself in his association of Asian commodity production with junk, he is critical of precisely those elements of the film's aesthetic that make it distinctive, finding it difficult "to focus the eye" on the film's "overcrowded" frames. In fact this visual dimension of the film is related both to a cell phone–inspired aesthetic of connectivity and to the mise-en-scène of girls' culture, the fragility of which the film so poignantly captures.

As the former schoolmates try to organize a get-together, the film multiplies an old-fashioned split-screen technique for showing telephone conversants simultaneously to link all the friends by cell phones (with the twins sharing their portion of the frame) (fig. 3.1). Hae-ju (second from left) wants everyone to come to Seoul to party. Resentful of their friend's arrogance and ensconced in their own spaces (Tae-hee, left, is looking for privacy from her family; Ji-young, far right, a would-be artist, is dyeing her hair), the friends urge her to come to Incheon instead. The split-screen device has often been used to render the contiguity, simultaneity, and intimacy—as well as the isolation and anomie—of telephony. These themes are recognizable amid the distracting clutter of dangling cell phone charms, and the intertextuality of the device rings permutations on female sociality and romance.

FIGURE 3.1 A split screen depicts the five friends talking on the phone in *Take Care of My Cat*. Frame capture. Kino International.

Expanding on two-way telephone exchanges, *Pillow Talk*'s (1959) party line laid bare the engineering of heterosexual coupling, and *Bye Bye Birdie*'s (1963) "Telephone Hour" dramatized high school girls' use of communication technology as a powerful force of social regulation, as the performers gossip about a couple that has been "pinned." In the scene from *Take Care of My Cat*, affective bonds are ignited in the ether. Although any erotic content is studiously avoided, the film's sensitivity to lines of communication that go against the grain registers jealousy and desire in these scenes and frames.

Nowhere is the fact of the film's taking cell phones, and the girls who use them, seriously, better or more elegantly displayed than in its distinctive and antirealist projection of text messages onto its mise-en-scène. These onscreen texts, which also accompany the poetry Tae-hee types up in her volunteer job for a young man with cerebral palsy, are not presented like subtitles but carefully fit into the frame as almost diegetic elements. Picking up from the credits design, onscreen text renders spaces of mise-en-scène readable in new ways, as if haunted by ephemeral human presence, use, exchange, and affect. Similarly the girls' cell phones enliven connections that are less predictable than the straight and rationalized lines of mass transit. These threads activate and bring into contact bodies that threaten to get lost.

In one striking example, Tae-hee tries unsuccessfully to reach the morose and alienated Ji-young, who had stormed away from the group outing to Seoul after Hae-ju insulted her. (Tae-hee asks Hae-ju why she's so harsh

FIGURE 3.2 Tae-hee's text message appears as she composes it while in transit. Bae Doona in *Take Care of My Cat*. Frame capture. Kino International.

with their friend: "In school, you two were the closest.") The text, signed with a cat icon (which isn't reproduced in the English subtitle but is visible at the end of the Korean text), scrolls across the window that frames Tae-hee as a subject in transit (fig. 3.2). Tae-hee is texting from the bus she's taking unannounced to Ji-young's neighborhood—this budding connection with her school friend will come to sustain Ji-young after the tragedy of her grandparents' death as well as the rejection by Hae-ju. A few shots later, a mail icon and then the text itself appear over an image of Ji-young outside at the new Incheon international airport, where she's gone to find work (fig. 3.3). The text, and the film, whose editing mimics its instantaneity, connects the two girls remotely in anticipation of their physical meeting back at Ji-young's home. And the two are ultimately paired: Tae-hee's text directs the film toward an ending whose promise is fueled by their homoerotic connection. The image of the airplane taking off on which the message is superimposed foreshadows the film's final shot. The film ends back at the airport; Tae-hee has finally acted on her dreams of running away, and she convinces Ji-young to come along. In the penultimate shot the two turn toward us after checking the listings on a departure screen: destination, unknown; journey, together. The final image shows a plane, superimposed with English text (fig. 3.4).[21] This time it banks and heads toward the horizon.

Without depicting erotic longing, the film ends with what feels distinctly like a romantic pairing.[22] Certainly the conclusion is one of protofeminist

FIGURE 3.3 Ji-young receives Tae-hee's text as she wanders around the airport. Ok Ji-young in *Take Care of My Cat*. Frame capture. Kino International.

solidarity, and, as I suggested above, of generic possibility: a road or buddy movie (Tae-hee is shown earlier trying to get a position on board a ship as a sailor). But there are clues to a deeper connection: Hae-ju's jealousy and petty cruelty toward Ji-young smack of soured romance, and Tae-hee and Ji-young are coded as more tomboyish than the other girls. The film situates emerging lesbianism within a homosocial world in a transitional time—in a queer time and place, to borrow the title of J. Halberstam's book. The "Good Bye" with which the film signs off both closes down its fictional world and leaves us guessing about the future of its characters. The use of English instead of superimposed Korean text suggests a transnational journey is beginning—like that of the film itself—but even as the film says "hello" to potential cross-cultural viewers, its final text shuts us out of full access, hanging a question mark over the romance as we attempt to decipher its gendered cultural codes.

Throughout the film, the texts that fade from windshields and the façades of buildings or panes of glass, and from our screen and the screens of the characters' mobile phones, are the traces of seemingly inconsequential contacts and stories that are nevertheless decisive for these characters. The film itself, with its story line in which "not much happens," partakes of this impulse to preserve the minor, the transitional, the emergent. After her grandparents are killed, Ji-young goes mute and is taken into juvenile detention for her refusal to cooperate with the investigation. (It is the most melodramatic twist of the story, even as the muteness itself—as Peter Brooks shows, a central trope of melodrama—keeps narrative histrionics

FIGURE 3.4 In the final image of *Take Care of My Cat*, the airplane becomes part of the friends' narrative. Frame capture. Kino International.

to a minimum.) When Tae-hee goes in search of Ji-young, the authorities explain that they cannot release her because she is a minor and has no one to take custody. Tae-hee replies, "I am not a minor." At the end of the film, her bags packed (including her own likeness cut out of the family portrait and the amount she would have earned had her father been paying her), Tae-hee returns to pick up Ji-young.

I have been referring to the protagonists as girls and young women interchangeably (*agasshi* in Korean); Tae-hee's comment insists on an adulthood that signifies among other things her capacity to love. Yet the film also preserves a connection with her schoolgirl past—Tae-hee was the photographer in the first scene. Both in the picture and outside it, she's director Jeong's stand-in. In *Take Care of My Cat*, the ensemble cast dynamics of the women's picture enact a culturally specific coming-of-age story. Unwilling to predict outcomes, the film is content to frame a moment—however unstably. The fact that *Take Care of My Cat* took time to build a following among young Korean women is appropriate to its interest in traces; it traces an indirect path, like a cat or a texting thread, to international audiences, especially female and feminist ones who are receptive to its messages.

Because *Take Care of My Cat* and *Caramel*—and this is true of *Water*, *Persepolis*, and a number of other films in this book—are positioned as authorial/art/festival films, they are not usually approached as chick flicks. But I argue that each of these films functions to a significant extent on the generic and affective level of the women's picture, and that this is part of their engagement with, not their retreat from, feminist geopolitics. By looking closely at the national contexts from which these films arise, I complicate the universalist reception of women's films as either problem films or as charming but apolitical. At the same time, I argue that structures of feeling common to women's genres provide a transnational and utopian dimension to female audiences' experience of these films. The female audience of quality cinema mentioned in chapter 2 is incorporated into this homosocial popular space, a dimension reflected in the thematics of female solidarity in these films. Taking a perhaps generous view of the audience as counterpublic sphere, my readings foreground the tensions between this common space and the emphasis on individual achievement associated with Western feminism as well as with auteurism.

Nadine Labaki's Celebrity

Nadine Labaki stars in her debut film, *Caramel*, as Layale, charismatic owner of a beauty parlor who is having an affair with a married man whose face we never see. But the film isn't restricted to her experience; she's surrounded and supported by an assortment of female employees, clients, and neighbors, played by an ensemble cast of nonprofessional actors. The salon is a chick flick topos par excellence and a microcosm of its concerns—at once homosocial (but not domestic) space, site of female bodywork, and neighborhood hub. The salon provides for an intersection of types (here Christian and Muslim, traditional and modern, successful and struggling, young and old), a focus on female desire, and the sharing of secrets (extending to cultural secrets such as the caramel depilatories that give the film its title).

These secrets are also entrusted to the viewer, as we are implicitly located as patrons of the beauty parlor. The credits sequence draws us in: opening with an extreme close-up of caramel that looks as though it is dripping off the screen, the camera sweeps forward accompanied by a tango and we see brief glimpses of caramel being made and tasted: the oozing substance drawn out by brightly polished nails, fed to a pair of bright red lips. The camera pushes forward although a curtain blocks its view. A scream: the curtain is drawn back and the beautician matter-of-factly checks her client's upper lip. With this convergence of romantic and comedic elements, we have arrived inside the generic space, and the film's cross-cultural seduction is complete.

Other story lines are interwoven with Layale's, involving sex before marriage, aging and divorce, lesbian desire, and family obligations. None is thoroughly resolved, and the romances mostly don't work out, though the film does end conventionally with a wedding. One of the stylists, Nisrine (Yasmine Al Masri) marries her fiancé, with the other women positioned in the newly respectable chick-flick character function of bridesmaids. While the wedding affirms a traditional female destiny, it doesn't offer closure, since Nisrine's marriage is just one of several plot threads. In fact the celebration and even the structure of married life as it's glimpsed elsewhere in the film sustain the homosocial bond so central to the film's spaces, plot, and address. At the same time, as a Muslim wedding with Christian guests, it is an occasion for intercommunal song and dance.

On the one hand *Caramel* was received internationally as universal in its emotions and situations, privatized by its interpersonal concerns. On the other, the film's success on the world stage was appropriated to discourses of the nation, softening Lebanon's image through the female director's humanizing perspective. Thus while making concessions to international viewers in the commodity form of the art house–friendly foreign film, *Caramel* also frames important questions about gendered authorship, genre, and trans/national address.

On the international film circuit, *Caramel* was launched primarily as an auteurist film—in competition for the Camera d'Or (for debut feature) in the Directors' Fortnight at Cannes—and as a harbinger of a Lebanese film renaissance. Cannes's Cinéfondation financed the script through the Residence program, which sponsors emerging world filmmakers. But neither auteurist nor national/regional designations could disavow the film's overtly female subject matter and sensibility. *Caramel* embraces both contemporary consumerist chick flick themes and the affective energies of traditional women's genres—while steering clear of overt framing in terms of contemporary Arab feminisms. I argue that this gendering facilitated the film's circulation and in doing so challenged masculinist discourses of the nation.

At the end of *Caramel*, a black title card displays the dedication: *A mon Beirut*. Like a number of other works of Lebanese cinema, this film pays tribute to the city's survival of the ravages of fifteen years of civil war. It also acknowledges Beirut's central place in the Lebanese (and a wider Middle Eastern) imaginary as a cosmopolitan city, "Paris of the Middle East."[23] After this dedication, the end credits then open over a shot of the streets outside the salon, a frequent location of the film, with two older female characters, the salon's laundresses, picking up pieces of paper, as if gathering shreds of communal memory in a shared living space. Thus the salon stands at the intersection of two discourses: the chick flick (and

FIGURE 3.5 The sign above Layale's salon holds double meaning in *Caramel*.
Frame capture. Roadside Attractions.

more generally the semipublic sphere of female cultural influence), and
the symbolic power of the capital (Beirut as cosmopolitan city). This intersection is inscribed with an authorial—female—signature: to MY Beirut.

The film's first exterior shot shows the salon's sign, Si Belle, which has
been damaged, by violence or regular wear and tear we don't know. But
with the B tipped, the sign, while still legible as "so pretty," becomes a conditional phrase: "Si elle . . ." (If she . . .) (fig. 3.5). Indeed, the city is not so
pretty as it once was, but the initial affirmation of beauty is still present in
the conditional assertion of potential. "If she"—that "she" read as a female
subject—were in a position of agency, would the city remain a symbol of
war? The film's focus on women and everyday life tests this proposition.
Caramel hangs a question on the salon as chick flick topos. It uses its gendered generic affiliation to explore questions of national/cultural specificity
and transnational legibility. The dedication *A mon Beirut* is at once a modest, feminized claim to particularity and an ambitious attempt to redefine
the cinema according to a female perspective.

Discourses of beauty and potential also define Labaki's authorial persona. The reflexive association of Labaki's name with the film is not only
consistent with the auteurist circuits in which it was launched but also
with her visibility as its star and as an actress more generally. At the time of
Caramel's release, Labaki had already made a name for herself in Lebanon
as a music video director for superstar Nancy Ajram and other Arab women
singers.[24] She was also a visible public presence, almost as glamorous as
Ajram herself. Fans followed personal details—her sister Caroline designed

the costumes for *Caramel*, and Nadine married the film's celebrity music director, Khaled Mouzanar, after the film wrapped. Labaki's profile—even star status—is achieved in a national and regional context with a relatively high number of women directors. But her music video successes, Coca-Cola Light ad contract, and social media proficiency locate her in a younger generation, one that is reviving the commercial prospects of Lebanese and North African / Middle Eastern cinema more generally.

While it has a rich cinema-going tradition dating to the period of French mandate, the Lebanese film industry before the civil war was largely associated with commercial genres and Egyptian styles and talent. During the civil war, a true independent cinema emerged, with such outspoken women directors as Randa Chahal Sabbag (1953–2008) and Jocelyne Saab (b. 1948) at its center. Both studied and lived in exile in Paris and produced political documentaries in the 1970s before moving into fiction film. Sabbag gained international prominence when her film *Le cerf volant / The Kite* (2003), a young girl's story set in a Druze village divided by the Israel-Lebanon border, received the Silver Lion at the Venice Film Festival. Saab explored female desire and genital cutting in Arab culture in *Dunia* (*Kiss Me Not on the Eyes*, 2005), an Egyptian/French coproduction, before returning to work in Lebanon.

Unlike her contemporary Danielle Arbid (b. 1970), Labaki (b. 1974) did not leave Lebanon during the war. She was among the first graduates of Beirut's St. Joseph film school in 1988, where her student film won a prize. In the absence of a solid infrastructure for Lebanese cinema, the filmmakers who returned after the civil war, as well as Labaki and her peers who came of age during the post–civil war period, remain dependent on foreign financing, traditionally from France, and only a small number of films are made each year. Anne-Dominique Toussaint is an experienced producer in France who put together *Caramel* as a French-Lebanese coproduction. Labaki has also benefited from and indeed contributed to a shift toward Middle Eastern financing, with the recent establishment of new festivals, institutes, and markets in Dubai, Abu Dhabi, and Doha stimulating Arab filmmaking regionally.[25]

Caramel topped the box-office charts in Lebanon and attracted international attention immediately after its Cannes debut. Its success on the festival circuit earned it release in thirty-two territories and a gross of $14 million (against a budget of under $2 million); it was the first Lebanese film to be released theatrically in the United States. A women's film from a peripheral film-producing country, *Caramel* nevertheless refuses marginalization. Instead it merges aspects of European and Middle Eastern film cultures and prestige, exemplifying the currency of women directors in twenty-first-century global film culture.

Labaki's insistence on opening her film in Lebanon before France and the use of nonprofessional actors and location shooting enhanced her authenticity as national spokeswoman. As a culturally oriented rather than a political film, *Caramel* also spoke to a diasporan population eager to see positive representations from Lebanon. Labaki commented in an interview with *Filmmaker*, "You have a very big sense of guilt because you're a filmmaker and you don't know . . . how your art can do something for your country . . . but then I understood that maybe it was my mission to make this film that shows something else . . . a new image."[26] This "new image" might refer to the slickness *Filmmaker* sums up as the film's "Hollywood aesthetic," but which may be more directly derived from Labaki's commercial and music video work. But it also invokes the makeover trope, the neoliberal postfeminist plot par excellence. And while some press accounts downplayed just how girly the film is in the interests of serious art cinema coverage, other sources had no problem calling the film a chick flick. *New York* magazine's Vulture column comments on *Caramel*'s beauty parlor setting: "The premise may evoke images of Queen Latifah tossing off one-liners with a blow-dryer in hand, but *Caramel* throws a few curveballs into the chick-flick mix: One woman falls for a female client, another has an affair with a married man, and a third finds love in the last stages of her life."[27] Interestingly, these so-called curveballs seem to have nothing to do with the national context in which the film is made. Yet these subplots do mediate key axes of national identification. The homosocial spaces of the film (the salon, the sleazy hotel room where the women end up partying together after the boyfriend is a no-show) are both postfeminist consumer spaces and an extension of gendered socializing in Middle Eastern culture.

The chick flick convention of the superficially different group of friends is here used to transcend Christian/Muslim and generational divisions. Themes of consumerism and beauty culture are articulated with those of tradition and modernity. For example, plastic surgery provides the occasion for what might be taken as a universal postfeminist story line: Jamale (Gisèle Aouad), a divorced mother of teenagers, competes against younger women for work as an actress in commercials. Meanwhile, the young Muslim stylist Nisrine turns to plastic surgery as a procedure to "restore" her virginity before marriage. While so-called virginity recovery is also widely practiced in the West, the film uses it to signal a culturally specific conflict—

and an accommodation—between modernity and tradition. The scene in which the three friends take Nisrine to the surgeon is comically leavened by Nisrine's adoption of the Christian name Magdalene when she signs in for the procedure. Perhaps the humor marks the film's awareness of its own limited engagement with sectarian divisions.

Layale too uses pseudonyms to take on an identity with more standing; she pretends she is a married woman when trying to book a hotel room in which to celebrate her lover's birthday. Living at home with her parents, she is infantilized by her pajamas and pink cell phone as she waits for her lover's call in the bedroom she shares with a younger brother. Women's culture attempts to bridge these painful divisions: Layale joins her mother gossiping with friends in the kitchen; the unmarried sisters Rose and Lily's shared home is also their laundry and tailoring business, though the former must sacrifice an autumnal love interest to preserve it. The salon, of course, brings everyone together, though in service to beauty standards that are set at least partially by the West.

Notably, the film addresses another form of difference—lesbianism—which paradoxically is used to sanction the community ritual of the wedding that closes the film. When the salon's hair washer, Rima (Joanna Moukarzel), offers a wedding song, it is a multivalent performance; though the identity is never spoken, Rima's clothing and stance have coded her throughout the film as a lesbian. The glances exchanged by her coworkers relay our own pleasure at being in on her secret. On one level, Rima's song sanctions the normative gender roles of the nation, as she's been rather forcibly made over to look femme for the wedding. On another level, her casting as guardian of culture strengthens the reading of the wedding not as ritual of heterosexual closure but rather as one of homosocial solidarity, even erotics—after all, her makeover involved one of the caramel depilatories.

Lesbianism functions more as thematization of an issue facing modern Lebanese women (like discrimination against postmenopausal women or cultural double standards about sex before marriage), a measure of the film's daring, than it does as a matter of sexual identity or practice. At the same time this curveball appeals to the cachet of the secret, the erotic promise of a female world—Rima is shown as hyperaware of the girl sitting next to her on the bus, and her rather minimal story line entails her attraction to a beautiful, unnamed client (Fatmeh Safa), who enters the salon with trepidation, not knowing quite what she wants. Labaki discussed the subject with *New York*: "[Homosexuality] is very secret, which is why I decided to

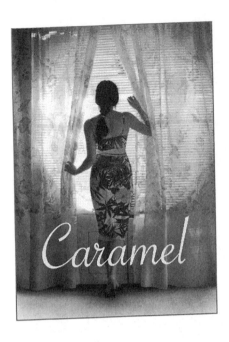

FIGURE 3.6 The poster for Nadine Labaki's *Caramel* combines an enticing orientalism with the melodrama's trope of the woman waiting by the window. Roadside Attractions.

write about that. I see a lot of homosexual women and men who just keep it to themselves, and they lead very unhappy lives where they end up hating their bodies and hating themselves. Many people live with it in secret, but there are also many victims and others who have problems dealing with it in public. It's the contradiction of the country."[28]

If homosexuality is posited as "the contradiction of the country," the film's tolerant treatment of lesbianism functions as an emblem of Lebanon's modernity.[29] The lesbian in the ensemble cast film has become a chick flick cliché. Her identity defuses a more generalized homoeroticism; the other women are just (her) friends. The Middle Eastern setting adds another twist. In an orientalist iconography of the harem or baths, the lesbian marks the diffusion of erotic possibility within such homosocial spaces. *Caramel*'s very title refers to a culturally specific female ritual.[30] The film's poster and marketing imagery beckon the viewer to a mysterious female-only space (fig. 3.6). In *Caramel* this nineteenth-century European iconography of orientalist female homoeroticism is supplemented by a late twentieth-century one, in which lesbianism is a metonym for feminism itself.

This burden of representation doesn't make Rima any less sexy; in a deployment illustrative of Eve Sedgwick's concept of the epistemology of the closet, the salon employee's cryptic identity may even make her more appealing, constrained as is her sexual expression within this diegetic reality.

Rima's nondisclosure also works in another way: for Labaki, the character is a stand-in for closeted Lebanese lesbians; her visibility as an erotic subject (or object) is a marker for the wider cultural recognition entrusted to the more tolerant, internationalized, and modern media this film strives to be and to bring about. Thus the film has it both ways—it thematizes lesbian identity while not having to be on the line itself as a lesbian film. It is knowing about the need for discretion while bracketing the lived reality of lesbian Beirut. There is a palpable eroticism in the scene in which Rima washes the mystery woman's hair (a well-worn trope of grooming as a stand-in for lesbian sex) as well as a failure of imagination; ultimately erotic desire falls back into line with discourses of empowerment.[31]

Rima's beautiful client is an even more versatile signifier. She has no lines or backstory or marker of religious identity; although the stylists recognize and whisper about her when she returns to have her lustrous hair cut short, she seems to belong outside the narrative, in some transmedial space. While Rima's wedding song could have ended the film, instead we return to the salon setting for this haircut. On the soundtrack, the song "Myrete Myrete / Mirror Mirror," composed by Khaled Mouzanar for the film and sung by Racha Rizk, plays as the woman exits the salon and looks at her transformed self in a shop window, a music video within the film. She smiles and tosses her bobbed hair, embracing a public self that implicitly challenges cultural expectations about appropriate femininity. If "Lebanese" has been used as a Western code word for lesbianism (cf. Lady Gaga's "Born This Way"), this scene appears to be a commercial for the opposite operation: Rima's lesbian desire authorizes a new Lebanese female image. In soft focus, slow motion, manicured, and wearing heels, this woman is not herself coded as lesbian; eroticism is consigned to Rima's gaze (and perhaps the viewer's), siphoned into female solidarity and Lebanese pop. Still, her haircut unmistakably signifies something new.

This cryptic figure of the Arab woman in public—to be looked at, perhaps, but first and foremost by herself—stands in, I suggest, for Labaki as director (fig. 3.7). Although she doesn't play the mysterious client (the part was likely too small for a filmmaker who asserts in interviews that acting alongside her nonprofessional casts yields the better part of her directing success), the director is cast in a similar role of confident public beauty on the red carpet at Cannes and in the media discourses that surround the marketing of her work in Lebanon and abroad. By linking this mirror scene with Labaki's celebrity status, I suggest that Rima's desire for her client, which catalyzes the latter's transformation, resonates with the affective charge in-

FIGURE 3.7 *Caramel's* director,
Nadine Labaki, in character.
Courtesy Roadside Attractions.

fusing the filmmaker's public persona and generated in large part by female audiences. Moreover, I believe that this scene of self-assessment figures Labaki's own reflexivity about her authorial image as a commercially successful yet serious female director within national, regional, and world cinema. She invites the gaze, and it is a gaze that figures possibility. Si elle . . .

Labaki used her symbolic position, as author and image, in the wake of the success of *Caramel*, to reframe issues of gender and nation in her next and more self-consciously important Lebanese film. In the epilogue to her book *Lebanese Cinema*, Lina Khatib tests Lebanese cinema against standard criteria for defining a national cinema and finds it falls short on every count. Concluding her study (published before Labaki's first feature), she writes, "one can go [as] far as saying that the Civil War has become the defining feature of Lebanese cinema."[32] And yet *Caramel's* press kit brags that it is the only Lebanese film that doesn't mention the civil war. As the director states: "I belong to a generation that wants to talk about something different, love stories for instance, something that is closer to the feelings that we know and the experiences that we have than to war."[33] The director's "we" refers to those who came of age after the civil war ended, but "feelings" and "love stories" also implicitly gender it female, in opposition to the masculine-coded subject of war.

Yet the habitual equation of masculine with war and feminine with home is challenged when one grows up during wartime, when public and private cannot be separated. If the female-cast homefront film is structured in opposition to war films in Hollywood, no such separation of spheres existed in the reality of the Lebanese civil war. In an English-language interview, Labaki describes being forced to stay indoors as a child; she grew up on *Dynasty* and *Dallas*, Egyptian films and French ones, influences that converge in her aesthetic.[34]

But the ambition to make a Lebanese film free of connotations of war was crushed by the fact that just a week after *Caramel* wrapped in summer 2006, war broke out again, this time between Israel and Hezbollah. The July war lasted thirty-four days, with a large number of civilian deaths in southern Lebanon and Israeli airstrikes in southern Beirut. Retrospectively, war can be seen as a structuring absence of *Caramel*. The younger characters don't mention it; and Lily, Rose's aged sister who suffers from dementia, is troubled by an inassimilable event in her past. But the unstable context into which the film was released made the national legacy of war impossible to disavow. "[Although] it wasn't my intention when I wrote it," Labaki admits, "because of the events, I would say yes [*Caramel* is a political film]. . . . In Lebanon, . . . politics slip into the most intimate areas of our lives. . . . I thought I could get away from it but the reality of the war caught up with me."[35] Labaki's remark illustrates the feminist claim that the personal is political and suggests that an "apolitical" or "postfeminist" concern with telling love stories might meaningfully mediate this context.

Despite her stated desire to change the national subject, in *Where Do We Go Now?* Labaki engages with sectarian conflict. The film was written, she emphasizes in interviews, after the 2006 Israeli air strikes and while she was pregnant with her son, scripting her authorial image according to another powerful discourse, the maternal. *Where Do We Go Now?* is a tragicomedy set in a remote village in an unnamed country, as news of sectarian violence threatens to endanger the village's sons, igniting conflict between Christian and Muslim neighbors. The combination of topicality and fable-like storytelling elevates Labaki to a mediator role, narrating the nation while avoiding specificities like Palestinian politics (fig. 3.8).

The film addresses politics, both feminism and sectarian violence, more directly than *Caramel*, while again employing the formula of a female ensemble cast of nonprofessionals—and the director in the lead role as literal mediator. And this time it's a musical. Again produced by Anne-Dominique Toussaint, and employing many of the same production personnel (cos-

FIGURE 3.8 In *Where Do We Go Now?* Labaki again casts herself at the center of a female community, which in this instance unites for social change. Sony Pictures Classics.

tume designer, cowriter, composer), the film shows the village's women banding together to keep the men from fighting. Christian and Muslim women gather in the café run by Labaki's Amale to bake hash brownies (Mouzanar composed the song "Hashishit Albe," with lyrics by Tania Saleh) to confuse them, bring in a busload of Ukranian strippers to distract them, and swap clothing across religious lines to confound them. If *Caramel* treats Muslim/Christian difference as primarily sartorial—a matter of Layale's cross—*Where Do We Go Now?* recognizes the link between clothing and identity as both performative and deadly serious. Like *Caramel*, *Where Do We Go Now?* relies on generic elements of the women's film for its power. These choices characterize Labaki's unique presence in world cinema as a filmmaker advocating women's point of view on geopolitical questions through entertainment cinema that will play to different audiences.

The surprise winner of the audience prize at the Toronto International Film Festival (the festival's major prize) and Lebanon's pick for the Oscar competition, *Where Do We Go Now?* failed to get the nomination, and its U.S. release through Sony Pictures Classics was unremarkable. But its box-office performance broke records in Lebanon, where it became the third-highest-grossing film after *Titanic* and *Avatar*. The film was distributed throughout the Middle East and North Africa; when theater chains refused to screen it in the UAE, other venues were opened up through Labaki's publicity. Labaki is emblematic of a new era of convergence media in the region. In an online media campaign sponsored by Johnnie Walker, Labaki recounts why she made the film: "I felt a responsibility as a mother, a citizen, a director, to convey this message [of coexistence] before it is too late."[36] The many media discourses that position her—commercial campaigns, red carpet appearances, music video awards, fashion coverage—translate this filmmaker's self-authoring to a world of potential fans.

Like the classic women's picture, Labaki's films are circumscribed in their political critique, and they should not overshadow the many other forms of experimental and engaged film and video practices in Beirut and beyond.[37] But as its chick flick tropes facilitate liberal inclusiveness (Muslim/Christian female friendship and alliance; crypto-lesbianism), they also challenge the gender politics of authorship in world cinema. For a woman director from a marginal film-producing country to make films that draw on popular generic sensibilities and art house protocols and achieve critical attention and audience approval from national, Arab, diasporic, and general audiences is to sustain a complex enunciative performance.

As women directors participating in world cinema circuits, Jeong and Labaki negotiate the constraints of the globally traveling commodity form of the festival film—signed by an auteur but inevitably positioned through regional and national frames. Their engagement with women's genres allows them to challenge both auteurist singularity and the dominant reception patterns of national cinemas. For example, lesbianism figures the utopian potential of homosocial narratives: *Take Care of My Cat* is animated by the unrepresentable horizon of the girls' love, and *Caramel* sequesters the lesbian in the story but can't fully contain the desire she represents for the audience. These films register shifting economic and geopolitical realities within intimately scaled stories that emphasize connections among women, and they address viewers on an experiential level within and across national borders. Feminist film appears to be alive and well in the age of the chick flick, including in the chick flick itself.

4. NETWORK NARRATIVES
Asian Women Directors

If any shift has rebalanced the world cinema equation since the 1980s, it is the rise in influence, both cultural and economic, of Asian cinema. This movement encompasses reenergized national cinemas like South Korea's and distinctly transnational phenomena, like coproductions among Chinese-language industries, or the acclaim received by Taiwan art cinema in international festivals.[1] Asian auteurs have cachet worldwide, their films garnering top prizes at exclusive European festivals even as festivals located in Asia have grown in global influence.[2] These phenomena are much more than trends.

Gender questions crisscross both critical and popular interest in this wide cultural field. Rey Chow's trenchant analysis of Chinese fifth-generation films looks at the "primitive passions" associated with images of feudal or rural femininity. Gender bending, encountered in *wuxia*, the transmedia storytelling of manga and anime, and the ways opera and other theatrical traditions have been adapted to the screen, has been the subject of robust scholarly and fan attention. National media industries and their transnational reception are shaped by the power of women's genres such as television dramas, as well as by that of female writers, producers, and audiences.

Nevertheless, in most instances, the credit and opportunities for women directors lag behind those of the male auteurs who are honored internationally and invested in domestically. Fifth-generation Chinese directors Peng Xiaolian and Ning Ying are nowhere near as well known or funded as comrades Zhang Yimou and Chen Kaige. While cinema cognoscenti might mention Kawase Naomi among Japanese directors to watch after her Cannes Grand Prize, the contributions of her contemporaries are just becoming known. In all of these contexts, individual directors' successes arise in the context of a wider shift in access for women in film.

Perhaps only in Hong Kong is a woman director—Ann Hui On-Wah—among the most prominent and respected film practitioners. Hui has made nearly thirty critically acclaimed and popular feature films and has won top honors at the Hong Kong Film Awards, a corpus unequaled elsewhere. The strength of Hui's record is due to historical and industrial factors as well as talent. At the center of the Hong Kong New Wave that emerged in 1979, she gained firm footing in the industry—she has made TV films, genre films, and independent films; her status affords her the opportunity to work on personal projects and anchor them with star power. Her extraordinary success should not be taken as an exception, however. Hui's fluency with the commercial industry and audience tastes and her commitment to a personal vision are shared by other women directors in East Asia whose career contexts have been impacted by feminism.

I invoke a broad range of practices and topics in gender and Asian cinema, to stress both the transnational nature of the phenomena (one example suggests another) and the specificity of each development (each example asks for explication). These centripetal and centrifugal forces are apparent in Ling-zhen Wang's benchmark anthology *Chinese Women's Cinema: Transnational Contexts*, with its range of approaches to the work of women directors in China, Hong Kong, Taiwan, and the diaspora: "It is in and through a diverse cinematic engagement with historical forces, whether of the market, politics, or patriarchal traditions at national, transnational, or diasporan levels, that Chinese women filmmakers, as historical and authorial subjects, have exhibited their agency," Wang writes in an introduction that interrogates Western feminist film theory though transnational feminism and Chinese intellectual traditions and politics.[3] Indeed, neither catalogs of women's contributions to national cinemas nor auteurist studies alone can account for the creativity and impact of Asian women's filmmaking today.

These regional, gendered dynamics in world film culture generate what I will call network narratives. A programming venue like the annual competition of short films by Asian women directors at the International Women's Film Festival in Seoul shows a polycentric burgeoning of talent as well as linked political and aesthetic agendas. Regional trends and links among filmmakers, films, scholars, and viewers cross national and linguistic boundaries. The network as a spatial model with which to approach Asian women directors is meant to map local and national nodes as well as regional and global flows.

The terminology of networks is common to feminist politics and theory, such as Donna Haraway's "Manifesto for Cyborgs"; to Foucauldian and related forms of social theory, including Bruno Latour's actor-network theory, which has helped unlock film festival studies; and of course to techno-society itself. I use the term to draw out multiple resonances, including a narrational one. David Bordwell introduces the concept of network narratives in *The Way Hollywood Tells It* to describe a narrative form (favored by filmmakers like Robert Altman and John Sayles) that features an ensemble cast and uses attenuated links between characters and story events to structure its episodes. Networks can be spatial or share an "event frame," or they may follow the popular culture version of scientific network theory: "six degrees of separation."[4]

Bordwell questions throughout his book the novelty of storytelling techniques in blockbuster-era Hollywood and concludes that narrative form remains intelligible within its style of "intensified continuity": "Whatever new shapes degrees-of-separation plots take, most remain coherent and comprehensible, thanks to the principles of causality, temporal sequence and duration, character wants and needs, and motivic harmony that have characterized mainstream storytelling (not just in cinema) for at least a century" (100).

My attempt to expand the denotative field of network narratives is not occasioned by a desire to be more precise, descriptive, or inclusive than Bordwell—who could be? Instead, it comes from discomfort with the sense that in such network narratives as *Crash* (Haggis, 2004) and *Babel* (González Iñárritu, 2006) the links among characters (the "converging fates device") present the social totality in a way that reinscribes social inequity and overdetermines closure. In contrast, I want to suggest that network narratives function as open structures in women's film texts and that these in turn link to the feminist and related cultural networks that sustain a growing number of women film practitioners.

Women's film festivals are the most obvious example of a transnational feminist film network. In Seoul, as we saw in chapter 3, the women's film festival has remained oriented to the country's culture of cinemania and at the same time committed to academic feminist inquiry, activist and community agendas, and queer visibility. Another important dimension of the festival's work as it grew became cultivating its constituency within Asia, as well as its connection to sister organizations, as longtime director Lee Hyae-Kyung notes in the first newsletter of the Network of Asian Women's Film Festivals, established in 2011.[5] Informal ties among allies thus strengthen into institutional ones. Whether they are internationally known cineastes or national figures who cross over between industrial and independent fields, the Asian women who make film their métier are impacted by each other and imbedded in connecting histories of film and feminism. Thus for me, the term "network" helps position several salient directions of Asian women's filmmaking: regionalism; politics; technologies; and experimentation with intertwined narrative forms.

Strikingly, several East Asian women directors have deployed the network narrative format, with multiple stories crisscrossing in time and space—and to different ends than "the way Hollywood tells it."[6] Their stories remain open in their temporalities and affects, for their characters and their audiences, and they suggest both women's vulnerability as a class and the multiplicity of their stories. Exemplary of this phenomenon in Asian women's cinema is the practice of Indonesian producer-director Nia Dinata (b. Nurkurniati Aisyah Dewi, 1970). In what follows I relate her film *Berbagi Suami / Love for Share* (2006), which uses a networked narrative structure, to the way she builds networks in her career. A fuller case study of Taiwan director Zero Chou and the networks in which her work travels follows. There are intriguing parallels between these two young women's careers. Both have shown their work at women's film festivals in Asia and at LGBT and mainstream festivals internationally. Both are active, public figures working in commercial but independent formats within national film industries that have been opened up by political, economic, and industrial reforms. The emergence of the young, feminist film director as a minor national celebrity (minor is not meant pejoratively) is itself a network narrative in Asian cinema. I underscore this connectivity but also emphasize differences in the contexts of their work and its reception. Nia Dinata's films are a vital site of post-Suharto progressive Indonesian cinema, directed primarily toward the national audience; Zero Chou's lesbian feature films balance their address to transnational queer audiences and domestic mixed ones.

Nia Dinata studied filmmaking in the United States and worked in music video and commercials in Indonesia before founding her own production company. Her second feature as director, *Love for Share*, is a gently satirical film about polygamy in contemporary Indonesia. In my reading, the film positions director Dinata both as one among a network of women, each with a story to tell, and as a cultural commentator who pulls the strings. Dinata's film showed at international festivals including the Tribeca Film Festival in 2006 after a successful though controversial domestic release. How did the simultaneous transnational and national address—or "two-timing" (to invoke a problematic but irresistible metaphor)—imprint the film? Discursively, the film doesn't want to be pinned down: two of the strategies Dinata employs in *Love for Share* are a three-part network structure that, even as it resolves each story, implies that much is left unsaid, and a healthy dose of irony (fig. 4.1). *Love for Share* is bold in attention to the issue of polygamy and vivid in its glimpses of contemporary Jakarta, a global city whose population of ten million supports a cosmopolitan cineculture and ethnic and cultural diversity amid class stratification and clashes between tradition and modernity.[7]

The first of the film's three story lines follows Madame Salma, a prosperous married professional woman with a dignified bearing. Yet without undermining the character, the film's tone satirizes her situation as first wife to a polygamist whose reputation as a charismatic holy man is exposed as hypocritical—not once, but multiple times, coinciding with the discovery of each of his ever-younger wives, all with babies in tow. The second story line is a classic tale of a country girl in the big city shot in a gritty, claustrophobic super 16 mm format. Siti comes to stay with her uncle to attend beauty school in the city, disappointed to find that he's only a driver for film productions, rather than the important film industry figure he had led her to believe. But despite his precarious economic status, he already has two wives and lots of babies; Siti moves into their two-room house, is soon conscripted as wife number three, and then in a delectable if predictable twist, falls in love with wife number two (fig. 4.2). At the end of the segment, the two women move out, taking the corresponding kids with them. In the third tale, Ming, a popular and chic ethnic Chinese waitress with acting ambitions, marries her boss for the comforts of cosmopolitan living and satisfying sex, only to recognize that she's no match for his first wife,

FIGURE 4.1 The network narrative is reflected in the poster for *Love for Share*. Courtesy Kalyana Shira.

FIGURE 4.2 Cowives in close quarters fall in love. Shanty and Rieke Dyah Pitaloka in *Love for Share*. Courtesy Kalyana Shira.

who we have known all along is the true boss—of the restaurant and the ménage. The film concludes with Ming's voiceover, a declaration of sexual independence in the big city, and her move to the crowded neighborhood where the polygamist uncle's remaining wife is just waking up to find her friends missing. Her offscreen voice calling out for the decamped cowives combines with a pop song about making a family on the soundtrack, as the camera rapidly tracks back down the narrow street, linking sight and a particular site—the neighborhood where such contradictions are playing out.

Three stories: multiple wives in each. While there is no intentional homology between the several narrative strands and the issue of polygamy, in fact the combination serves the film well. Depending on point-of-view, polygamy singles out one wife at a time. But this narrative does not follow conjugal time, and surprising connections among the women keep turning up. And of course, the orchestrator of these convergences and the one who maintains the balance among the stories—the director herself—is on the women's side. The result is a wider portrait of Indonesian women's lives that suggests the breadth of a social problem as well as the potential for self-determination, resistance, and solidarity. Dinata critiques this widespread, socially tolerated practice; she also uses the pretext of polygamy to generate play with space, time, and common destinies.

We find out at the end, in the sequence that I just described, that the cab in which Ming moves back to the overcrowded neighborhood is the same one that carries away the two lovers and kids when they move out. The transition links the characters' fresh starts through the trope of circulation. The cab driver remarks, "Everyone is moving this morning"—urban density that protects the polygamist also affords women social mobility. The overlap reveals that the three stories are convergent in space and time; this simultaneity is reinforced in each segment by news coverage of the aftermath of the devastating tsunami of 2004 in the Aceh province of northern Sumatra. Sharp indictments of hypocritical humanitarianism are painted in brief scenes: Madame Salma refuses her husband's request that she accompany him for a photo opportunity—his second wife is only too willing to go. In the second segment, Uncle drives a documentary film crew to the site, and comes back with a fourth wife. In the third segment, Ming, in the capital, reads about the disaster in the newspaper.

The tsunami is one of the primary globally mediated images of Indonesia in recent years. Dinata builds this devastating event into the texture of the film without exploiting it.[8] The tsunami is a powerful figure through which to explore the interaction between the address to national and global audiences. International viewers may be more or less aware of Aceh's history of separatist armed struggle; in the wake of the crisis the remote province became better known through the coverage of celebrity humanitarian visits. Of relevance to the film's feminist politics are the striking disproportions in male and female survival rates, with women numbering two-thirds of the dead.[9] This appalling statistic—women were thought more likely to be at home, burdened down with children and the elderly, or less able to withstand the force—takes on grim irony in the context of polygamy. But rather than making an appeal to international humanitarianism—even one shaped by a feminist gaze such as the one I just deployed—the film links the tsunami to the thematizing of the media and filmmaking in Indonesia. Besides the documentary crew in the second segment, the news comes when Madame Salma's husband is being interviewed for television, a female director in charge. This embeds in Dinata's film ethical questions of how to frame images of Indonesia—natural disaster, Islamic militancy, polygamy—for transnational consumption.

In turn, the treatment of other issues in the film is geared more to urban and international rather than national audiences. Feminists organizing around polygamy in Indonesia who were primed to embrace Dinata's film criticized the lesbian subject matter of the second section, and Dinata points out that the film's success was centered in Jakarta. The thematizing of film production figures the very question of what we imagine the filmmaker's job to be (in other words, the aesthetic and political problem of how a feature film can be about a feminist issue) while showing her actually going about her work—quite literally, in the case of the production stills punctuating the credits (fig. 4.3). When Ming expresses her desire to be the Indonesian Zhang Ziyi, she situates Indonesian national cinema within regional East Asian and world cinema cultures. *Love for Share* refuses to claim a transparent relationship between storytelling and polygamy as an issue, but it also assumes a certain burden of representation, linking individual women's lives to bring a big picture into focus.

The film's use of multiple narrative strands, mediated and connected by chance and social and historical context, finally goes beyond the metaphor of infidelity suggested by the polygamy theme. Rather, its rhythms resonate with aspects of feminist narrative theory—defying closure (like a soap opera), it relies on the contiguous and accidental in the syntagmatic connections among stories and builds up to the generalizable, in the paradigmatic relationships among parallel lives. By presenting Madame Salma first—telling a first wife's story—the film maintains a certain loyalty to this

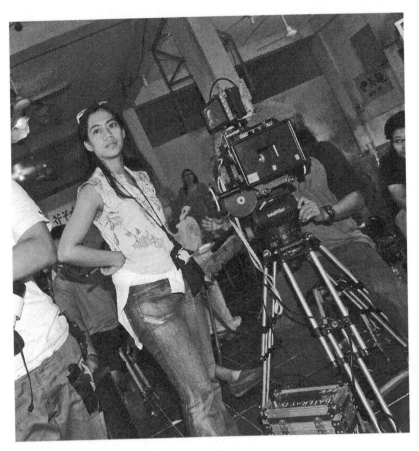

FIGURE 4.3 Nia Dinata. Courtesy Kalyana Shira.

mother figure (who is also a gynecologist who treats the second segments' cowives for sexually transmitted diseases).

For ultimately the film is primarily concerned with polygamy not as a trope, but as a social reality. While the stringently moralistic Suharto regime kept polygamy in check, the practice became more widespread in Indonesia during the post-Suharto reform starting in 1998. Today, while there is a movement in the government to make the practice illegal, there is little confidence that this will be effective given that some high-ranking officials themselves have multiple wives.[10] There is also vocal feminist opposition and cultural debate. *Love for Share* partakes of what Fatimah Rony describes as an exciting post-Suharto film culture in Indonesia in which young women play a central role.[11] Dinata's very active career as producer (thirteen features plus shorts and television through her company, Kalyana

Shira) is central to these national networks. At the same time, the film incorporates a postmodern, Pan-Asian aesthetic while addressing an issue that is the focus of transnational activism in the Islamic world.

Love for Share shows polygamy as an aspect of patriarchal Muslim culture that is taken advantage of by non-Muslim men and as part of the structure of village life that adapts to the overlapping spaces and intersecting lives, as well as the anomie and anonymity, of the city. Dinata uses humor and melodrama, rather than gritty realism, to usurp the platitudes about the practice that are given voice in her film in the hypocritical holy man's radio broadcast. Again, she speaks within and to a nation about and through a transnational issue and medium.

Dinata's work is a significant feminist intervention in the national media culture of Indonesia, and it is committed to the theatrically exhibited feature as a way to engage conversations about the role of women in public culture—through the content of each film, debates around reception, and the persona of the director. An ensemble of interviews, media appearances, and other projects contributes to Dinata's vocal presence.

After *Love for Share*, Dinata's production company produced several omnibus films featuring Indonesian women directors, extending the open-endedness of the multipart structure to a collectivity of cultural producers.[12] As Fatimah Rony details in her richly textured essay on the documentary *Pertaruhan / At Stake* (2008), Dinata's work as producer and her focus on collaboration are precedent setting. The different segments in *At Stake* highlight sexuality, class, and migrant labor. In the fiction film *Perempuan punya cerita / Chants of Lotus* (2007), four women directors, including Dinata and Rony, explore various aspects of women and sexuality in fictional scenarios about trafficking, abortion, and HIV/AIDS. Although it was subject to significant censorship, the film opened the Jakarta Film Festival. As a U.S. filmmaker-scholar of Indonesian descent participating in and writing about these projects, Rony exemplifies in her own practice the richness of networks of transnational feminist cinema.

As we have seen, in the case of Dinata, "network narrative" denotes *Love for Share*'s narrational strategy and her work as producer—especially of omnibus films on women's issues. But like many global women's films, her works have not entered the distribution networks of North American theatrical release due to language barriers and the hierarchies of value and distinction analyzed throughout this book. But in the flexibility of the current mediascape, Dinata's work travels through transnational circuits that bring it into contact with diasporan and general audiences at festivals, as well as with overlapping feminist and queer counterpublics. *Love for Share* showed in Taiwan at Women Make Waves, and the International Women's Film Festival in Seoul highlighted Dinata's work in a series on post-1998 Indonesian women's cinema in the Asian Spectrum section and invited her to serve on the jury. Her previous hit, *Arisan!* (2003), Indonesia's first gay-themed film, was widely exhibited in global LGBT festivals and circulates in and beyond Asia on DVD—it is so well loved it prompted a sequel, *Arisan! 2* (2011), eight years later. Olivia Khoo develops the concept of "minor transnationalism" to illuminate the affinities between queer networks and women's filmmaking in Asia.[13]

The discussion of Zero Chou that follows attends in detail to these networks of economic and information exchange as well as political and affective affiliations. Both cases show how women's and queer film festival circuits remain vital cultural hubs that contest globalization with local organization and regional alliances. In Chou's case, subcultural lesbian networks in transnational China are particularly crucial. In order to situate her success, I first contrast how questions of authorship and identity are mobilized in the reception of her work with the discourses of prestige that frame male auteurs in world cinema today.

Zero Chou and the Spaces of Chinese Lesbian Film

In an indelibly romantic image just before the halfway point of Apichatpong Weerasethakul's *Sud pralad / Tropical Malady* (2004), two lovers ride together on a motorbike, accompanied by the addictively sweet song "Straight" by Thai band Fashion Show. An image of freedom that precedes an abrupt narrative switch, the motorbike ride, in this syntagmatic placement, traces a Deleuzian line of flight, an unpredictable swerve into the unknown. In the film's strange, fantasmatic second half, the soldier Keng (Banlop Lomnoi), on some weird walkabout in the desert, is stalked by a beast of prey, who may or may not be Tong (Sakda Kaewbuadee), the village boy he'd courted so charmingly in the film's first half. Resisting territorialization by narrative succession, the motorbike ride is an image of the virtual, in which past, present, and (open) future coexist.

In a similarly romantic scene near the ending of Taiwan director Zero Chou's *Piao lang qingchun / Drifting Flowers* (2008), the tomboy Diego, protagonist of one of the film's three parts, takes Lily, a showgirl, for a spin. Although this pair too will be separated, in a future that the film has already dramatized, their paths cross here in a time and space marked by its poten-

FIGURE 4.4 Diego comes into her erotic identity through the romantic trope of riding double. Chao Yi-lan and Herb Hsu in *Drifting Flowers*. Frame capture. Wolfe Releasing.

tial (fig. 4.4). A ride on the back of a scooter is a romantic cliché, seemingly ubiquitous in Asian films, so there is no reason to see this similar scene in the third fiction feature by Chou as quoting *Tropical Malady*. But what if we hold these two queer cinematic flights together for a moment? Chou's image could be an homage, either to the sublimity of queer emotion, or to the formal structure of Weerasethakul's film, given Chou's film's use of a multipart narrative. But the images, the films that contain them, and the authorial signatures they carry do not circulate in the same way, even if they encounter each other on the road. I locate Chou's work and persona at the transnational horizon where Chinese-language, women's, and queer cinemas intersect, where ardently desired lesbian futures are cautiously projected.

Queerness is an oft-remarked theme in the Asian cinema boom of recent decades, running the gamut from cross-dressing in Chinese opera films and comedies to schoolgirl romances, gay rom-coms, and art films, with audiences for these films' theatrical runs, DVDs, downloads, and festival presentations divided into different niches of reception, more or less gay or straight, geographically proximate, Asian-identified, or linguistically and culturally competent.[14] Within the contrary currents of this mediascape, the two films just invoked might, however reductively, be said to correspond to auteur and identity categories. In both cases, the authorial persona signifies strongly in determining value, but to different audiences and ends.

Tropical Malady received the Jury Prize at Cannes and a berth in the New York Film Festival as well as on many international critics' top-ten lists. The inclusion of *Drifting Flowers* in the Panorama section of the Berlin Film Festival confirms that what we might consider more populist gay Asian fare also has international designs. However, while *Tropical Malady* has been widely written about and all but canonized (with Weerasethakul's 2010 Palme d'Or for *Uncle Boonmee Who Can Recall His Past Lives* vindicating any Cannes boos), *Drifting Flowers* has followed a different path. After a modestly successful run in Taiwan, the film played the global LGBT and women's film festival circuits, received a brief theatrical release in Hong Kong, and was acquired by lesbian-owned Wolfe Video for DVD distribution in the United States. The transnational circulation of her films has brought Chou a degree of attention among cinephiles and lesbian and gay audiences within Europe, North America, and Asia. In Taiwan, she has brought her vision to mainstream film and television projects that have also traveled beyond boundaries. If not the first out non-Western lesbian director to be recognized in the West, Chou is perhaps the first to meet the auteur critic's criterion of a body of work (i.e., multiple theatrical fiction features) across which to trace common themes and styles.

While there are a number of world-class Asian gay male auteurs—Lino Brocka, Stanley Kwan, Tsai Ming-liang[15]—the persona of the Asian lesbian director is more likely to be localized, linked with activism more readily than aesthetics. Indeed, is there reason to talk about the "persona of the Asian lesbian director," given the size of the pool, as well as the Western identity categories it appears to impose? As we've seen, women, including a number of quite young ones, are active in industry and independent filmmaking across Asia, but, not surprisingly, fewer women directors have gained access to the art film / coproduction sector and the aesthetic habitus of the internationally heralded Asian new waves.[16] I show how discourses of sexuality, feminism, and filmmaking in transnational China (the PRC, Taiwan, Hong Kong, and the Chinese-language diaspora) construct female authorship and women's cinema in terms of networks rather than within the aesthetic, celebrity, and genre determinants focused on in previous chapters.

There is a growing body of Chinese lesbian filmmaking from which to draw out these arguments. One of the few women among the underground or sixth-generation Chinese directors to achieve notable success, Li Yu made her fiction film debut in 2001 with the low-budget *Jīn nián xià tiān / Fish and Elephant*, touted as mainland China's first lesbian film. While

Li is not a lesbian, her film cast Beijing lesbian artist, programmer, and activist Shi Tou in one of the main roles, and the latter gained some international recognition as the film circulated abroad.[17] Hong Kong lesbian experimental filmmaker and scholar Yau Ching has also received attention in Anglophone queer academic and cultural circles, and her 2001 feature *Ho Yuk / Let's Love Hong Kong*, touted as Hong Kong's first lesbian film, is a key text in Chinese-language lesbian cultural production, with international exposure in LGBT venues and circuits. Yan Yan Mak's *Hu die / Butterfly* (2004) was a more mainstream lesbian narrative, though still a personal one. And in 2010, Ann Hui achieved new visibility for Hong Kong lesbian film with her comedy casting well-known actresses as pregnant former lovers who reunite, *Duk haan chau faan / All about Love*.

In this context Chou is a significant, though not anomalous, figure. Although she can't be credited with Taiwan's first lesbian film, she made two lesbian-themed, theatrically released feature films in a two-year period— both were shot, as were her previous gay male–themed feature *Yan guang si she ge wu tuan / Splendid Float* (2004), her documentary about the Taipei gay bar, *Si jiao luo / Corners* (2001), and her expensive costume drama *Hua yang / Ripples of Desire* (2012), by her partner Ho Ho Liu. Her record comes close to qualifying Chou as a lesbian world cinema auteur.

What is the significance of such a figure, and what more specific definitions of lesbianism, connection to the world, and cinema can be gleaned from her career to date? These questions are relatively novel ones, as the lesbian auteur remains rare enough in any era or region of film history. And they are important ones, as such a figure is accorded considerable standing through identity politics or what Catherine Grant calls "the identificatory pleasures of auteurist reception."[18] In this chapter, I attend to discourses of uniqueness and priority—marks of distinction—around Chou even as I attempt to locate her within wider networks. Her films should be seen not simply additively in relation to the firsts just mentioned, but intertextually, as part of a vibrant moment in Chinese-language lesbian visual culture and community.[19]

Insofar as Chou's authorship is tagged by the terms "lesbian" and "Asian woman" as social identities, it is not easily abstractable to expressive individualism. Her background as a documentarian (shared by mainland directors Li Yu and Guo Xiaolu) supports a grounding in the social. What might in some cases be considered the baggage of authorial gender, sexual, national, and ethnic identity can be read not in terms of biography but rather as traces of the other contexts, audiences, and films that shape a filmmaker's work. These times and spaces and scales interact—arguably this happens in any filmmaker's oeuvre—however, I suggest that Chou's films themselves make room for those exchanges.

I begin by reading Chou's first lesbian feature, *Ci qing / Spider Lilies* (2007), in the context of recent Taiwan cinema. Then I consider the global market for lesbian feature film programming (mainstream, queer, and women's film festivals, lesbian consumers) and follow the kinds of gazes that structure this circuit, particularly for Asian films. Finally, I return to situate the national and regional (sub)cultural dimensions of *Drifting Flowers*, offering a reading of the fantasy and work of initiation in Chou's films.

Contemporary Taiwan Cinema

Taiwan cinema is the object of considerable critical attention within Chinese- and English-language academic and critical circles at present. Chou's third feature, *Drifting Flowers*, was released in 2008 just a week before the sensational hit *Cape No. 7*, which ushered in a return of audiences to locally made films. This was a much remarked-upon development after a crisis in the domestic industry driven by Hollywood films' dominance in the 1990s.[20] Cinephiles speak with hushed tones the names of the Taiwan New Cinema auteurs heralded on the international festival and art house circuit since the 1980s. Yet in Taiwan, art film directors like Hou Hsiao-hsien and the late Edward Yang had been criticized for neglecting local audiences' sensibilities and for relying on foreign money and festival exposure. Such criticism was also aimed at Tsai Ming-liang, who launched what some call a second new wave in the 1990s.[21] (U.S.-based, Oscar-winning director Ang Lee is the outsized figure against which these vicissitudes of loyalty and repudiation are plotted.) The revitalized domestic production that has emerged alongside the auteurist coproductions combines an eye for commercial viability with an independent and entrepreneurial spirit. SPOT-Taipei Film House, the film center of the Taiwan Film and Culture Association, with Hou as president, is one site of this resurgence.

The fact that the building that houses SPOT served as the U.S. consulate and ambassador's residence before the severing of diplomatic ties between the United States and Taiwan in 1979 in favor of mainland China reminds us that Taiwan's is a film context in which questions of the national cannot be bracketed even as they are unusually fraught. These questions are of course geopolitical ones, as Taiwan's political status in the international community remains as undecided as its economic one is central. And they are questions that arise in the transnational context of Chinese film more generally, in which shared culture and language have in recent years been strengthened by closer ties in film financing, production, and distribution, especially since the turnover of Hong Kong to mainland China in 1997. Finally, queerness challenges national boundaries, both in the formations that are sometimes pejoratively referred to as "global gay" and in those that the editors of the volume *Asiapacifiqueer* describe in Foucauldian terms as "'discontinuous, particular and local critiques' based on the (re)emergence of 'subjugated knowledges'" that make intraregional links and connections possible.[22] A national queer Taiwan cinema is both an impossibility and a de facto reality.

In the context of democratic reforms and the lifting of martial law in the mid-1980s, an outspoken lesbian and gay culture emerged in Taiwan, especially in Taipei. Fran Martin explores in *Situating Sexualities: Queer Representation in Taiwan Fiction, Film and Public Culture* the "knotty entanglements of appropriation and translation in regard to sexual knowledges and cultures" that this emergence entails.[23] Martin teases out the strands of signification in a local lesbian magazine's multiple translations of the U.S.-originated term Queer Nation in 1994. The use of the localized term *tongzhi*, "comrade," for gay and lesbian allies it with the egalitarian ethos of communist address and bears a resemblance to the more clinical term for homosexuality, *tongxinglian*. Significantly introduced by Edward Lam in the title of the inaugural Hong Kong LGBT film festival, *tongzhi* has been widely adopted in Taiwan (a Google search for *nütongzhi*, the term for lesbian, yields a hit for Chou's *Spider Lilies*). *Tongzhi* exists alongside other terms, Martin points out, with the magazine passage also deploying *guaitai* (freak or weirdo) as well as several differently inflected terms for nation. The word *ku'er* (cool kid) was also introduced in Taipei circles as a more cutting-edge term that sounds like "queer."[24] As the multiplication of translations indicates, queer Taiwan culture flourishes at the intersection of local, regional, and global discourses. As Martin details, its cultural imaginaries and practices are informed by Republican China under the Kuomantang, indigenous Taiwan, imperial Japan, and postcolonial Hong Kong as well as Western or "global gay" identity politics and consumer culture. In Taiwan, university programs draw on, translate, and hybridize English-language queer theory; numerous gay- and lesbian-themed novels and other cultural artifacts have gained acclaim; and homoerotic television dramas have achieved popular success, all forces of "glocalizing" *tongzhi*.

In this context, gay-themed films have contributed to a desirable external image of Taiwan as progressive, as readings of Ang Lee's *The Wedding*

Banquet (1993) have argued.[25] Arguably, recent films have also played a key role in the nationalizing of Taiwan's gay culture. The gay rom-com *17 sui de tian kong / Formula 17*, the domestic box-office winner of 2004, is regularly invoked among the hits that registered a resurgent interest among youth audiences in nurturing domestic film culture in Taiwan. As Brian Hu concludes in a discussion of the film and the phenomenon of its success in *Senses of Cinema*, "the fact that mainstream Taiwanese cinema is still untreaded [sic] territory means that filmmakers, distributors and marketers have the opportunity to produce meaningful products which project a multiplicity of voices, especially in a time of great political and social uncertainty. Is a radical mainstream cinema possible? The infant industry can certainly try."[26] It isn't the film's subject matter or its music-video style that Hu finds potentially radical, but its successful appeal to an audience. He locates particular promise in the fact that *Formula 17*, with its vision of gay utopia and lack of diegetic female characters, was directed by a woman, then twenty-three-year old DJ Chen Yin-jung. The film's production company, Three Dots Entertainment, founded by young women with a background in marketing and distribution, has become a significant force on the Taiwanese film scene.[27] Yu-Shan Huang and Chun-Chi Wang note that these box-office successes by young women filmmakers "established a marketing model independent of government support." They are "commercially oriented but retain uniquely Taiwanese social, cultural and historical characteristics."[28]

Interestingly, the same year's Golden Horse winner for Best Taiwanese film was also a gay-male-themed debut feature by a woman director. *Splendid Float*, Zero Chou's first fiction feature, shot on 16 mm, tells the tale of a transvestite Taoist priest longing for his lost lover. Tonally distinct from *Formula 17*'s comic and breezy urban love story, it is interested in rendering an authentic, regional gay milieu (the Splendid Float is a traveling drag troupe). Previously, Chou's feature-length documentary *Corners*, her most personal film, memorialized a Taipei gay bar forced to close after a police raid. The film's self-reflexive style is heralded by Kuei-fen Chiu as sign of the maturity of Taiwan documentary, particularly in the hands of women directors, and its evocation of a vanished yet present space, a memory that lives in the now, are themes to which Chou returns.[29] If Chou's *Splendid Float* played to the international LGBT film festival network that embraced *Corners*, as a deliberate turn to feature filmmaking it also had its eye on a domestic and regional Chinese-language audience.[30] *Splendid Float*'s award at the island's most prestigious film festival earned it a theatrical release.

The film's interest in queer intersections with traditional culture, as well as its high drama, link it to Chou's later features.

While *Splendid Float* received aesthetic recognition, Chen's *Formula 17* connected with audiences, and Chou would expand in this direction with her next release. Hu and others cite *Formula 17*'s youth-oriented, music-video aesthetic, urban middle-class demographic, and cute (straight) male stars (from Hong Kong and Taiwan) for its success. Young women were a significant audience for the film despite its exclusively gay male world. The film played at SPOT; gay cultural consumption was both niche and trend.

Into this climate came Chou's next film, *Ci qing* (Tattoo), with the English release title *Spider Lilies*, a glossy lesbian art romance with its share of melodramatic hokum that became the island's breakthrough *nütongzhi* (lesbian) title. Lesbian onscreen content in mainstream films was not entirely new—the French/Taiwanese coproduction *Lan se da men / Blue Gate Crossing* (2002) about a three-way high school friendship won popular audiences and critical acclaim at home and abroad. That film is a key example of what Martin calls a "flexible" text, which emulates in a scaled-down fashion Hollywood's attempt to maximize audiences by including something for multiple users. A teen pic with art film elements, *Blue Gate Crossing*, Martin argues, is intentionally multicoded, allowing for global queer audiences to "respecify" the main character's rite of passage as coming out and for Taipei audiences to recognize it as a local film, at the same time that its friendship themes and shallow-focus, urban backgrounds can travel as universalized signifiers of big-city youth romance (the obligatory motorbike date is complemented with multiple bicycle scenes).[31]

But *Spider Lilies* goes further than *Blue Gate Crossing*. Directed and produced by an out lesbian director collaborating with her partner and cinematographer, the film features true love; butch/femme—or more apt to Taiwan, T/po (tomboy/wife)—gender play; tasteful (that is, tantalizingly short) sex scenes; and the promise of romantic closure. It tells the story of Jade, a naive young girl who works from home, where she lives with her grandmother, offering private chats with male callers over a webcam. When she reencounters the female tattoo artist she remembers from her lonely childhood, she attempts to revive their love in the present. Described by Elsa Eider as "a trippy hybrid of traditional queer Asian tragedy and magical realism" in the 2008 Frameline (San Francisco International LGBT Film Festival catalog), *Spider Lilies* was nevertheless a breakthrough for local lesbian realities.

The hook for mainstream Chinese-speaking audiences was the casting:

Spider Lilies features Taiwanese pop star Rainie Yang as Jade, steadfast in her crush on Takeko, played by Macau-born Hong Kong actress-on-the-rise Isabella Leong. Advance publicity about the casting of Yang, a popular TV personality, played to her fascinated Pan-Asian fan base eager to see her acting in a more mature role, with the kiss between the stars received as humanistic revelation or soft-core come-on, depending on one's inclination. In either case, the pairing was a considerable box-office draw.[32] The domestic distribution campaign appealed directly to youth audiences and the film's success as a local independent was stoked by word-of-mouth and promotional events—including fans sporting Jade's signature green wig. After the film's release, YouTube clips and fan movies as well as discussion board postings attest to strong responses from nongay Asian audiences outside Taiwan, some of whom were able to see the film in theaters, while others accessed it later on DVD, VCD, and over the Internet. Though the male gaze is certainly solicited by Jade's job as a sex worker, Yang's fandom, consisting largely of young girls, was rewarded by her "cute" character and the opportunity to hear her sing (the karaoke-ready theme song "Xiao Mo Li" is prominent on the soundtrack) as well as by the titillations of tattoo and lesbian love.

Zero Chou is out as a lesbian in the publicity for and press coverage of the film, and grassroots efforts effectively targeted both Taiwanese queer audiences for the theatrical release and Chinese-speaking queer audiences elsewhere for word-of-mouth interest in the film. As Martin indicates, transnational nütongzhi discussion boards were just as active in dissecting *Spider Lilies'* kisses, sex scenes, and casting choices as were those frequented by "Rainie's" more mainstream fanbase; she even cites a thread discussing the ethics of circulating the film since it could not be released in mainland China.[33]

Spider Lilies thus played to intersections of queer, gendered, generational, and genre-based regional circuits, activating counterpublics across fandoms and subcultures. In this regard *Spider Lilies* qualifies as a flexible text like *Blue Gate Crossing*; while here the content is unmistakably lesbian, the context is less so, and its breakthrough success can be recoded as stunt casting or voyeurism (a theme that the webcam trope inscribes in the film). However flexibly defined, the formula worked: the *International Herald Tribune* reported in June from Singapore as the film opened there that it was the top-grossing local film at the Taiwanese box office of the year to date; the article was headed "In Taiwan, *Spider Lilies* Fuels a Small Gay Renaissance."

If domestic box office is international English-language news, it is also enhanced by international recognition. *Spider Lilies'* award at the Berlin film festival provided just that. Taiwan film programmer Sophie Shu-yi Lin, who managed the film's early marketing, recounted that Chou was even recognized by her taxi driver on the way home from the festival because of the publicity her film had received. The fact that the award was in a competition for lesbian- and gay-themed films didn't seem to matter: the Teddy worked for marketing purposes much as a Golden Bear (Berlin's top prize) or Horse (Taiwan's) would have done. This box-office boost is ironic given the reluctance of many major distributors in the United States to premiere gay features in LGBT contexts for fear of ghettoizing them when first reviewed. Is the Taiwan box-office phenomenon indicative of a mistranslation of the tags of global identity politics into national pride? Or is the identity category trumped by film politics—the prestige Berlin/Europe confers on a film? Certainly the anecdote speaks to a cinema consciousness in Taiwan that Chou, Chen, and other filmmakers are using to their advantage to connect with an important youth demographic imagined as antihomophobic and potentially queer.

With regard to national recognition, Chou can again be regarded as a flexible author. Her films signify as authentically lesbian and authentically Chinese, without being so specific that they cannot travel. While since *Splendid Float* her feature films have been notably set outside Taipei, the markers of locality are not emphatic. Like many Chinese-language films today, *Spider Lilies* pulled its cast from Taiwanese and Hong Kong actors. The lives of the film's protagonists have been tragically marked by the earthquake that struck in their youth, and while the characters' ages mark this as the devastating "921" earthquake of September 1999 that struck central Taiwan, the event is not specified for foreign viewers. Nor do unmistakable markers territorialize the film's symbolic spider lilies and jasmine blooms in a specific region.

But rather than seeing these as generic and even self-orientalizing images, we might see Chou's films as choosing not to put everything up on the screen for outsiders to decipher. If they bear limited traces of the specific place and time of contemporary Taiwan nütongzhi subcultural politics and history, her films nevertheless emerge from local and queer cultural milieus, connections secured through Chou's own lesbian community identity and her history as a documentarian (source material for *Spider Lilies* came from work on a documentary on the earthquake's legacy). Yet markers that seem to be specifically, even mythically, Taiwanese, such as the family puppet troupe of *Drifting Flowers'* main characters, can be understood in the context of localism as negotiations, not mystifications, of this identity. A more consciously political syncretism in Chou's work is the drag queen Buddhist priest of *Splendid Float*. Chou localizes Taiwan's queer culture outside of, but not in isolation from, the urban centers in which global gay discourses circulate most insistently.[34]

One mark against authenticity claims around Chou's depiction of lesbian identity is raised by the gender presentation of *Spider Lilies'* central couple. While Jade is very much a girl—even a case of arrested development who uses a lookalike doll as part of her webcam mise-en-scène—the half-Japanese Takeko's gender identification, although visually signified only by button-down shirts and ponytails, is taken for granted, not as puzzlingly masculine, but as legibly "T" or butch lesbian.[35] The punk youth Ah Dong, a frequent visitor to her tattoo salon, first jokingly hits on Takeko and then asks, with sincerity, why she doesn't have a girlfriend. Later, he and Jade exchange a joke about Takeko's being "too much like a man" (as the subtitle renders it) to excuse her behavior as PMS. The dialogue may ring false when applied to the willowy, long-haired Isabella Leong, but the discourse of lesbian gender complementarity, or "secondary gender" as Martin calls it, is enlisted to guarantee the central couple's destiny.[36]

Melodramatic vicissitudes intervene: Takeko's flight from commitment is accounted for in flashback as a consequence of having abandoned her four-year-old brother the night of the earthquake in order to visit a schoolmate's bed; their father was killed rescuing the boy and her brother has not remembered her, or anything besides the spider lily tattoo on their father's severed arm (the "real skin" on the wall of Takeko's parlor), since that night. Meanwhile, Jade is under surveillance in an internet sex sting operation, but her real problems were caused long ago by her mother's running off to Taipei after the earthquake, taking only the girl's brother. The nine-year-old took consolation in the small kindnesses of her neighbor, whose own spider lily tattoo allows us to recognize her as the younger Takeko, who got the tattoo, and became a tattoo artist herself, in order to connect with her brother through the memory of a signifier of their dead father's body. Jade tries to provoke Takeko's memory by digging out and wearing the bright green wig she first wore as a little girl in an attempt to attract Takeko's attention. Already a keen reader of codes, she had waited by the side of the road for the older girl to bike past in her school uniform. And there are side plots for the male characters, appealing to girl fans' sympathies: Ah Dong is gay-bashed; Takeko's brother Chen runs away from his care facility and is lost among the spider lilies (did I mention the myth that spider lilies line the path to hell?) before being struck by a car and falling into a coma from which he awakens with his memory restored; and a stuttering detective-cum-cyber stalker tries to tip off Jade about the impending raid of the website's operations that his boss has ordered.

The pileup of parallel childhood traumas, oedipal thematics, performative genders, and physical impairments all intertwined with the trauma of natural disaster portend a tragic queer romance littered with narrative debris. But all ends happily with Takeko declaring a halt to the madness—with a text message: "I'm sorry, meet me at the studio." Pathos swells again as the film ends, Rainie's jasmine flower song playing on the soundtrack as the two women walk toward the rendezvous in slow motion. Jade wears her childhood wig but has a new maturity in her stride. Fade to black: if it means we don't get that final sex scene, at least we don't have to see the film scrambling to integrate the trail of wounded males into the reconstituted family.

In *Backward Glances* Fran Martin describes a "female homoerotic imaginary" that cuts across contemporary Chinese public cultures. Female same-sex love is depicted in a pervasive "memorial mode"; a schoolgirl romance is remembered but renounced, evoked everywhere while ostensibly consigned to the past. The affective triumph of *Spider Lilies'* happy ending trades on the memorial temporality. As Martin notes, the film's narrative and symbolic preoccupation with memory and forgetting, jasmine and spider lilies, position it as an explicitly lesbian rewriting of this structure of feeling.[37] As she notes, Chinese lesbian films that revisit the dominant memorial trope "dramatize the radical potential of that narrative by literalizing memory's enactment within, and power to transform, present experience."[38] *Spider Lilies* is certainly deeply invested in questions of temporality (to the point of confusion: unless Takeko suffers from amnesia like her brother, why doesn't she remember Jade from events that happened less than a decade earlier?). However, Jade's reclaimed wig in the final shot suggests that *Spider Lilies* may be content to offer lesbian role-playing fantasy, both to its protagonists and to its audiences, rather than definitively moving on. Its embrace of the doomed-to-repetition nature of the schoolgirl romance (of genre itself) as part of its pop legacy makes the film harder to distinguish as a lesbian text (critical or not) from a mainstream homoerotic one except with recourse to the author figure. I don't mean that we should overvalue Chou's intentionality, but rather that we should attend to the markers of what Kaja Silverman calls the "authorial fantasmatic"—a set of libidinally invested figures and scenarios ("nodal points") that characterize a director's oeuvre.[39] I return to this in my discussion of Chou's follow-up feature.

The critical notice and financial success of *Spider Lilies* enabled Chou quickly to go into production with *Drifting Flowers*, which she opted to make on a more modest scale. Although Chou is quoted as having plans for a rainbow series, with a movie for each color of the flag, she is not exclusively interested in queer subject matter, and in interviews plays the universality card.[40] I suggest that her very productivity recodes *Spider Lilies'* success: a domestic box-office mini-phenomenon, a sign of Taiwan progressivism, new product source for the global LGBT festival network as distribution alternative, and part of a lesbian director's oeuvre. An interviewer at the Berlinale asks Chou how she could be back the very next year with a new feature. The director seems stumped: "I have nothing else to do except make films."

Film Festival Circulation:
Value Addition, Identity Crises, and Orientalism

As my discussion of *Spider Lilies'* regional reception has suggested, the itineraries of Chou's work bring it into contact with different systems of value and different audiences. In this section I discuss various international film festivals as destinations for her films, considering how the relationship between a global gaze and global gays receives different emphases in the programming and consumption of lesbian versus gay male work.[41]

Spider Lilies debuted at the 2007 Berlinale, where, as noted, the film collected the Teddy Award for Best Feature. Instituted in 1987, the Teddy recognizes the festival's best LGBT-themed feature, documentary, and short. Chou was the first Asian lesbian director and the first director from Taiwan to win the award. The film was invited to Berlin by programmer Wieland Speck, who screened a cut while scouting in Taiwan; after the invitation to Panorama was secured, Three Dots, the production company that formed to make *Formula 17*, signed on as international sales agent. One year later, Chou's *Drifting Flowers*, also represented by Three Dots, was invited to the Berlinale and promoted as the work of the previous year's Teddy Award–winning director, garnering good ticket sales and generally favorable reviews.

Although third in the hierarchy of Europe's A-list festivals (established in 1951 as a Cold War Western cultural foothold in the East), Berlin is a preferred destination for programmers of the bigger LGBT festivals (San Francisco, LA, London, Melbourne, Toronto, Hong Kong).[42] As a competitive festival, Berlin is both gatekeeper and feeder (given its February dates) for the global network of such festivals clustered around gay pride month in June. At the same time, the prestigious context of the Berlinale puts individual LGBT titles on the wider film market in a way that festivals branded as LGBT do not, with distributor, press, sales, and propaganda efforts surrounding festival appearances.[43] As Marijke de Valck and Thomas Elsaesser emphasize, the process of "value addition" through a film or director's recognition on the festival circuit is self-sustaining. Although *Drifting Flowers* was not as successful as *Spider Lilies* at Berlin, its selection there signaled prestige and potential commercial viability.

Still it is via the dedicated queer festivals that such work makes contact with audiences, potentially on a global, if grassroots, scale.[44] Most of the more than two hundred LGBT festivals currently in operation worldwide are audience, not industry, oriented, and critical opinion is often less important in programming decisions than is pleasing a local constituency. The buzz from Berlin was certainly helpful, but the mere fact that *Spider Lilies* and *Drifting Flowers* were competently made lesbian feature films guaranteed Chou's work a spot on this circuit (no disrespect to Chou's talent or curatorial vision intended). The festivals' mushrooming growth was coterminous with the New Queer Cinema boom in independent American cinema, and LGBT film festivals continue to struggle with the identity crisis of being community-oriented versus film events brought into focus by New Queers Cinema's commercial and critical success.[45] Programming reflects both mandates, drawing on queer cinema's rich history and high degree of experimentalism on the one hand, and the democratization of video, in the service of activism and seeing oneself on screen, on the other. As Jenni Olson stresses, the festivals are an ecosystem; production feeds the festivals, and the festivals encourage production.[46] LGBT film festivals serve local communities—in Minneapolis or Mumbai—as site-specific calendar-driven festivities that link audiences with the global images they view in a mutual traveling. But they are defined by wildly discontinuous local realities and political agendas that make their circuit less self-regulating than that of the prestigious international festivals, which arguably aims to reproduce a comparable cosmopolitanism and even tourist economy in each of its sites, a uniformity that has started to inform festival film aesthetics. The kind of reception a film like *Spider Lilies* receives on the LGBT network, in contrast, will vary greatly.

The LGBT festivals provide occasions for many forms of cross-cultural spectatorship. The most established North American festivals have long highlighted international programming, from storied queer European art film directors and contemporary heirs to the tradition like François Ozon, to homosexual heritage films, to breakout queer films from the Global South like Brocka's *Macho Dancer* (1988) or Tomás Gutiérrez Alea's *Strawberry and Chocolate* (1994). Gay-friendly offerings from a number of different Asian cinema trends—Hong Kong genre films, Taiwan art cinema, Korean horror—travel the Western LGBT festival circuits. Audiences may bring their own contextual frames—if they are diasporan subjects from the filmmaking nations, such frames are likely to differ greatly from those of Hong Kong swordplay film aficionados or cinephiles seeking out the latest Tsai Ming-liang.[47] Often queer audiences are quite sophisticated spectators and have indeed been trained as such by the festivals. Yet the reality is that non-Euro-American works are often received through universalizing discourses of oppression versus rights, consumerist criteria of entertainment, humanist concepts of positive images and visibility, or dynamics of sexual tourism that can be objectifying, orientalizing, or otherwise unimaginative. Mimetic spectatorship is a dominant mode, with subtitles regarded more as code for the universality of whichever dimension of the film—sex, romance, family, or coming-out—enables cross-cultural consumption than as markers of a film's origin or reminders of the way in which all films are foreign.[48]

There are gendered dimensions to these viewing dynamics and the programming choices that feed them. Most LGBT festivals are committed to gender equity in what is otherwise a fairly asymmetrical cultural realm, and lesbian audiences are vocal in their demands for realist and entertaining representations. Because of the paucity of nonpornographic feature-length lesbian programming, which remains underresourced and underdeveloped in the United States despite important breakthroughs, international art films have historically filled the lesbian feature programming slots. The lesbian content of such films is either characteristic of the art film tradition's branding as sexually daring or functions as a code for female emancipation and social progressivism, or both.[49] Many such films are directed by men. Only with the advent of digital technology were lesbian producers able to make feature-length films in any significant numbers. Yet even when they were, they did not have the production values of industrial or art house filmmaking or the publicity of theatrical release.

Given this confluence of circumstances, a film by and about Asian lesbians, and a glossy feature to boot, was a perfect plug-in to the global LGBT festival network in 2007. *Spider Lilies* was screened in dozens of such festivals, and *Drifting Flowers* followed, programmed at metropolitan queer fests like Turin, Oslo, and Barcelona as well as the biggest North American venues, Frameline, Outfest, New Fest, and Inside/Out. The films did not secure theatrical distribution in the United States but were released on DVD by the lesbian-owned company Wolfe Video, with Jenni Olson, former programmer of Frameline's storied festival in San Francisco, in charge of marketing. The consumer market for the DVD includes Chinese-language and queer audiences. Any public nontheatrical events that programmed the films are hard to trace.

If Chou's earlier work was shaped by the existence and structure of the global LGBT festival circuit, it was *Spider Lilies* that matched lesbian content (including sex), female authorship, and scale (feature film of relatively high production values, with stars) to its specifications. It is true that many audiences will consume such work with little understanding of cultural or subcultural specificities, genre conventions, or even the gender of the director. Homogenizing aesthetic and spectatorial vision may structure such interactions. *Spider Lilies* delivers tradition (flower symbolism) and techno-modernity (Net sex) with tattoo, providing a balance of oriental exoticism and subcultural currency. Queer audiences' consumerism—of lifestyle and cultural difference—can be objectifying in its very sophistication.

And yet, as I argue in my introduction to a 1999 collection of short essays on lesbian and gay film festivals published in GLQ, "Queer Publicity," queer festivals also function as a counterpublic sphere in which the interests and pleasures of diverse nonhegemonic subjects are articulated to a specific time and space. The degree and nature of the "counter" vary according to geopolitical location and other factors, as much writing on the increasing commodification of gay life under neoliberalism shows. But simply by virtue of the attempt to address at once gay, lesbian, bisexual, and trans constituencies and their allies, as well as film fans and special interest groups for particular films, the public for such events cannot be imagined as homogeneous. At festivals, local interests confront the circulation of global gay aesthetics and politics, contesting representations, generating debate and even counterimages.[50]

GLQ subsequently hosted a series of round tables devoted to three sets of actors in the LGBT festivals: filmmakers, critics, and programmers. These polyvocal texts challenge thinking that relegates LGBT events to the category of thematic festivals without understanding the dimension of queer world making they involve. But the festivals are not innocent instances of "glocalization." As Ragan Rhyne notes in her contribution to the curators' round table:

Festivals are the primary markets for international queer film, but they do not simply acquire and screen the films they show; they actually create the economic conditions that enable their production. This is not to imply that queer internationalism is merely inauthentic or commercial and thus without any kind of political viability. Rather, what it indicates is that scholars, activists, and festival directors must begin to look at the economy of queer cultural production as an essential element of queer collectivities and the institutions they form. Conceiving of an international queer community through cultural circulation and consumption begs significant questions about how U.S. audiences understand the role of the festival in defining a gay and lesbian class identity within this global economy.[51]

Across the global network, the flows of images and the power to determine meanings are much more likely to be from the West to "the rest." While oppositional media spaces like the LGBT festivals are a site to contest these imbalances, they may also emulate these uneven flows, with white muscle-boy films and corporate sponsors headlining events from the cosmopolitan to the grassroots. A brief look at how Chinese lesbian films and filmmakers have networked with festivals in Asia to redirect these currents will bring some of these questions into relief.[52]

Intersections of Feminist and Queer Film Culture in Transnational China

The number, scale, and longevity of LGBT film festivals in Asia—in Tokyo, Bangkok, Manila, and Mumbai—attests to thriving queer and movie cultures and their intersections as well as to the potential for disjuncture in this global queer image economy. The oldest festival in the region is the Hong Kong Lesbian and Gay Film Festival, founded in 1989 by Edward Lam and Wouter Barendretch. As mentioned, the festival's first edition coined the now-prevalent term *tongzhi* as a Chinese, gender-inclusive nomination for gays and lesbians. After more than twenty-five years, spanning the decriminalizing of homosexuality in 1991 and the return of Hong Kong to China in 1997, the festival has undeniably served a counterhegemonic and political purpose. However, as Yau Ching outlines in her contribution to the *GLQ* critics' round table: "LGBTQ film/video festivals in Asia suffer from the triple burdens produced by the globalization of Euro-American white gay culture, the colonial histories of our own social contexts, and the chauvinism embedded in our queer communities. . . . Hong Kong's film festivals and their audiences, including the HKLGFF, have been 'programmed' to take the white, mainly gay—with a little bit of lesbian recently—culture as 'natural,' 'desirable,' and 'progressive,' contributing to further suppression and marginalization of a localized and regional queer culture."[53] Do Asian LGBT festivals necessarily reinforce hegemonic global gay discourse or are they a significant articulation of local, already hybridized queer identities and globally circulating, already hybridized images? Whether the queer Asian films shown at the fests are forms of self-representation aimed at local subcultures or represent the cultural and economic significance of Asian cinemas regionally and across contemporary world cinema, their production and reception show the ways that sexual citizenship and subjectivity and global belonging are continually being recast. Yau concludes with the mandate "to relocalize LGBTQ issues and strategies within and against the global gay economy."

Audiences, curators, and filmmakers are all faced with these paradoxes. Film scholar and curator Denise Tang, who served as director of HKLGFF in 2004–2005, turned toward the future in her introduction to the twentieth anniversary edition in 2009:

> I imagine a selection of films and videos that are controversial, warm and fuzzy, local, with lesbians, inter-Asia based and at the very least, pornographic. I imagine media coverage that stretches beyond web forums, pop magazines and the festival website but on the 6:30 news and Ming Pao headlines.
>
> Okay, so maybe the future is partly here and partly there.

This complicated spatial-temporal figure "the future is partly here and partly there" resonates with Chou's images of lesbians living passionate lives limned with tragedy in nebulous times in which contemporary political movements are evoked but not depicted. Taken on a more practical level, the phrase might refer to perspectives on the different areas within "cultural China." While Hong Kong's future may lie in China, mainland gay and lesbian culture looks to both Hong Kong and Taiwan.

Although after the lifting of martial law in 1987 Taiwan quickly became a regional center of lesbian and gay culture, the island still lacks a regular LGBT or tongzhi festival. Perhaps mainstreaming has been successful—locally made queer-themed hits like *Eternal Summer* (2006) get exposure in the high-profile Golden Horse festival and robust theatrical release. Or perhaps it is partly because, for lesbian work, there is a viable alternative. Taipei is the site of the longest-running women's film festival outside Europe. In Taiwan, feminism is central to lesbian film culture as well as lesbian identity formation, literature, and politics.

Women Make Waves was founded in 1993 by a group including filmmaker Huang Yu-Shan, whose *The Twin Bracelets* (1991), a Hong Kong–produced period drama about the friendship between two girls, was, to the best of my memory as a programmer, the first Chinese-language film directed by a woman to be featured in the New York Lesbian and Gay Film Festival. The Taiwan festival (its title echoing that of New York–based distributor Women Make Movies, which initially provided films to screen) has been held annually with one exception in the intervening period.[54] Asian women's work and lesbian work are not explicitly part of the mission, but the festival is an indispensable forum for both. *Corners* showed at the festival (credited to Zero and Ho-Ho, no surnames), and *Spider Lilies* and *Drifting Flowers* showed in the festival in addition to having theatrical runs. Chou's subsequent feature, the public television production *Wavebreaker*, was the domestic opener in 2009. Chou's persona as a community-based, commercially savvy, out lesbian and feminist director is to a significant extent congruent with and exemplary of the festival's philosophy.

Despite—or enhanced by—the presence of an established annual women's event, Taiwan was also host to the first Asian Lesbian Film and Video Festival in 2005. Organized by prominent activist Wang Ping and scholar Chen Yu-Rong of the Gender and Sexuality Rights Association of Taiwan, the festival was a showcase for locally made and Pan-Asian women's film and video, a mark of the coming of age of the movement. One participant writes, "The ALFF was a breakthrough event for the Asian lesbian community, as it brought together media art, social activism and cultural exchange.[55] Although there has not yet been a second such festival, regional organizing among Chinese lesbians in film and video has continued. The circulation of commercially viable works like Chou's is crucial in this context.

The clashing politics of transnational networks intersecting with locally organized events are perhaps most visible in mainland China where, as Lisa Rofel's work details, the mobilization of Western-style sexual identity and rights politics serves a complex function in relation to both communist and globalization ideologies.[56] Since the authorities shut down Beijing's first lesbian and gay film festival in 2001, efforts to support regular exhibition of queer work have been continuous. The first event was organized by prominent filmmaker, writer, and film professor Cui Zi'en and activist and artist Shi Tou, the same pair who claimed the distinction of being the first gay man and lesbian to come out on Chinese television. The program of the 2001 event included *Fish and Elephant* and the first mainland gay film, *East Palace, West Palace* (Yuan Zhang, 1996). These films subsequently received university screenings but only became widely viewed in China on pirated DVDs. The 2005 follow-up event was also interrupted by the authorities. Finally, in 2009 the festival was pulled off successfully, soon followed by a Shanghai pride event with a film component. The distance traversed in the decade since 2001 can be seen in the Beijing-based webcast Queer Comrade's 2010 segment on the top ten Asian lesbian feature films. Included were works by Chou and mainland independent lesbian director Zhu Yiye.[57]

Drifting Identities: Circulating Lesbian Histories

This top-ten feature demonstrates that the Internet is a crucial element of Chinese queer (post)modernity,[58] but it also foregrounds, in its restriction to fiction features—many of which are described citing their festival appearances or critical accolades—the importance of this format to the circuits of queer culture. These circuits are built around the agency of cultural workers, the creativity and contribution of other formats such as documentaries and shorts, performance and installation work, and the material spaces of programming venues and publications. But feature films help lay the tracks, not just for consumption, but also for the networks that build identities and audiences across spaces and over time.[59] The Queer Comrade segment quotes Chou on the difference between her two features: "*Spider Lilies* is a dream; *Drifting Flowers* is reality. We live in both dreams and reality." Not a documentary, *Drifting Flowers* (2008) uses the feature film format to depict a more personal reality, addressing Taiwan lesbian history in three intertwining story lines.[60]

Drifting Flowers lacks the box-office stars of *Spider Lilies*, but its casting of newcomer Chao Yi-lan in the role of Diego, a sad-eyed accordion player, goes some way toward redressing Leong's lack of butch (T) credibility in the earlier film. The three parts are loosely related and of varying lengths. The first tells of the romance between Diego and the blind singer Jing (Serena Fang) from the perspective of Jing's jealous ten-year-old sister May (Pai Chih-Ying). Economically insecure, Jing is shamed into allowing May to be adopted by a childless bourgeois couple. The second, seemingly anomalous, part of the film tells of an older lesbian suffering from Alzheimer's, Lily (played by Tsai regular Lu Yi-Ching), who is reunited with Yen (Sam Wang), the gay man she'd married years earlier as a cover. Yen, who is HIV-positive, has been dumped by his lover and shows up at Lily's door with a suitcase. Lily misrecognizes Yen as her former female partner Ocean and the two go on to find a measure of comfort together under this premise. The third part tells Diego's backstory as a tomboy coming of age, struggling to find her place in the world and in her family's business, a village puppet theater.[61] Meeting a showgirl from a rival puppeteer family helps give shape to some of Diego's inchoate longings, and, when the viewer figures out the girl is the young Lily (Herb Hsu), to the film's multipart structure. The film affirms a range of lesbian possibilities in its tentative resolution of stories of painful separation, without resorting to the romanticized closure of *Spider Lilies* or its traumatic events.

Variety gave *Drifting Flowers* a negative review at Berlin: "[The film] . . . moseys along for 90-odd minutes, seemingly content to speak largely in lesbian cliches. Centered on a group of femmes struggling with that old gay chestnut, 'identity,' three-parter looks to bounce into fest dates on the strength of Chou's niche success with last year's 'Spider Lilies.' But without Asian name leads behaving transgressively onscreen this time, theatrical biz looks far weaker, especially in the East."[62] Whether we should credit a publication that uses its dated slang for women, "femmes," to encompass literal butches in its dismissal of "lesbian clichés" is questionable.[63] But notable here is an attribution of authorship that is repeated across reviews, blogs, and catalog descriptions of the film, whether or not Chou is identified as a lesbian. Also prominent is the use of a developmental scale arranging Chinese sexualities on the way to fully realized Western definitions. I'd suggest that the seeming naïveté of the film's politics should be reframed in relation to culturally specific modes of queer gender performance and sexual definition, as well as to the trope of initiation, which challenges a linear progress narrative.

Thematically, both of Chou's lesbian films are centered on stories of young girls with intense crushes on older butch figures. The girls are quite young (nine and ten)—that these crushes are not innocent is suggested by Jade's telling her lesbian origin story as part of a live online chat. Her male clients are voyeuristically attuned to what they want to hear as a prurient loss-of-virginity tale; instead Jade tells a very girly story of getting a lift on the back of a bicycle by a neighbor (Takeko, who she hopes is signed in and listening to the session). May in *Drifting Flowers* falls in love with Diego at first sight (something her blind sister cannot literally do), and the film underscores the importance of the girl's gaze with a point-of-view construction (figs. 4.5–4.7).

FIGURE 4.5 *(top)* May looks on as Diego performs with her sister in *Drifting Flowers.* Frame capture. Wolfe Releasing. FIGURE 4.6 *(middle)* Gender performance converges with musical performance. Chao Yi-lan and Serena Fang in *Drifting Flowers.* Frame capture. Wolfe Releasing. FIGURE 4.7 *(bottom)* A shot of May anchors the previous image in her point-of-view shot in *Drifting Flowers.* Frame capture. Wolfe Releasing.

It is hard for me not to extrapolate these girls who fall in love with tomboys to the figure of the spectator; at the same time, the repetition across both films points to Chou's authorial signature or fantasmatic. The director projects images of young girls attempting to decipher (their feelings for) charismatic tomboy figures for audiences that include, but are not limited to, young female consumers of popular culture. Second in importance to the schoolgirl romance, another subgenre of Chinese female homoerotic representation Martin defines is the tomboy melodrama (ch. 4). In the examples she cites, the viewer is positioned as a sympathetic friend to the tomboy, who often meets a tragic end. *Drifting Flowers*, with its charismatic butch hero, combines this empathic address to the viewer with an inscription of authorial, erotic desire that refuses to sacrifice or isolate the tomboy.

The spell is effectively cast. An early conversation in which May quizzes Diego about her gender—with the blunt curiosity natural to a ten-year-old—is echoed later in the film in a scene representing Diego's own past. The outcome of the latter scene (discussed below) is erotic initiation, and so, in a sense, is that of the former. We catch glimpses of an older May that indicate that she does become a lesbian (when she's away at school, of course).

Perhaps the narrative trope of initiation also facilitates the film's transnational mobility. Evidently Chao Yi-lan as Diego was as warmly received on the North American LGBT festival circuit as she was in Taiwan. *Drifting Flowers'* temporal scheme allows for the resolution of individual stories while keeping a larger network open, and its migrating lesbian plots are spatially correlated as well. The film's "clichés"—which arise in part because of the limited narrative time allotted each of its stories—signal its translatability on the international market but also invite more stories.

Images from a train traveling through a tunnel in the forested mountains serve as a connecting device among the film's three parts. Each of the film's principals appears on the train. The teenage May's journey home from boarding school is diegetic, with her reflections along the way, rendered in flashback, leading to her resolution to reconcile with her sister and Diego. The presence of elderly Lily and Yen on the train is less explicitly narratively motivated; we do see them on a platform at the end of their segment, at peace with each other and graced with a rainbow marking their joint queer journey. And we find Diego standing outside on the platform behind the train's rear car; thus all of these bridging shots retrospectively take up her optical point of view. Whether hers is the travel of a trouba-

dour or a linear journey to Jing, her destiny, we are not sure, and her accordion, whose rhythms accompany these sequences, supports both interpretations with its up-and-down rhythms. Endless transit and circulation,
foregrounded by these interstitial train sequences, frames the film's own
disjunctive encounters.

In the final segment, Diego takes Lily, headline act of the rival puppet
troupe in town, for the spin on her scooter that I mentioned at the beginning of the chapter. This exhilarating image of a freer form of motion and
flight than the train permits comes near the end of the film. As they speed
along, Diego confides that her family would like her, too, to perform as a
showgirl to attract audiences. "How can that be possible?" Lily jokes, grab-
bing Diego's chest—we know that Diego binds her breasts. When Diego
repeats, as if it is a liberating mantra, "How can that even be possible?"
the phrase condenses several meanings. Diego can't be a showgirl—she is
a tomboy (she can be a musician); Lily can't grab her breasts, as they are
disavowed (but she can touch her). This intuition of im/possibility allows
her an ecstatic moment, acknowledging her desire for girls and the body
image she projects. It is in this sense that I suggested the scooter ride is a
"line of flight," Gilles Deleuze's figure for creative evolution through the
encounter with something new.

After their ride, it begins to rain, and the pair takes refuge in the cab of a
truck. Attracted to Lily but reluctant to be touched and unsure of the codes,
Diego asks, "Am I a boy or a girl?" Lily's answer is quick, "A girl of course,
but one who doesn't like her body."

DIEGO: Can a girl love a girl?
LILY: Yes, love is love. But can you love a showgirl like me?
DIEGO: Can you love a tomboy like me?
LILY: Yes, that's always been my type.

This conversation about "that old chestnut" identity, however didactic,
emphasizes, by ending with the timeless allure of the tomboy type, that
it is just as much about desire. Although Western-style transgender and
coming-out discourses clearly inform both the construction of the scene
and viewers' readings of the film, the subtitles cannot convey all that is
at stake here. Moments later, the kiss between Diego and Lily breaks off
in laughter. Does this interruption signify relief of tension, excitement at
their intimacy, or amusement at the tangle of tropes (gender inversion, humanist transcendence, tomboy melodrama) they've just tugged at? We are

FIGURE 4.8 After their kiss, Diego and Lily gaze at what looks like a movie screen. Chao Yi-lan and Herb Hsu in *Drifting Flowers*. Frame capture. Wolfe Releasing.

left gazing at the screen, which soon fades to black, much as the pair look through the windshield, not knowing whether it is an urgent eroticism, an identity lesson, or something new that we've just witnessed (fig. 4.8). We know already that this couple does not last, though the two remain queer kin through their mutual friend Yen (Diego and Jing perform at the wedding). Overlapping codes of Chinese gender presentation and lesbian desire authorize flexible readings of the film.

If Chou has cannily framed a moment of multivalent reception in the scene in the truck, she elsewhere includes a blatant authorial inscription, one that locates her films in what Helen Hok-Sze Leung, adapting the term from Gordon Brent Ingram to the Chinese context, calls a "queerscape."[64] In the middle segment of the film, Yen wanders the city after a conflict with Lily, encountering a line of posters for the film *Spider Lilies* (Berlinale logo visible) (fig. 4.9).[65] As Leung explains, "Queer space is . . . a 'locality of contests' between normative constitutions of identity and less acceptable forms of identification, desire, and contact" (14). "What is this place?" Yen mutters, aptly. While one might read the poster placement as Chou's shameless self-promotion, this local encounter with a globally circulating commodity resites both *Spider Lilies* and the film in which it appears in a queerscape, as queer Chinese public culture in a tangible form. If *Spider Lilies* signifies on one level Taiwan's box-office revival, both trans- and subnational queer spaces echo with uncanny effect within that national discourse.

Underscoring this theme of the uncanny is the film's Alzheimer-like

FIGURE 4.9 A wall of posters for director Zero Chou's *Spider Lilies* serves as queerscape for Yen. Sam Wang in *Drifting Flowers*. Frame capture. Wolfe Releasing.

temporality: not only are the segments out of order, but the ages of the characters just don't add up. In the brief coda set on the train, May has aged at most ten years while Lily, who grew up with Diego, is in her seventies, and Diego appears on the train platform as she did when May was a child. This convergence of the film's multiple temporalities may suggest a disregard for a precise historicizing of Taiwan queer culture, a postmodern sense of its rapidly accelerated timeline, or just incompetent plotting. But in Brian Hu's reading, "the result of the temporal inconsistency is a magical folding together of the lesbian community's past, present, and future, allowing tradition and destiny to commingle in one spectacular gasp of air."[66] What might seem like continuity problems finally appear to be intentional simultaneity. We experience the stories' closure and the plot's open-endedness and implied dispersal. Without fully untangling its investments in the memorial mode or the tomboy trope or including much by way of mise-en-scène (with the exception of the *Spider Lilies* poster) that could definitively date the film in a post–identity politics present, *Drifting Flowers* asks what's next.

Refusing closure, the film eventually achieves something like *Tropical Malady*'s image of the virtual, despite its more conventional plot. Opening up the narrative world through its multipart network structure, *Drifting Flowers* is a different kind of flexible text, with multiple encounters possible along all its lesbian story lines. Chou overstuffs her films, it is true, perhaps to make up for lost time, but also to allow each world to multiply.

Zero Chou's oeuvre resonates within Chinese-speaking lesbian cultures and plays within the economy of lesbian and gay film festivals and their demand for product. It traces contours of a transnational lesbian audience without conforming to global gay tropes and genres. For the purposes of my argument about the circulation of a set of thematics, affective experiences, and associations evoked by her name, it is also important to stress Chou's successful breach of the independent/popular barrier with an address to female and youth audiences. Before the big-budget *Ripples of Desire*, Chou directed the successful TV drama *Gloomy Salad Days / Death Girl* (2010). Unlike most (but not all) of the gay male Asian auteurs, Chou enters transnational spaces with local identity and community politics trailing—if she doesn't quite gain the status of art film auteur, she is able to travel these networks without having to transcend nationality, queerness, or feminism.

Shaping careers that defy standard pathways limiting women's achievement, Nia Dinata and Zero Chou are feminist icons. They connect with audiences through their incorporation of popular and youth-oriented idioms without relinquishing their political affiliations. Their network narratives use multipart structures not to pose formal challenges but to open up women's spaces and temporalities. A regional rather than an exclusively national perspective on Asian filmmaking and flows makes these patterns and possibilities more apparent.

5. IS THE WHOLE WORLD WATCHING?
Fictions of Women's Human Rights

The title of this book juxtaposes two keywords—"women's cinema" and "world cinema"—and suggests a parallelism between them. Both are singular terms for plural phenomena; both are terms in need of ideological interrogation. Yet a qualitative connection is also suggested—the implication perhaps that women's films are worldlier than some other types of film, that they travel outside national boundaries more freely, on a particular kind of passport. Previous chapters have explored a number of ways in which women's films access the global dimensions of current art cinema culture while maintaining their cultural identity. In this chapter I turn to films that make this dynamic visible with some urgency, as they concern women's human rights violations and attempt to convey the specificity of the perspectives from which they are experienced. Narrative films concerning women's human rights appeal to the world in different ways: some promote universal subjecthood as grounds for redress; some expose the fictive nature of this construct; still others are more concerned with fictions and aesthetic worlds than with rights. Moving beyond national borders to be heard, these films nevertheless refuse to give up local idioms, making a significant feminist impact on world cinema's current contours.

Many of the most insistent issues of twenty-first-century feminist politics—migrant women's labor, femicide, rape as a tactic of war, sex trafficking—exceed the bounds of the nation-state, and feminist media including fiction films are increasingly addressing these concerns. These representations take place within the context of what Inderpal Grewal describes as the rise over the past several decades of the framework of "women's rights as human rights" among nongovernmental organizations and activists.[1] By conceiving of women and girls as rights-bearing human subjects rather than citizens of a particular nation, this approach seeks to guarantee protections under international or postnational conventions. In 1979 the UN General Assembly adopted the Convention on the Elimination of All Forms of Discrimination against Women, extending the provisions of the Universal Declaration of Human Rights (1948); to date the United States has not ratified this document. While there is no single representational regime corresponding to this paradigm of women's human rights, public appeals using images of women and girls from around the world have become more pervasive during this period. In her study of the visual rhetoric of humanitarianism, Wendy Hesford investigates "how human rights principles are culturally translated into a visual vernacular that imagines Western audiences . . . as moral viewers."[2] She shows how images of women's suffering deployed in humanitarian campaigns and documentaries evoke a sense of recognition on the part of the Western viewer. This visual culture proliferates online and across nonfiction formats, rendering other strategies of feminist representation both necessary and complex to achieve.

Multisited cultural production by and about women has a key role in ensuring that context, differences, subjectivity, and situated politics don't get lost in globalizing discourses, whether of suffering or empowerment. For women trouble the category of the universal, a contradiction that informs the "women's rights as human rights" paradigm, under which women need specific protections to attain general rights. This contradiction also informs the role of the fiction film in human rights discourse, since specific narratives complicate the humanist aspiration to depict universality. Fiction films by and about women from the Global South have the potential to challenge the generalizing frame of reception. They are not taxed with resolving the contradiction between universal and particular. However, such questions are broached in how their stories are told and their audiences addressed.

World cinema can itself be thought of as a postnational formation in its aesthetics, economics, and address. A number of twenty-first-century women's fiction films expose traumatic national narratives, and their costs for women, in the world cinema arena. They address audiences outside the nation not to universalize women's stories but, perhaps paradoxically, to prevent any one of them from being taken as exemplary. The films I discuss negotiate the universals of human rights discourses with the particulars of their narratives rather than functioning as advocacy or didactic works. Such fictions of women's human rights work in conjunction with other forms of feminist media and activism to bring global women's issues into public discourse.[3] They use the spaces of world film culture as stages of accountability, each in its own way bearing witness to traumatic national and regional histories and asking spectators to witness in turn.

This chapter thus brings into political focus a dynamic relating women and world that is present in each of this book's chapters. These women's stories, although particular to them, are not isolated; it is on the higher-level, global realm of human rights frameworks that they are recognized as the basis of feminist activism. However, they risk being overwritten by the universal story of woman as victim. Similarly, film from the margins needs to function on the level of the global to sustain itself, but risks being deterritorialized when received in that realm. By correlating these two sets of tensions between particular and general, I hope to show that women's cinema is world cinema—whether we want it to be or not. In other words, universalist frames snap into place in certain contexts of reception. Our readings of the diverse and growing practices of women's filmmaking help global connectivities to emerge as well.

Pakistani director Sabiha Sumar's (b. 1961) debut feature film, *Khamosh Pani / Silent Waters* (2002), a German/French coproduction (ZDF/Arte), achieved widespread recognition after winning the Golden Leopard and several other prizes at the Locarno Film Festival in Switzerland in 2003. Distributed in the United States by First Run Features, it is one of the most significant feminist films of the early 2000s. *Silent Waters* is a complex indictment of patriarchal violence in the context of nationalism and fundamentalism, set during General Zia's rise to power in Pakistan in 1979. It is also one of the only Pakistani films to circulate in international festivals in recent decades.[4]

The paradox of enunciation the film's prominence presents is worth considering. In "Translating Silences: A Cinematic Encounter with Incommensurable Difference," Priya Jaikumar links *Silent Waters* to Moufida Tlatli's great *Silences of the Palace* (1994) in the canon of filmic critiques of gender and the postcolonial nation. The films' theme of women's silence is echoed in the question of their filmmakers' right to speak. Tlatli's film drew attention internationally to Tunisian cinema, and some critics accused it of using an orientalist representation of women's oppression to appeal to the West. For others, it was the film's feminist politics that its wide reception cast into relief, a challenge to the unitary narrative of the nation. At stake is the symbolic power of woman in relation to national narratives—and the difficulty of a woman's exercising that power to tell her own story. I show in this chapter how Sumar and other women directors complicate world cinema's scripting of female oppression both in their films and in their own representativeness.

In her genealogy of "post-Third-Worldist" cinema, Ella Shohat critiques Eurocentric feminism's neglect of women filmmakers outside the Euro-American canon. The legendary women involved in postcolonial cinemas of liberation or Third Cinema in the 1960s and 1970s include Sarah Maldoror (*Sambizanga*, 1972, Angola), Assia Djebar (*La nouba des femmes de Mount Chenoa*, 1977, Algeria), and Sara Gomez (*De cierta manera*, 1964, Cuba). In their political use of the feature-length film form, these filmmakers can be considered predecessors of Tlatli and Sumar. As Shohat writes, "post-Third-Worldist feminist cultural practices also break away from the narrative of the 'nation' as a unified entity to articulate a contextualized history for women in specific geographies of identity."[5] Shohat discusses how filmmakers of the 1980s and 1990s also often break away from narrative to work in documentary, experimental, and video formats. For reasons of scale and address, such films are less susceptible to the allegorizing of woman and/as nation than the feature films. Shohat's research provides multiple genealogies of the contemporary feminist art film in both Third Cinema and multicultural media. By considering Sumar's turn from documentary to feature film form with *Silent Waters* alongside the work of somewhat younger directors, I foreground the strategic use of the art film format by women directors negotiating the space of world cinema in the 2000s.

As the examples I have been tracking throughout the book indicate, it is becoming a more frequent occurrence that a woman director will emerge in international festivals as the representative of a "small-nation" cinema.[6] Small-nation cinema, according to Mette Hjort and Duncan Petrie, functions between the mandate to preserve language and mediate the nation to its citizens and the address to audiences outside its borders required to sustain itself economically.[7] Women's access is in many cases facilitated by transnational funding practices that reward emerging artists. These women-directed features could be considered post-Third-Worldist films in that they go beyond national liberationist narratives to foreground gender, sexuality, the local, and the regional, and their works may draw on transnational feminist thought and activism. But since films produced in very different media industries may be similarly positioned in terms of international consumption, the successes of these younger women directors can still be seen through the discursive frame of woman as symbol of the nation.

Women—as directors and protagonists—may be even more likely to be taken up as representative when the recent national history is traumatic. In Bosnian director Jasmila Žbanić's *Grbavica* (2006) and Peruvian director Claudia Llosa's *The Milk of Sorrow* (2009), the central women characters have been directly affected by rape as a tactic of war and terror in 1990s civil conflicts. The first limns the relationship of a Bosnian Muslim mother and a young daughter who doesn't know that she was conceived by rape during the nationalist conflicts in the former Yugoslavia. The conceit of the second, very stylized, film is that an indigenous mother's trauma—rape during the conflict between Maoist rebels and government-backed paramilitary in Peru in the 1980s and 1990s—has been passed to her daughter through breast milk. Very different in tone and historical context, both films were recipients of the Berlin International Film Festival's top honor, the Golden Bear. In fact, both films received support from the World Cinema Fund administered through the Berlinale, whose regional targets are defined by development zones. We might see a pattern of international acclaim (flowing in the wake of international financing) for creative treatments of shattering examples of violence against women in nationalist conflicts.[8]

Rather than viewing the solicitation of women's voices from the Global South cynically, I want to argue that the filmmakers do more than stand in for national problems. Fostered by feminist histories and networks of both politics and film, their works push back against objectifying funding directives and exhibition patterns. These filmmakers question and complicate their status as national subjects representing troubling human rights concerns to international audiences through marks of enunciation and aesthetic choices in their films. Whether the films are realist or stylized, their protagonists resist preconceived notions of victim and survivor. Their bodies are imprinted with history and their voices herald new futures. The filmmakers interrogate the symbolic freight of femininity through the kinds of heroines they create, the stories they tell, and the construction of their own personae.

Crucial to Jaikumar's argument about *Silent Waters* is that "the woman is explicitly *not* a metonymy or allegory for the nation"; the film's main character is, from its first images, embedded in networks of sociality, exchange, and contestation over the meaning and future of Pakistan.[9] I argue that we think of women directors like Sumar, Žbanić, Llosa, and others in a similar way, while diagnosing the discourses that still attempt to position them as representative.

In a manner similar to the works of the diasporan filmmakers discussed in chapter 2, the awards conferred on these films and the acclaim accorded their directors are at least in part due to the gravity of their subject matter. Sumar was a participant in a transnational documentary project for public television called Why Democracy? In the obligatory interviews at her film's festival dates, prizes, and nominations, Llosa makes statements about Peru's national character. And the success of Žbanić and Aida Begić, writer director of *Snijeg/Snow* (2008) and *Children of Sarajevo* (2011), bears out Balkan cinema expert Dina Iordanova's position: "I am more and more often inclined to think that it is women who represent the viable and vocal critical alternative in former Yugoslavia today."[10] The moral authority attributed to the female director grants her publicity—something resembling a voice in the democratic public sphere.

Unlike Western celebrities who bring attention to humanitarian issues "over there," Sumar, Žbanić, and Llosa speak from "here," places and histories that have been marked by violations of women's rights.[11] The films have in common the fact that their women directors intervene in a symbolic way in cinema's function as national imaginary around these violations and in a material way in its restructuring as an industry by foregrounding women's stories. While she may also be interested in branding an authorial persona or vision (Llosa), shaping public opinion through a mixed documentary and fiction practice (Sumar), or addressing a transitional society (Žbanić), each of these directors is directly concerned with bringing women's lives and subjectivity to the center of attempts to redefine the nation critically in a globalized context of post–Cold War nationalisms, the U.S.-led war on terror, and neoliberal economic policies. This is accomplished through the subject matter of the films and through the directors' own standpoint as figures on an international stage.

While fiction films about grave violations of women's human rights comprise only a small number of the women's films made in the first decade of the twenty-first century, the genre has a more direct tie to feminist politics than many of the films discussed in this book. Although they still focus on individual protagonists and offer no programmatic vision for change, these films engage with feminist futures by telling the story of two generations of women. On the one hand, the passing of time required for this fiction to make sense takes the film out of the realm of immediate action in response to harm. On the other, as I shall argue, the generational device allows for questions of historical reconciliation, including those of gendered citizenship, to be posed within the form of the film. While the filmmaker does not stand in for the fictional aggrieved woman in films about women's human rights, she arguably stands as her ethical support, projecting a society accountable to women's experience.

As much as these films seek a world stage as redress for violations of women's rights, they are equally invested in revising national narratives and reinventing national cinemas. As each of these countries has been riven by internal conflict in recent decades, their film cultures have declined accordingly. Thus the national narrative is as important to production and reception as it is to the film's content. Participating in the transformation of these industries, and countering dominant news images of regional conflicts, women filmmakers may be strategically positioned as harbingers of a new film culture. For example, in the case of films from the former Yugoslavia, strengthening film industries and cultures in each of the republics involves matters of financing, casting, and festival publicity and reception, which become ways of mediating and sometimes of enacting tensions. Thus a feminist voice, advocating for women whose rights have been violated and for a generation marked by conflict, both represents and troubles the category of the nation in each case. Beyond setting out to represent the nation or right historical wrongs, such films are about (re)building an industry and infrastructure.

At the same time, as I've noted, the films reference the postnational appeal to universal women's rights. Moreover, the entities that fund the films are supranational: European film funds favor projects on human rights issues and a number of collaborative funding arrangements seek to redress colonial legacies of mis- and underrepresentation. Finally, their audiences are "the world"; they are committed to "approaching a kind of positive understanding of globalization," as the World Cinema Fund FAQ puts it, and the woman director's reputation is part of this positioning.[12]

Sabiha Sumar's Democratic Cinema

I want briefly to situate what I will argue is *Silent Waters'* principled address to viewers in relation to Sumar's work in documentary. Beginning with *Who Will Cast the First Stone?* (1988), a film funded by Channel 4 in the United Kingdom about women imprisoned under Islamic law in Pakistan, Sumar has produced a significant body of documentary work on cultural shifts and

Islamicization in Pakistan. Both *For a Place under the Heavens* (2003, ZDF/Arte) and *Dinner with the President* (2007, ITVS, codirected with Sumar's producing partner, Sachithanandam Sathananthan) center her own experience and questioning as a secular Pakistani feminist. The first film explores the paradoxes of the increasing adoption of hijab and the second the contradictions of a democratic government headed by a general. *Dinner with the President*, one of ten films produced for the international broadcasting initiative Why Democracy?, was finished shortly before Benazir Bhutto was assassinated and President Pervez Musharraf left office, leaving its questions about Pakistan's future hanging. While Pakistani television declined to air *Who Will Cast the First Stone?*, *Dinner with the President* was shown by satellite and provoked lively debate. Funded by European and U.S. agencies and broadcast—though not exclusively—to audiences living in the West, Sumar's documentaries position the filmmaker transnationally, and the conversations about gender, freedom, the future, and Pakistani media that are conducted within the films are informed by these contexts and audiences.

Sumar's own situation as a cultural producer is also determined by multiple locations and efforts. Born in Karachi and educated at Sarah Lawrence College and Cambridge University, she has worked with Sathananthan on Sri Lankan as well as Pakistani topics. She is also an executive producer of *Saving Face*, the 2012 Academy Award–winning documentary made by Daniel Junge and Sharmeen Obaid-Chinoy on surgeries for acid attacks on women in Pakistan. She struggled to make her second feature, envisioned as an entertainment film that would instill a sense of collective identity—a Pakistani Dream akin to the American Dream and the Bollywood sensibility. Sumar overcame the lack of industry resources and freedoms in Pakistan and completed *Rafina* (2012) with outside funds (ZDF/Arte) and local talent in Karachi.[13]

Although not explicitly concerned with the entertainment value of fiction filmmaking, *Silent Waters* used the fiction format to attain a higher profile and to reach different audiences than the television documentaries. Made with French and German television funds, *Silent Waters* was geared to audiences beyond the subcontinent, although it was released in India and its producers brought it to Pakistani audiences with a projector and screen.[14] The film unveils a mother's traumatic past and grave present dilemma through her adult son's growing attraction to Islamic fundamentalism. What could be seen as an individual, even Oedipal drama of separation is entwined with the history of Pakistan as a nation, although the

FIGURE 5.1 Kiron Kher in *Silent Waters*. Courtesy First Run Features.

film is set predominantly in one small Punjabi village and doesn't deal in epic or iconic imagery. The violation of women's rights and personhood is traced to a traumatic past of sectarian violence—significantly, however, the main character, Ayesha (Kiron Kher) is, as Jaikumar emphasizes, more than a symbol of violence against women. Her present existence is rich; she teaches village girls the Koran and helps her neighbor prepare for her daughter's wedding (fig. 5.1). If the film identifies the woman's story with that of the nation, it is not didactic. The narration of women's choices instills a historical subjectivity in the viewer and insists on accountability from its present-day audience. It is the silencing of the past that predicts a violent, even unlivable, future.

The identity of the main character is a divided one, as the viewer and soon the other characters discover: as a young girl at the time of Partition in 1947, the heroine, then called Veero, refused to consent to male elders' demand that the village's Sikh women and girls commit suicide to escape communal violence and abduction. While the preponderance of the film is set in the late 1970s during General Zia-ul-Haq's rise to power, there are flashbacks to the harrowing primal scene when the women jumped into the village well. After fleeing from the well, the young Veero is sheltered by Muslim neighbors. She takes the name Ayesha and eventually marries into the village community.

The transformation of her grown son Saleem (Aamir Malik) from a dreamy youth into an Islamist ideologue not only calls up imagery of this primal violence for his mother—a return of the repressed past signaled on the formal level by the flashbacks—it also leads to its historical repetition. When Saleem discovers his mother's ethnic origin, he calls upon her to renounce her past. Refusing, she returns to the village well for the first time since her childhood—to jump.

A brief epilogue set roughly in the film's present shows that Saleem has come to a position of power with the Islamist government; yet a trace of a different outcome remains. In a wordless scene, we see his former fiancée, Zubeida, turn away from his televised image; instead, she embraces his mother's memory in the form of a locket bearing the likeness of a young girl—Veero.

The extent of violence against women—the deaths, abductions, and rapes —during the massive and contested relocation accompanying the partition of the Indian subcontinent has become more widely discussed in recent years, including through English-language narratives like Bapsi Sidhwa's *Cracking India* (1991) and its film adaptation, Deepa Mehta's *Earth* (1998). Sumar drew on Urvashi Butalia's study *The Other Side of Silence: Voices from the Partition of India* (2000). The book collects testimonies from around Rawalpindi where the film is set, including an account from a survivor of a now-notorious incident in which more than ninety women jumped into a village well. Unlike the more melodramatic *Earth*, *Silent Waters* keeps the violence largely in the past. The style of the flashbacks signals these events as other, as inassimilable to present experience. Ayesha's repetition is not a compulsion—it is an ethical decision. The film contrives to give subjectivity (even to grant optical point of view—of the depth of the well in the flashbacks [fig. 5.2]) to a character whose death, and refusal to speak publicly, are narrated in the film. At the moment of the suicide, however, the camera maintains a long shot as Ayesha disappears from the frame; this objective distance turns the viewer back on herself to interpret the action (fig. 5.3).

Jaikumar links the film's staging of the question of the narratability of violence to the larger problematic of cinematic communication across difference. Pertinently, she draws on Gayatri Spivak's questioning of the intelligibility of a woman's act of resistance in the latter's famous essay, "Can the Subaltern Speak?" It is at a time of renewed fundamentalism that the heroine completes the act whose suspension granted her a productive life. It is a fatal paradox that this act, refusing her son's authority to secure her participation in a ritualization of female and thus community purity, echoes

FIGURE 5.2 The protagonist's flashback includes a point-of-view shot of the well in *Silent Waters*. Frame capture. First Run Features.

FIGURE 5.3 We are removed from Ayesha/Veero's perspective when she jumps into the well in *Silent Waters*. Frame capture. First Run Features.

her childhood flight from the well, refusing her father's command. But, as Jaikumar argues, a reading of the suicide in terms of a secular critique of Islamicization is inadequate, in part because of Ayesha's own Muslim faith (222). Jaikumar understands audience debates over how to interpret the suicide not as confirmation that the subaltern cannot speak but as a productive extension of the thematic of incommensurable experience marked by Ayesha/Veero in the film: "I read this disagreement as a space constituted between the film and its audiences, between a representative system and its interpretive acts, where a series of arguments unified in their opposition to religious fundamentalism struggled to find expression when their recourse to the language of secularism was made deeply problematic" (221). The "space . . . between the film and its audiences" is opened by the film's fictive mode, by its deployment of particular codes of narration, by its address, by its travels. The film's urgent political message is not delivered by its relation of facts about the past; rather, it directs us to the present time of reception, an attempt to interrupt a narrative of return.

As a story of the historically disempowered and silenced set within a family, the film draws on the codes and affects of melodrama. But despite casting an actress with Bollywood experience (*Devdas*, 2002) as her lead, Sumar sees *Silent Waters* as a neorealist film related to her documentary practice. The film uses location shooting, a nonintrusive score, and song and dance are diegetically motivated by a wedding sequence. Combining melodrama and art house realism, the film might also be seen as addressing both regional and international audiences. Touted as the only Pakistani film in thirty-five years to receive worldwide release, *Silent Waters* poses the question of national identity both within the temporal folds of its story and in the vectors of its address.

Such a question is figured in the film itself. In Jaikumar's reading, the protagonist's death is not futile even on a narrative level because Zubeida arguably "recognizes [Ayesha/Veero's] resistance" (221). It is in the address to this next female generation that the film figures alternative futures. But if Zubeida is a stand-in for the viewer, she does not represent a mere consumer but rather a social actor, perhaps one like Sumar. As Jaikumar notes suggestively, "Zubeida's community is not in her immediate vicinity," thus necessitating an appropriation of media forms (222). *Silences of the Palace* ends on a similar note of potential communion between generations of women.[15] Jaikumar notes that these endings "do not appeal to audiences through a unified emotional message, but allow a dialogic social collective to form by taking viewers to the silenced counterparts of national and global modernity, while leaving room for debate over its content and significance. The collectivity of audiences and subjects thus constituted through encountering and debating an unwritten history becomes one of many transnational feminist communities" (223). We are accustomed to the way documentary films open up dialogic space for their audiences. After *Dinner with the President* aired on PBS in the United States, online comments ranged from gratitude for showing Musharraf as reasonable to rage at the filmmakers' breaking bread with a dictator. But those fiction films that eschew a "unified emotional message" go beyond documentary immediacy and historicity to allow for a projection of this dialogue, symbolized here and in the films about rape warfare that I turn to next by the depiction of generational legacies of female trauma. Sumar's mixed documentary and fiction practice multiplies these encounters with "incommensurable difference."

As a film about women's human rights issues that is also an international breakthrough for a marginalized national cinema promoted under a woman director's signature, *Silent Waters* sets a precedent for *Grbavica* and *The Milk of Sorrow*. But changing political contexts and film practices privilege different dimensions of promotion and reception. The politics of Sumar's films challenge Pakistan's prevailing ideology, and they have been directly shaped by second-wave feminism (*Don't Ask Why, For a Place under the Heavens*) and by human rights and national liberation struggles (the documentary on women Tamil Tigers, *Suicide Warriors*). Jasmila Žbanić and Claudia Llosa grew up during their countries' conflicts and are positioned as part of a process of cultural renewal. While Žbanić is also a documentarian and an outspoken feminist, Llosa is a film stylist whose mystical heroines are held aloof from rights-based claims. The success of their first features in the international art film circuit have placed both directors at the forefront of their respective national cinemas and given them the opportunity to make multiple features in a few years. The politics of globalized art cinema mark the content and the aesthetics of their films, which resonate with Jaikumar's compelling but cautionary vision of transnational feminist film's potential.

Jasmila Žbanić's *Grbavica* and Balkan Cinema's Incommensurable Gazes

In her debut feature *Grbavica: The Land of My Dreams* (2006), Bosnian director Jasmila Žbanić (b. 1974) explores the legacy of the mid-1990s Bosnian war though the story of a woman survivor of detention and systematic rape during the siege of Sarajevo. Like *Silent Waters*, *Grbavica* combines realist narrative conventions emphasizing the individual and familial with questions of collectivity—including accountability, testimony, and generational legacies. The surprise winner of the Golden Bear at the Berlin Film Festival, the film was released in the United States by Strand Releasing in spring 2007 and played in a number of European markets. An Austrian, German, and Croatian coproduction with Bosnia and Herzegovina, Žbanić's film addresses an international audience for whom the Balkan wars are a living media memory. At the same time, the film speaks to local and regional audiences who experienced the conflict directly. These audiences are differentially confronted with public accounts of the legacy of mass rapes; the film taps into Serbian denial, Bosnian shame, and a conflicted mix of other positionalities.

The geopolitical and human rights background of Grbavica is the systemic rapes perpetrated by Bosnian Serb paramilitary on as many as 20,000 Bosnian Muslim (Bosniak) women as part of a strategy of ethnic cleansing during the Yugoslav wars. Local and transnational feminist response to the Bosnian rapes included lawsuits before international criminal courts, activism, documentaries, artworks, and writing, including a play by Eve Ensler.[16] The extent of outside involvement became a source of concern for some feminists working on the issues regionally. As Grewal writes, in reference to the discourse of "women's rights as human rights": both "representational practices—that is, the ways in which the objects of violation [are] depicted—and . . . subjectifying practices need to be examined. Who [is] speaking for whom? What [are] the knowledges that enable them to speak for others?"[17] As a Bosnian feature film entrusted with the task of telling a woman's story of rape, Grbavica is a high-stakes project, but Žbanić does not pretend to speak for Bosnian women. In positioning the film in the transnational space of world cinema a decade after the crisis, and foregrounding themes of silence and the specificity of place, the filmmaker locates both her own subjectivity and the limits of her knowledge.

Žbanić was born and lives in Sarajevo. She attended Sarajevo's Academy of Performing Arts, which prominent Bosnian filmmakers Danis Tanović and Aida Begić also attended, but comments, "There was a war raging in the country while I was studying, and we did not have neither [sic] electricity nor cinemas for three and a half years. The studying itself was quite absurd. . . . We actually studied by imagining films."[18] She made shorts and documentaries through Deblokada, an artists' organization she founded in 1997. After Tanović's Oscar-winning No Man's Land (2001), Grbavica became the most widely circulating film from Bosnia and Herzegovina's fledgling national cinema. Begić's Snow, about a village of women war survivors, soon followed, winning the Critics' Week grand prize at Cannes. Both women followed their debuts with other feature films with female protagonists, putting women at the forefront of the region's cinema, including in its critique of postwar realities.[19]

But while it marked a new beginning, Grbavica also built on international acclaim attained by Balkan cinema in the 1990s, notably by its casting in the lead role of the Bosniak victim the Serbian actress Mirjana Karanović, who was featured in such acclaimed Balkan films as *Cabaret Balkan* (Goran Paskaljevic, 1998) and Emir Kusturica's *Underground* (1995) and *When Father Was Away on Business* (1985). This casting provides an example of the tension between regional and international address. As the director reports, the actress received hate mail for taking on the role of a "Bosnian whore"; at the same time, the film's potential reception as an indictment of the Serbs was mitigated by casting Karanović in the lead. Karanović's performance carries the film's tone of quiet realism, a striking departure from the black humor associated with the aforementioned touchstones of Balkan cinema.

Set in the present, *Grbavica* explores the relationship between a woman, Esma, and her twelve-year-old daughter, Sara, who was conceived by a rape in a detention camp during the siege of Sarajevo. The film avoids generalizing blame to all Serbs, using the (derogatory) term Chetnik for the occupiers and shifting questions of disclosure and reconciliation to familial terrain. The question of Sara's patrimony is directly raised in the narrative: she must provide documentation of her father's status as a *shaheed* (war martyr) in order to receive a fee waiver for a school trip; Esma takes a second job to earn the fee.

Eschewing direct representation of Esma's trauma, *Grbavica* instead dwells in the silences and absences that echo in and shape the present. I emphasize "dwells": the film takes its name from the occupied neighborhood where rapes were committed. It is a name that is both notorious and strange, especially as memories of news coverage fade for international audiences. Esma still inhabits Grbavica, struggling in this scarred space as she follows her quotidian routine and works nights to support her daughter. The film conveys a tension between the everyday and the weight of history— as Žbanić points out, Grbavica's etymology is "woman with a hump," a figure that could evoke Esma's secret (the film's U.K. release title). The pressure eventually tips the film's realism over to melodrama.

Esma finally tells Sara of her origins when her daughter, who's been flirting with delinquency and with a young man whose father did die a war hero, pulls the boy's borrowed gun on her mom. While the tonal shift here could be seen as a flaw, it is also a source of affective power, linking the film with fraught explorations of mother-daughter relationships in so-called women's genres from soaps to Lifetime movies to serial dramas. This physical confrontation is prefigured by the film's memorable opening scene, in which mother and daughter tussle affectionately, only to have

FIGURE 5.4 Esme holds the viewer's gaze before the title comes up. Mirjana Karanović in *Grbavica*. Frame capture. Strand Releasing.

Esma freeze up, seized by a physical memory she cannot disclose. The gun, seemingly out of place in their modest home and a metonymic emblem of the state of war, so recently past, momentarily assigns these female kin to opposite, untenable sides of a civil, ethnic conflict. In the film's final scene after the revelation, daughter and mother meet each other's gaze as Sara departs on the field trip, joining her schoolmates in the popular secular song "Sarajevo, Land of My Dreams." The film's U.S. subtitle is borrowed from this paean to a city known for its cosmopolitanism and ethnic tolerance; however, "dream" conjoined with "Grbavica" must also connote Esma's nightmares of her experience in the camp.

In a chapter on gender and Balkan film in *Cinema of Flames*, Iordanova beautifully diagnoses "the specific 'feminization' of the critical discourse on resistance to nationalism which established itself as an alternative to the popularly mediated perception of 'macho' Balkans" and argues against this feminization's "confining nature" (197). She argues that the way "the mass rapes became a *cause célèbre* for feminists in Croatia, Serbia, Germany and the USA" (198) blunted "subtle problems of interpretation which arised [sic] at the intersection of feminism and nationalism" (197). Historically, "rape as a metaphor has been extensively used in Balkan cinema," she writes, "where one's own nation is usually identified with the rape victim" (204). Assessing the representational landscape in the wake of the conflict and writing before the release of *Grbavica*, she argues that in fiction films the subject of mass rape is broached as "just one of the many violent aspects of the war" (202), while the specificity of women's experiences was developed in documentaries. Žbanić's feature film changed this landscape. While rape is kept offscreen (*ob-scene*) in *Grbavica*, it is neither metaphor, as with rape of a country, nor metonymy, one of many aspects of violence, but a woman's story, one of "incommensurable difference" in perspective from stories told from any other point of view. Rather than representing the violated woman's body as national trauma, the film looks askance at rising nationalism, peopling the screen with competent, reticent women and men divested of economic or patriarchal power.

The film opens with an image of a state-run women's group that Esma attends, a recurrent space that evokes the collective experience the narrative otherwise holds at a distance. The use of nonactors in these scenes evokes documentary treatments of the issue, and the slow panning shot over the women's still, crowded bodies eerily evokes a site of detention. The shot ends as Esma opens her eyes to look into the camera; the screen goes to white and the film's title appears (fig. 5.4). Esma's own testimonial gaze meets ours and seems to call for what Meta Mazaj, in an astute review of the film, describes as a "patient, responsible and responsive listener/viewer, not a passive witness."[20] Thus from the opening sequences address is carefully staged; we are challenged to return this gaze. The women's center sequences foreground a therapeutic scenario: the social worker says that in her experience healing can begin only when people speak their stories. But the fully privatized solution is not sufficient: at one point the proceedings are undermined by one woman's demand for jobs or money instead of therapy and then by another's hysterical laughter. Mazaj convincingly links this laughter, which spreads to include the other women, Esma, and finally the therapist, to a similar moment of dialogical, gendered laughter in the feminist classic *A Question of Silence* (Marleen Gorris, 1982).[21] In that film, laughter spreads out into the courtroom from a working-class female defendant who has previously remained mute, deeming speaking out in a hostile system to be futile. Her codefendants, female bystanders, jury members, and defense attorney join in, finally engulfing—and dividing—the court and the movie theater into whose space the scene thus extends.[22] Both films transform public spaces of reckoning though acknowledgment that male justice will not serve. After the climactic confrontation with her daughter, Esma finally does begin to share her story with the women's center group. The film does not position this as a cathartic moment, but rather as the beginning of a narration that will implicate its listeners, as the film does its audience.

Feminist activists have successfully intervened in the realms of international law around the issue of rape as a war crime in the Balkan conflict. This activism includes powerful independent documentaries like *Calling the Ghosts: A Story of Rape, War, and Women* (Mandy Jacobsen and Karmen Jelincic, 1996), which traces two women's stories of torture and systematic rape at the Omarska concentration camp and their subsequent participation in the ultimately successful campaign to have rape prosecuted as crime against humanity in the International Criminal Tribunal for the former Yugoslavia. Patricia Zimmerman writes, "*Calling the Ghosts* engages the rapes of the women only to disengage them from private suffering. The tape does not simply evidence the rapes in Bosnia but imprints with its structure the form of witnessing itself."[23] The tribunal's groundbreaking prosecutions were achieved only after the tape's completion. Analyzed in Iordonova's book as well, *Calling the Ghosts* was a relatively high-profile documentary for international audiences. It was produced by actress/activist Julia Ormond, shown on the premium cable station Cinemax, and distributed in the United States by Women Make Movies.

Made twelve years after the end of the war on a different scale and perhaps with a different audience in mind, the 35 mm fiction feature *Grbavica* lacks *Calling the Ghosts'* direct politicization and immediacy; it doesn't allude to the ongoing war crimes tribunal, offer statistics, or document the camps. The passage of time is what makes this particular narrativization of the repercussions of these war crimes possible: the twelve years that have passed are measured in Sara's adolescence. Moreover, the film's very production registers the material cause of this deferral of narration: during the war filmmaking was impossible and the industry has been slow to recover. As Žbanić notes: "BiH [Bosnia and Herzegovina] is the only country in Europe that does not have a 35 mm camera, or a film laboratory." The film was facilitated by regional efforts to make narrative film production viable. Speaking neither of nationalism nor as a representative of its feminized critique, Žbanić's debut feature emerges on the global film circuit to confront an issue of national and regional importance—the fate of the children of forcibly impregnated women.

Writing on the Balkan women directors who have made an intervention in world cinema in the 2000s through their films' visibility and acclaim, Mazaj diagnoses the "importance of the transnational not so much as a spatial but as a visual territory that displaces the viewer and the processes by which we accommodate and appropriate the threat of the foreign."[24] In *Grbavica*, the subject matter of rape compounds this process of displacement by evoking incommensurable, gendered positionalities and an international framework of redress. The film tries not to resolve the issues it raises but to open a space and a future; like the scene of infectious laughter, it communicates unspoken and diverse dimensions of women's experience.

Geographically proximate and historically entwined, the Balkans are a site of investment for German cinema in both a financial and psychological sense, and as we have seen German feminists were prominent in bring-ing the mass rapes of Bosnia to light and to justice.[25] *Grbavica*'s Golden Bear at Berlin was thus an important symbolic statement about cultural priorities, as well as a material boost to production in the Balkan region. In 2009 the Berlinale awarded its top prize to another film about the legacy of mass rapes in a civil conflict: Peruvian filmmaker Claudia Llosa's *La teta asustada / The Milk of Sorrow* (2009). Although the geopolitical connection is less direct, Llosa's film was also the recipient of German coproduction money, and the German sales company and distributor Match Factory rep-resents both Žbanić and Llosa.[26] While foreign financing for Latin Ameri-can filmmaking has been a long-standing feature of its international suc-cesses, this relationship with the Berlinale's World Cinema Fund maps a North/South axis characteristic of twenty-first-century global art cinema that distinguishes Llosa's authorship.[27]

Claudia Llosa's Trans/national Address

Celebrated almost immediately as an auteur as much for her style as for her subject matter, Llosa departs from the realism and political urgency of Sumar and Žbanić. I explore how the festival circuit frames Llosa as a national subject whose relation to human rights, feminism, and the exotic is appealing but difficult to decipher. Indeed, in its self-consciousness about aesthetics and its trans/national address, Llosa's work inhabits the spaces of contemporary world cinema in a way that is emblematic for this book. Un-like Lucrecia Martel, who, I argued in chapter 1, deploys auteurist style in part to block easy cross-cultural consumption of her explorations of class, race, and history in Argentina, Llosa seems to emphasize her films' "Latin American-ness." Her first two feature films have young Andean women pro-tagonists and are set in colorfully rendered indigenous communities. But Llosa is almost as elliptical in her historical references as is Martel. Her second feature, *Milk of Sorrow*, directly relates to women's human rights vio-lations during Peru's internal conflict. But while Sumar and Žbanić depict their female protagonists' subjective experience of trauma during Partition and the Bosnian War, respectively, *Milk of Sorrow* fancifully registers the effects of the recent past on the body of the next generation. Llosa's films make a spectacular play for international attention on behalf of a national cinema and narrative in dispute.

Born in Lima in 1976, Claudia Llosa currently resides in Barcelona. She studied filmmaking in Peru, at NYU, and in Madrid. Her gorgeously mounted and provocative debut feature *Madeinusa* is set in an isolated, fictional town in the Andes. Its title character—"My name is on your shirt label," she says to a baffled visitor from Lima (residents of the coastal capital, Limeños, are regarded with suspicion in the highlands)—becomes the center of the town's carnivalesque Holy Week rituals and of the attention of the visitor, significantly named Salvador. Between Good Friday and Easter Sunday, the villagers believe, God is dead and all laws are suspended. Madeinusa (Magaly Solier) and her sister live alone with their father, the town's mayor, and it becomes increasingly apparent that his incestuous desires are due to be fulfilled during the festivities. The outcome—for the father, Madeinusa, and the Limeño—is more shocking still. Developed at the Sundance Screenwriters' workshop, the film debuted in the festival's world cinema competition in 2006, received extensive festival exposure, and was Peru's official submission to the Oscars.

In the wake of Llosa's sensational debut, *Milk of Sorrow* anointed its young director as a world-class female auteur in the sense I discussed in chapter 1: an aesthetic brand with international currency. Echoing responses elsewhere in the trade and cinephile press and blogosphere, Boyd van Hoeij declares in *Variety* that "with her sophomore effort *The Milk of Sorrow*, Peruvian director Claudia Llosa (*Madeinusa*) bolsters her reputation as one of the most interesting femme helmers working in the Americas today."[28] A Spanish/Peruvian coproduction, with funds from the World Cinema Fund and other sources, the film moved from its Golden Bear in Berlin (the jury was headed by Tilda Swinton) to an Oscar nomination for Best Foreign Language Film, Peru's first shot at the award in the history of the competition, and significant box-office success at home.

Llosa's authorial persona is thus strongly identified with Peru's national cinema. At the same time, her success shows how the construction of national cinemas has changed with current media globalization. The New Cinemas of Argentina and Mexico can be cast as an edgy resurgence of longtime international cinema players from the region. But according to film critic and historian Ricardo Bedoya, "the history of cinema in Peru has always been one of crisis. . . . The instability of crisis has been the normal condition at all stages of its intermittent existence."[29] While cinema legislation was introduced in 1994 to strengthen the national cinema, only ten features were produced between 1997 and 2001. With the new coproduction arrangements opened up by the establishment of Ibermedia—a fund sponsored by Spain, Portugal, and more than a dozen countries in Latin America—a shift became possible. In little more than a decade, Ibermedia was funding sixty to seventy features annually—Llosa's films among them.[30] Given her films' international publicity and domestic notoriety, the thirty-something director can be taken as a metonym for Peruvian national cinema at this juncture.

In Llosa's first two feature films, national identity is associated with indigeneity, with the mystery and endurance of the Andean people, particularly Andean women. Complicating the gaze this representation solicits is the fact that this perspective is articulated from a coastal Lima, European-identified location and marked as such. Interpreting indigenous culture for international audiences is not an unfamiliar role for the Latin American intellectual elite. Indeed, a towering precedent is the Nobel Prize–winning novelist Mario Vargas Llosa, the director's uncle (filmmaker Luis Llosa, of *Anaconda* [1997] fame, is also an uncle). Vargas Llosa is a politically polarizing figure, not least for his role on the commission investigating a 1983 incident in which eight journalists were murdered in the Ayacucho region, where *Madeinusa* is set.[31] Critics felt Vargas Llosa's report characterized indigenous Peruvians as barbaric. The massacre in Ayacucho's resonance with the story line of *Madeinusa* complicates interpretations of the film and of Llosa's familial and political legacies.

Although *Madeinusa*'s depiction of indigenous culture was the subject of heated debate in Peru, rarely did the international cinema press greeting its release question these portrayals. The made-up rituals and vividly rendered miserabilism—the opening scene is a tour de force in which Madeinusa performs the quotidian chore of poisoning rats—were read in terms set by Llosa's interviews as her homage to Buñuel. The most vociferous Peruvian critics, on the other hand, attacked its stereotypes of "highlanders who appear on screen raping their children, getting drunk until they fall down, and betraying the candor of an upper class young man from Lima who had dared to bring his beautiful humanity to this Hell on earth."[32] The critical public sphere in which the film was debated in Peru was all but lost in translation. As John McGowan points out, "The debate around *Madeinusa* has much more to do with the country's historic internal tensions than with some Machiavellian distinction between a poor, misrepresented Latin American nation faced with an Orientalist West."[33] Yet although her film engages memories of the massacre, Llosa departs from previous generations' political scripts and national narratives in her emphasis on gender and sexuality, which informs her positioning both nationally and transnationally. Her youth and gender define her authorship, as do aesthetic strategies that reject passive portrayals of female suffering in favor of distinctly provocative ones.[34] Marvin D'Lugo details how "film authors have reemerged as key players in this Latin American audiovisual cultural scene." Of the transnational funding models introduced in the 1990s he claims, "the most serious and significant of these co-produced films challenge the assumption of the core/periphery model by generating cultural texts that have as their underlying project the co-production of newly emerging cultural identities."[35]

In this light the film's favorable international reception is more than a cued response to typical gestures of exoticization. The film concludes with an exhilarating feminist line of flight: Madeinusa's point of view of the road to Lima as she decisively leaves behind both her father and the visitor as well as all responsibility for her actions. Certainly, as Iliana Pagan-Teitelbaum points out in "Glamour in the Andes," the real story of migration the conclusion gestures toward is far from a utopian one. But the heroine's story of departure, which ends the film's fairy tale—if not the lurid events that take place in the village—is interestingly echoed in lead actress Magaly Solier's own itinerary from Ayacucho, where she is from. The DVD biography informs us that being cast in the film "completely changed her life. She moved from the city where she was born to Lima and created a fictional character without any previous experience." The "fictional character" could be read as her persona as well as her role, her collaboration with Llosa as a "co-production of newly emerging cultural identities." Building on her exposure in Llosa's film, Solier launched a successful singing and acting career. While she lacks the director's cultural capital and degree of control over the film's discourse, I read her as coauthor, in part, of the film's construction of a new image of indigenous femininity.

Solier's starring role in Llosa's second film, *The Milk of Sorrow*, uses her singing centrally as her character is otherwise all but mute. At the Berlin awards ceremony, Llosa introduced her film's star onstage, and Solier, in a galvanizing performative gesture, delivered a song in Quechua.[36] Avant-garde or primitivist, earnest or opportunist, the performance articulated the two definitions of culture, the anthropological and the highbrow, in a way that is shared by, if not as explicitly foregrounded in, other internationally circulating women's films.

The surreal picture of Andean culture in *Madeinusa* carries over to *Milk of Sorrow*'s theme of sexual violence against indigenous women. The film opens with a novel and terrifying invocation of such crimes; over a black screen a female voice begins to sing in Quechua of her memories of rape and torture. As the image comes in we see that the voice belongs to the

FIGURE 5.5 Fausta listens to her mother's terrible deathbed song. Magaly Solier and Bárbara Lazón in *Milk of Sorrow*. Match Factory.

heroine's mother, Perpetua (Bárbara Lazón), framed on her deathbed from directly overhead in medium close-up. Her beautiful daughter Fausta (Solier) leans into the frame, ministering to her mother in song (fig. 5.5). A cut to the window curtains billowing softly signals that the mother has passed away. A fade to black prepares for the film's dramatic title card.

In the next scene, Fausta exhibits symptoms—headache, a bloody nose, fainting—of a malady her uncle calls *la teta asustada* (literally, "frightened teat") when he consults with a Lima doctor. His niece was born in a village "during the time of terrorism"; her mother's trauma was passed on to her via her breast milk. Both matter-of-fact and poetic, naive and resonant, the myth he offers is indicative of the film's tone, through which horror is uncomfortably, figurally displaced. We learn that Fausta keeps a potato in her vagina to ward off sexual assault like her mother and the women of her generation endured. The film's fable-like quality erases historical specificity while highlighting (at least the notion of) localized cultural meaning.

Milk of Sorrow doesn't blame—or name—Maoist Sendero Luminoso (Shining Path) guerillas, or government security forces, as perpetrators of this crime, although both groups were responsible for sexual violence and human rights violations. Peru's bloody internal conflict of the 1980s and 1990s, in which 75 percent of the estimated 69,000 people who died were indigenous, is not referred to again in the film. Instead the conceit of la teta asustada is offered as both alternative genealogy that binds mother and daughter over and against sanctioned state narratives, and a crippling legacy that Fausta must overcome. The mother's preserved body literally remains a presence, as Fausta is unable to bury her until the end of the film. For international viewers, the film's symbolism is powerful, but it cannot evoke the experience or extent of the violence against indigenous women.

Milk of Sorrow was made five years after Peru's Truth and Reconciliation Commission report on the crimes, when the generation born after the internal conflict was coming of age.[37] The film's Spanish title takes poetic license from the work of Harvard medical anthropologist Kimberly Theidon, who provides the term as a translation of a Quechua phrase used in one of the many women's *testimonios* gathered in her study of the conflict, *Entre Prójemos*.[38] The title raises its own issues of cross-cultural reception. The English translation introduces a poeticism the Spanish title lacks, and reviewers tend to take the concept as a widespread folk belief. The connection to transnational feminist human rights scholarship through Theidon is important; at the same time it evokes an outside expert. Llosa was drawn to the term as a powerful figure of the embodied, generational memory of violence. She makes an analogy between history conveyed through sensory experience and her own cinematic narration: "What for many was foreign—therefore rare or enigmatic, due to the differences of language, culture, etc., was unconsciously recognized and understood with the logic of the senses."[39]

The opening images of the film—the mother's face and the horrific image conjured by her words, or rather by the subtitles that translate her Quechua song—evoke and function as originary trauma. Perpetua sings of being gang raped while pregnant with Fausta, then forced to swallow her dead husband's penis. Like the affected breast milk and the potato, these images of introjection map the indigenous female body as site of multiple symbolic transactions, between outside and inside, violence and reparation, the social and the subjective. Without historical footage, analysis, or statistics, the film attempts to engage the imaginary and the extent of crimes against women. The mother's actual body in its mummified state stands in for the racialized and class-specific nature of these crimes.

A member of the next generation, Fausta is not simply an allegorical figure of a violated Peru. Making her body host to the food source native to Peru, she could be said to have a rhizomatic relationship with the nation. As the potato grows and sprouts, it counters Fausta's positing as an empty vessel symbolizing a violated indigenous culture. Instead the tuber serves an apotropaic function—it is meant to deflect a would-be attacker by overwhelming him with disgust. Yet it is Fausta who is sickened by it, and only at the film's conclusion consents to have it removed. The film's last image is of a blooming, potted potato plant—no simple image of rebirth, as its roots cannot be disavowed.

Given such imagery, it is no wonder that *Variety*, with characteristic bluntness, describes *Milk of Sorrow* as an "ultra-arthouse item." Surreal touches, like the bizarre behavior of the wealthy composer and pianist who hires Fausta for domestic work, Mrs. Aída (Spanish actress Susi Sánchez), the mother's mummy appearing when the bed upon which Fausta's cousin's wedding dress is laid out is slid away from the wall, and mysterious landscapes like the dunes of the penultimate scene, where the heroine finally buries her mother, could be lifted from a catalog of art film highlights. Can the film's interest in women's human rights and art house aesthetics be reconciled in reception?

Each of the films discussed in this chapter speaks differently to audiences who are familiar with the histories to which they refer and those who aren't, but Llosa's style makes this double address central. The village architecture in *Silent Waters* bears marks of the past before religious differences exploded into communal violence. The Sarajevo of *Grbavica* is leaden and silent; the scars of the recent past are everywhere. In *Milk of Sorrow*'s brightly painted, picturesque mountain slums, only Fausta and a gardener who speaks to her in Quechua seem to remember the past. Llosa fits uncomfortably into a transnational feminist framework: while she intervenes in a public discourse of human rights abuses and links a salvage discourse around the Quechua language and Andean identity to testimony about crimes against indigenous women, her work favors art film ambiguity over political coherence.

The film is nothing if not aware of the dynamics of global reception, and it foregrounds markers of cultural enunciation and address. The ethnographic-seeming scenes in *Milk of Sorrow* of Fausta's aunt and uncle's wedding business give a vivid sense of the material culture cum pop art of the inhabitants of the outskirts of Lima (fig. 5.6). Yet in considering whether the scenes are objectifying, we do well to recall that the sensational anthropological ritual at the heart of Llosa's *Madeinusa* was made up from whole cloth; the wedding scenes too foreground the production of folkloric culture. The doubleness of local terrain is signified in the image and thematic of burial. Fausta has asked her uncle to wait to bury her mother while she earns the money she needs to transport her body back to the countryside. Fausta's gaze registers panic when she returns home to find a hole dug in the yard. The reverse shot of her little cousins enjoying a makeshift swimming pool almost satirizes our desire to find buried secrets.

FIGURE 5.6 Imagery of Fausta's uncle's family wedding business combines the ethnographic and the surreal. *Milk of Sorrow.* Match Factory.

The figure of the Europeanized, high-culture Mrs. Aída illuminates another crucial dimension of art cinema as an institution: its characteristic address to cultured rather than mass, frequently foreign rather than domestic, audiences. While the film accedes to realities of coproduction like financing deals that require the participation of Spanish actors and other personnel in Latin American films, it turns them to its own purposes. *The Milk of Sorrow* acknowledges questions of cultural appropriation in a central scenario of barter and aesthetic syncretism, in which Mrs. Aída, lacking inspiration for an upcoming concert, coaxes Fausta to sing, with a promise of a pearl for each song. The maid, whose singing was previously used only as a mode of communication with her Quechua-speaking mother and, after the latter's death, as a means of consoling herself, agrees to the arrangement and begins to accumulate pearls that she plans to use for her mother's burial (fig. 5.7).

After a successful performance of a work inspired by Fausta's music, the white woman turns on her servant, cheating her not only of creative credit but also of her pay. On the way back from the concert hall, she orders the car to pull over and puts Fausta out into the night on unfamiliar city streets, the height of terror for a young woman who has refused to go anywhere alone in her life. An allegory of the selfish extraction of an authentic national culture from indigenous Peruvians by the elite agents of high culture, the scenario unavoidably implicates the filmmaker herself as a European-identified cultural producer who collaborates with an indigenous actress. At the same time, the sensuality of the pearls and the songs

FIGURE 5.7 Mrs. Aída (Susi Sánchez) and Fausta in *Milk of Sorrow*.
Match Factory.

recall nothing so much as the sexual barter around music in Jane Campion's
The Piano, adding a level of engagement in the portrayal of relationships
between women. The tension between white women and indigenous domestic workers has risen to the fore in recent Latin American films; it is at
the center of the Chilean *La nana / The Maid* (2005), and depicted as erotic
in *La Ciénaga* (2001) and *El niño pez / The Fish Child* (2009). Here the two
women's power-saturated alliance at the very least indicates a scenario of
collaborative female creativity, one that has its origins with Fausta's mother
singing about her pain and that extends to comment on the relationship
between the film's director and its star.

Collaboration between women structures the film's production and reception. The film was shot in wide-screen by Argentine cinematographer
Natasha Braier, who also shot Puenzo's xxy (fig. 5.8). And as I have suggested, Solier's contribution in the lead role alters the terms of authorial
discourse around the film, turning a transnationally financed art film into
a national phenomenon. Solier's 2009 debut album *Warmi*, the Quechua
word for "women," released in the wake of her screen success, found regional audiences the films might reach only by reputation. As an icon of
twenty-first-century indigenous femininity, Solier complicates Llosa's status as national spokesperson—at the very least by sharing it. Images of the
two side by side signify class and ethnic difference, but also a shared glamour and creativity based on gender, age, and involvement in an industry
that is a source of national pride. The intertextual resonances of Solier's two
roles with Llosa contribute a postmodern spin to her star persona, although

FIGURE 5.8 Natasha Braier, cinematographer, with Claudia Llosa, writer/director. *Milk of Sorrow*. Match Factory.

her career does not remain circumscribed by this association. Llosa's films' politics are post-Third-Worldist in their interest in gender and sexuality over consolidation of a national narrative; they might also be construed as postfeminist in their stylization and refusal of social analysis. Yet their contradictory attempt to redefine indigenous femininity beyond victim or emblematic status leaves her heroines open to contestation, including from Solier's own "reverse discourse" of pop stardom.

In Llosa's work, national identity and femininity are articulated and dis-articulated as much in relation to transnational film culture as they are to an authentic Peru. In imagining indigeneity, this film comes closer than most I've analyzed to making the world cinema spectator's desire for an "other" culture explicit. At the same time it uses performativity and styliza-tion to jam that desire—its heroine remains inaccessible. In his account of the infrastructure and ideological effects of transnational European film productions, Randall Halle identifies "the strategy of national appearance" in films made outside Europe with such funds. To international specta-tors, such films "offer a sense of engagement with a foreign culture be-cause there is little to indicate . . . that national cinema now gives way to the transnational."[40] Such arrangements are today endemic to film financ-ing and festival circuits, and antirealist styles like Llosa's foreground these transactions. Her "strategy of national appearance" is concentrated in her authorial image.

Llosa's films' visibility is shaping current expectations of Peruvian cinema; to what extent do they shape transnational perception of post–Truth and Reconciliation Commission Peruvian national identity? They have at best an oblique relationship to women's human rights activism in Peru and in Latin America more generally.[41] In a human rights framework, one tells one's story to prove one's humanity and entitlement to universal rights. In *Milk of Sorrow*, there is little evidence of the impulse to testify; Fausta continues her mother's legacy by singing, but she does not pass on her words. Llosa, in turn, alludes to her own relationship to Solier in the appropriation of Fausta's voice by Mrs. Aída. Invoking precedents like Buñuel and Campion, Llosa claims the position of auteur. She turns the internationally circulating art film's anticipated display of the signifiers of exotic national identity and trauma into a performance. I would like to read it, in the context of the careers of her star and her expanding cohort of Latin American women filmmakers, as a collaborative one. But *Milk of Sorrow* does not represent indigenous communities or the sexual violence perpetrated against women during the internal conflict in Peru. *Milk of Sorrow* articulates auteurism and aesthetics, the construction of the nation in gendered and racialized terms, and transnational modes of production and reception. It is an excellent example of how women's filmmaking inhabits the spaces of contemporary world art cinema; insofar as it doesn't leave room for other accounts, is also a cautionary one.

While the commodification of fiction films on human rights issues can entail a depoliticization of both their feminism and their critiques of the state, the emerging genre is one through which women directors participate in a significant way in the remapping of world cinema. This occurs quite literally in the cases of Pakistan, Bosnia, and Peru, where film culture is undergoing significant change in the early twenty-first century. Bringing these films together, I attempt to foreground how gender informs "the potential ways in which the periphery can function as a critical paradigm that allows for a commonality of meaning to emerge from what are, effectively, radically diverse historical processes."[42] The events of Partition and the civil conflicts in the former Yugoslavia and Peru cannot be made equivalent; nor can patterns of attacks on women based on ethnicity and religion be ignored. I have considered these works with the aim less of critiquing how they address massive violations of women's human rights than of exploring their directors' role in bringing women's stories to the transnational public sphere. On a narrative level, all of these films end with a connection—however fraught or tenuous—between generations of women. These daughters are figures of futurity and thus of the filmmakers' own creativity.

Jaikumar, in her essay on *Silent Waters*, says that work on transnational women's film culture should be a "search for alliances and solidarities that acknowledges potentially incommensurable difference" (223). These three films foreground incommensurability: within audience experiences and interpretations, between the films and the contexts from which they arise, among the heroines' predicaments. The well is a complex signifier in *Silent Waters*—the village's source of sustenance, grave, and aporia. *Grbavica's* stubbornly untranslated, nearly unpronounceable title is a marker of place, a name once freighted with meaning from coverage in international news media, but then largely forgotten internationally until a feature film reinscribes it in/as a woman's story. Fausta's songs communicate different messages when incorporated into another woman's compositions and into the actress's repertoire. The films thus "tak[e] viewers to the silenced counterparts of national and global modernity" while communicating on their own terms.[43]

Address and enunciation are carefully marked in all three films: Zubeida confronts her own image in the mirror, with Veero's locket around her neck. As I've described, the heroine of *Grbavica* opens her eyes to engage ours in that film's pretitle sequence. In the opening song of *Milk of Sorrow* the mother addresses her daughter and, through her, us: "This woman who sings was raped that night," she begins. When she finishes her song, she closes her eyes and dies. This gaze of engagement is, I suggest, crucial to fiction films about women's human rights. It makes a claim on the viewer. Not a legal claim, but a claim on attention—attention to language and location and all that film is capable of revealing of the world, but also attention to the frame itself, so prominent in these compositions. It is the frame through which the viewer acknowledges her difference and displacement as well as her potential for ethical engagement.

AFTERWORD

A number of factors came together by the first decade of the twenty-first century to articulate gender and cinema with geopolitics in new ways. During this period, training opportunities expanded; transnational financing for art cinema reached more women directors in more countries; costs of feature film production decreased with digital technologies; festival economies—of taste as well as sales—proliferated; and cinephilic criticism and digital streaming exploded on the Internet. Documentary's prestige and institutional supports increased worldwide, accessing political formations and forms of creative labor in which women and feminism flourished. While U.S.-dominated postfeminist popular culture consolidated its hegemony, women and girls became targets of national and international development discourses, affecting the content of films as well as opportunities for women in media making. Starting from and analyzing the U.S. art house as a reception context, this book has argued for an updated, transnational concept of women's cinema that makes visible feminist countercurrents within the neoliberal context behind many of these changes.

Each case study has ranged from close reading to global claims, and it is time to take the measure of these travels. I have attempted to track the systems of value that position the films encountered in the North American art house–academy–feminist public sphere and to detail the historical, cultural, and aesthetic contexts from which those films emerge. I have argued that gender informs not only the images and stories on screen but also the terms of film financing, production, distribution, exhibition, and evaluation. Methodologically, each chapter traced a salient discourse that positions women's filmmaking within world cinema and displays tensions between ideologies of individualism and privatization and more expansive social claims.

It may be helpful to summarize these discourses and tensions here. I began by showing how the categories of art and auteur are deployed to dismiss questions of gender equity in filmmaking and how women filmmakers in turn deconstruct the association of woman with the aesthetic. I then analyzed how diasporan directors may become placeholders for particular concepts of culture but are able to engage in transnational cultural politics from this position. I also considered how women filmmakers negotiate their place in reinvigorated national and regional cinemas through progressive uses of women's genres that have found global audiences. I went on to detail how Asian women directors draw on the politics and erotics of networks as approaches to authorship, narration, and audience, and finally I illuminated how work by women filmmakers positioned as authentic national subjects goes on to counter portrayals of women as universal victims of rights abuses. Through textual analysis, I attempted to navigate the dynamics of particular and general that activate each discursive field. In aggregate, these films and filmmakers mobilize gendered perspectives as a challenge to prevalent views of value and address in world cinema. They allow for a transnational theorization of women's cinema that is an important counter to approaches to women and film in the United States, where gender disparities have become more visible while seemingly remaining intractable in the face of liberal demands for inclusion.

We've seen how the concept of women's cinema first arose in the 1970s to advocate for women's independent production and their greater participation in film and media industries and to project cinema's feminist future. The concept was neither prescriptive nor totalizing. But unlike the term "world cinema," which has weathered political and technological changes and is widely used by scholars, distributors, viewers, and even airlines—if not always in the same, at least in mutually intelligible ways—the term "women's cinema" is not in wide circulation today despite the richness of the terrain I've mapped. Scholars, programmers, and audiences of the women's film festivals that take place around the world may still use the term as a part of their feminist vision; but for mainstream critics and audiences, a "woman's film" is likely to be a love story or other sentimental tale. But such so-called women's genres attract audiences across national and regional film cultures; these viewers will help to define the future of transnational women's cinema as they come to embrace the expanding corpus of critical work by women filmmakers.

If women's cinema today cannot be defined in terms of Western texts and theories, we have seen that it is also poorly served by older national cinema models. Women's film culture crosses geographical borders, scales of production, political commitments, and the magical threshold between production and reception. By considering the contributions and positioning of women directors in this way we get a fuller picture of how they are both privileged and constrained by present articulations of gender and world cinema. The aesthetic, political, and institutional frameworks of transnational women's cinema have decentered a hegemonic vision of feminism and film and interrupted an illusory progression toward equal opportunity. Contemporary cinema studies must now contend with a critical mass of films by women directors; doing so could change the world.

Notes

Introduction

1. Streisand made a feminist speech when accepting the first Golden Globe for a woman director for *Yentl* (1984). But even with *Prince of Tides* (1991), a nominee for Best Picture, she was passed over in the director category at the Oscars.

2. Appadurai, "Disjuncture and Difference in the Global Cultural Economy," 33.

3. Lauzen, "The Celluloid Ceiling." From the online executive summary: "In 2008, women comprised 16% of all directors, executive producers, producers, writers, cinematographers, and editors working on the top 250 domestic grossing films. . . . Women accounted for 9% of directors in 2008, an increase of 3 percentage points from 2007. This figure represents no change from the percentage of women directing in 1998." The 2008 figures were quoted by the mainstream press during the Oscar buildup. In her latest study, Lauzen found women were 8 percent of directors. "The Celluloid Ceiling: Behind-the-Scenes Employment of Women on the Top 250 Films of 2013," http://womenintvfilm.sdsu.edu/files/2013_Celluloid_Ceiling_Report .pdf.

4. These stories also shared space with the coy coverage of the rivalry between Bigelow and ex-husband James Cameron among the nominees. A low point, earlier in the season, was marked by *Variety* editor Peter S. Bart's comparisons of Bigelow's looks with Jane Campion's appearance: "Unlikely Rivals on the Oscar Circuit." His piece was reported by Women and Hollywood blogger Melissa Silverstein, "Sexism Alert: The Catfight Begins," September 24, 2009, http://womenandhollywood.com/2009/09/24 /sexism-alert-the-catfight-begins/.

5. At the same time, Catherine Grant wonders whether feminist criticism of the 1970s–1990s went far enough in reconceptualizing authorship. Grant, "Secret Agents," 115.

6. Judith Mayne's *Directed by Dorothy Arzner* presents these arguments compellingly.

7. See, among others, Jermyn and Redmond, *The Cinema of Kathryn Bigelow*; Lauzen, "Kathryn Bigelow"; and Tasker and Atakav, "'And the Time Has Come!'"

8. Virginia Woolf has stated this problem most pithily: "Speaking crudely, football and sport are 'important'; the worship of fashion and buying of clothes 'trivial.' And these values are inevitably transferred from life to fiction. This is an important book, the critic says, because it deals with war. This is an insignificant book because it deals with the feelings of women in a drawing-room." *A Room of One's Own*, 34.

9. Note, for example, that of the 2012 list of films submitted for consideration for the category by a record number of seventy-six countries, sixteen were directed or co-directed by women.

10. Miriam Hansen, *Babel and Babylon: Spectatorship in American Silent Cinema*, 8.

11. Questions about female colonial power and Bigelow's films' ideological alignment with U.S. imperialism are raised even more pointedly in her follow-up project with screenwriter Mark Boal, *Zero Dark Thirty* (2012), which puts a lone and single-minded woman at the apex of the extraordinarily costly hunt for Osama Bin Laden. For a response, see Fawzia Afzal-Khan, "The Heart of Darkness in *Zero Dark Thirty*," *Counterpunch*, December 12–14, 2012, http://www.counterpunch.org/2012/12/14/the-heart-of-darkness-in-zero-dark-thirty/.

12. Nagib, "Towards a Positive Definition of World Cinema," 35.

13. There is much to recommend Nagib's definition of world cinema, cited above, as "simply the cinema of the world," and work on world cinema that encompasses popular films consumed nationally and transnationally is highly productive. However, this book looks at the festival and art house ecosystem as a privileged one for the cinema of women directors.

14. Fiachra Gibbons, "They Just Thought I Was a Kid with a Video," *Guardian*, October 26, 2003. Because this book refers to a new generation of filmmakers who became active in the twenty-first century, the filmmaker's year of birth is given at first mention or if otherwise relevant to the discussion. Film titles are given in the original release title at first mention, using spelling or transcription from the Internet Movie Database for simplicity, followed by the English title.

15. Belinda Smaill in "The Male Sojourner, the Female Director and Popular European Cinema" identifies the similarities in a trio of the Danish director's films. *In a Better World*, as well as *Brothers* (2004) and *After the Wedding* (2006), all written with Thomas Anders Jensen, revolve around what Smaill calls Danish "male sojourners." These men bring their problems home with them when they return from serving in aid roles in Third World locales. Smaill reads Bier's trilogy of male melodramas as portraying a crisis in Europe's patriarchal authority in a newly ordered world. Paradoxically, it is the Western woman's perspective that both identifies and redeems the impotence of the privileged male.

16. See Chow, *Primitive Passions*; Wang, *Chinese Women's Cinema*; Dove, "New Looks."

17. Among the recent publications on world cinema, including *Screening World Cinema* (edited by Catherine Grant and Annette Kuhn), *Rethinking Third Cinema* (edited by Anthony R. Guneratne and Wimal Dissanayake), *Remapping World Cinema* (edited by Stephanie Dennison and Song Hwee Lim), *World Cinemas / Transnational Perspectives* (edited by Nataša Ďurovičová and Kathleen Newman), *Global Art Cinema* (edited by Rosalind Gault and Karl Schoonover), *Theorising National Cinemas* (edited by Valentina

Vitali and Paul Willeman), *Transnational Cinema* (edited by Elizabeth Ezra and Terry Rowden), and *Theorizing World Cinema* (edited by Lúcia Nagib, Chris Perriam, and Rajinder Dudrah), only *Remapping World Cinema* uses gender as an organizing rubric. This does not mean that individual essays do not attend to gender and sexuality, just that we see a paradigm shift in a field that has made feminist thought central at least since Laura Mulvey's "Visual Pleasure and Narrative Cinema" in 1975.

18. Media feminism in the early 1970s was both local and transnational. To name just a few of the organizations that flourished: In 1972 in Britain, Claire Johnston co-organized the Women's Cinema Event at the Edinburgh Film Festival from which *Notes on Women's Cinema* arose, and the Women's Film Group and the distribution organization Cinema of Women were established in London. *Women in Film* began publication in Berkeley (a group of its editors left to form *Camera Obscura* in 1975), and Women Make Movies was incorporated in New York. The Sydney Women's Film Group was formed in 1971; and Women and Film in 1973. Studio D, the powerfully influential women's studio of the National Film Board of Canada; La femme et le film (later Video Femmes), a Quebec women's film organization; Amsterdam's Cinemien; and the journal *Jump Cut* were established in 1974. Groupe Intervention Video (GIV), a distributor of women's video in Montreal, and Cine-Mujer, a group of feminists and women filmmakers at the Mexican national film school, were set up in 1975. Colombia's Cine-Mujer was established in 1978, as was the Films de femmes festival in Creteil, France. The term "cinefeminism" is used by E. Ann Kaplan in "Interview with British Cine-Feminists." For two of the many possible and valuable genealogies and mappings of the formation of feminist film culture, see Mellencamp, *A Fine Romance*, and Rich, *Chick Flicks*. On *Camera Obscura*, see *Camera Obscura* Collective, "*Camera Obscura* at Thirty." On feminist distributors in the 1970s, see *Camera Obscura* Collective, "*Camera Obscura* Questionnaire on Alternative Film Distribution." On Women Make Movies, see the dossier "Women Make Movies at 40," *Camera Obscura* 82 (2013): 125–164.

19. This question echoes Teresa de Lauretis's formulation in "Rethinking Women's Cinema": "If we rethink the problem of a specificity of women's cinema . . . in terms of address—who is making films for whom, who is looking and speaking, how, where, and to whom—then what has been seen as a rift, a division, an ideological split within feminist film culture between theory and practice, or between formalism and activism, might appear to be the very strength, the drive and productive heterogeneity of feminism," 135.

20. This abbreviated history of the field focuses on the concept and term "women's cinema." While I isolate a few of the most prominent interrogations of the term, its use has been too widespread to include them all.

21. Johnston, "Women's Cinema as Counter Cinema," 211. On the status of this essay in the genealogy of feminist film studies, see White, "The Last Days of Women's Cinema," my contribution to *Camera Obscura*'s An Archive for the Future. For a moving assessment of Johnston's contribution, see the preface to Meghan Morris's *Too Soon Too Late*.

22. Mulvey, "Visual Pleasure and Narrative Cinema."

23. Doane, "The 'Woman's Film.'"

24. De Lauretis, *Technologies of Gender*, 26.

25. De Lauretis, "Rethinking Women's Cinema," 135. Subsequent references to this work given in the text.

26. The conferences Console-ing Passions (founded 1989, http://www.console-ingpassions.org/about-cp/), Women and the Silent Screen (founded 1999, http://wss2013.arts.unimelb.edu.au/), and Visible Evidence (founded 1993, http://www.visibleevidence.org/) were established to offer international scholars working in these subfields of feminist film and media studies a more welcoming environment than the larger professional meetings. (Visible Evidence focuses broadly on documentary, but it is strongly identified with feminism.) While some of the international women's film festivals hold scholarly forums, there is not yet an established international academic infrastructure for scholars working specifically on contemporary women's filmmaking. "Contemporary Women's Cinema: Global Scenarios and Transnational Contexts," organized by Veronica Pravadelli and E. Ann Kaplan in Rome in 2013, was planned as the first of regular meetings in different countries.

27. Another longstanding European event, the International Women's Film Festival Dortmund/Cologne merges two biannual festivals founded in 1984 and 1987. A wave of festivals that started in the 2000s, including London's Birds Eye View, Filmmor in Turkey, and Citizen Jane in Columbia, Missouri, responds to new forms of feminist and film festival culture. The importance of the network of women's film festivals in Asia is discussed in more detail in chapters 3 and 4. Despite the burgeoning of film festival studies, the history of women's film festivals is still insufficiently documented and theorized; Kay Armatage, as a programmer and scholar, has done significant work to redress this. See her "Toronto Women and Film International 1973," and the panel "Women's Film Festivals: 40 Years On," held at the Toronto International Film Festival, September 10, 2013. See also White, "Last Days of Women's Cinema."

28. The first films to emerge from the lab, held in Jordan, Cherien Dabis's *Amreeka* (2008) and Najwa Najjar's *Al-mor wa al rumman / Pomegranates and Myrrh* (2008), were by women, and *Wadjda* is another recent success. "RAWI Middle East Screenwriters Lab," Sundance Institute, http://www.sundance.org/programs/middle-east-screenwriters-lab/. Women Make Movies partnered with the event in Sierra Leone as part of forty international exhibitions honoring its fortieth anniversary ("WWM@40," http://www.wmm.com/40for40/#sierra). The Santiago festival, established in 2010, gives a needed boost to regional connections among Latin American women filmmakers. Nick MacWilliam, "Calling the Shots: Chile's New Wave of Female Filmmakers," Sounds and Colours, April 4, 2013, http://www.soundsandcolours.com/articles/chile/calling-the-shots-chiles-new-wave-of-female-filmmakers/.

29. My emphasis is on work that takes on traditions and practices outside the United States, but important works on American independent filmmaking like Valerie Smith's *Not Just Race, Not Just Gender*, Jacqueline Bobo's *Black Women Film and Video Artists*, and Peter X. Feng's *Identities in Motion* also influence how these issues are taken up in feminist film studies. These debates spurred work by critics central to cinefeminism, for example, E. Ann Kaplan's *Looking for the Other*.

30. Among English language texts, see Tarr and Rollet, *Cinema and the Second Sex*; Rashkin, *Women Filmmakers in Mexico*; Rebecca Hillauer, *Encyclopedia of Arab Women*

Filmmakers; Austin-Smith and Melnyk, *The Gendered Screen*; Laviosa, *Visions of Struggle in Women's Filmmaking in the Mediterranean*.

31. Wang, "Introduction," in *Chinese Women's Cinema*, 2.

32. Shohat, "Gendered Cartographies of Knowledge," 2. See also Shohat and Stam, *Unthinking Eurocentrism*; Shohat and Stam, *Multiculturalism, Postcoloniality, and the Media*.

33. Butler, *Women's Cinema*, 21. Subsequent references to this work given in the text.

34. Deleuze, *Cinema 2*. See also Lionnet and Shi, *Minor Transnationalisms*. Priya Jaikumar critiques the "assimilationist" model of Butler's text, which uses "postcolonial or national cinemas and exilic or diasporic filmmakers and theorists as instructive extensions of existing notions of women's cinema," in "Translating Silences," 208.

35. See White, "Lesbian Minor Cinema," for a related discussion of Butler's concept.

36. See Jameson, *The Geopolitical Aesthetic*.

37. Kaplan and Grewal, "Transnational Feminist Cultural Studies," 358.

38. Guneratne and Dissanayake, *Rethinking Third Cinema*; Hjort and Petrie, *The Cinema of Small Nations*; Iordanova, Martin-Jones, and Vidal, *Cinema at the Periphery*.

39. Nataša Ďurovičová, "Preface," in Ďurovičová and Newman, *World Cinemas / Transnational Perspectives*, ix.

40. Andrew, "An Atlas of World Cinema," 19.

41. Drawing on the work of Franco Moretti and Fredric Jameson, Andrew asks, "Why not examine the film as map—cognitive map—while putting it *on* the map. How does a fictional universe from another part of the world orient its viewers to their global situation?" "An Atlas of World Cinema," 24.

42. Kaplan, "The Politics of Location as Transnational Feminist Cultural Practice," 139.

43. Nagib outlines her "positive, democratic, inclusive approach to film studies," acknowledging Stam and Shohat for the term "polycentric," in *World Cinema and the Ethics of Realism*, 1.

44. Shohat, "Post-Third-Worldist Culture," 62.

45. Kaplan, Alarcón, and Moallem, *Between Woman and Nation*.

46. The letter to the French Embassy in Tehran stated, in part, "*Persepolis* presents an unrealistic face of the achievements and results of the 'glorious Islamic Revolution' in some of its parts" and queried whether its programming was a "political or even anti-cultural act." Lawrence Van Gelder, "Vexation from Cannes," Arts, Briefly, *New York Times*, May 22, 2007, http://query.nytimes.com/gst/fullpage.html?res=9E0DEED B1F31F931A15756C0A9619C8B63&scp=1&sq=persepolis%20farabi&st=cse.

47. Shohat and Stam, "Introduction," in *Multiculturalism, Postcoloniality, and Transnational Media*, 1.

48. The longtime (male) festival directors of Cannes, Venice, and Berlin clearly stamp the programs with their preferences. Each festival's mix and history deserve individualized study. For more on Cannes, see chapter 1; on Toronto, see chapter 2; on LGBT and women's festivals, chapter 4; and Berlin, chapters 4 and 5. See also de Valck, *Film Festivals*; Wong, *Film Festivals*. See Loist and de Valck's bibliography of festival scholarship, "Film Festivals / Film Festival Research."

49. McHugh quotes Woolf's claim that "as a woman my country is the whole world"

and her comparison of the thin soup served at women's colleges with a rich lunch at Oxbridge in *A Room of One's Own*. McHugh, "The World and the Soup," 115. Subsequent references to this work given in the text.

50. Grant, "www.auteur.com?," 107.

1. To Each Her Own Cinema

1. For the now robust literature on film festivals, see Loist and de Valck, "Film Festivals / Film Festival Research." This bibliography and the number of participants in the research group coordinated by Loist and de Valck have grown exponentially during the drafting of this book, and I am unable to do justice to the insights of all the scholars. Good places to begin include de Valck, *Film Festivals*; Elsaesser, "Film Festival Networks"; Porton, *Dekalog 3*; Iordanova, "The Film Festival Circuit"; and Wong, *Film Festivals*.

2. Elsaesser, "Film Festival Networks," 88.

3. Funds like the Rotterdam Film Festival's Hubert Bals and the Berlinale's World Cinema Fund offer formal structures for coproduction agreements (see chapter 5). Cannes Cinefondation's Residence and Atelier programs do not have a specific geographical mandate but have frequently sponsored filmmakers from the developing world. The Centre National du Cinema's Fonds Sud specifically fosters filmmaking in developing countries, especially Francophone.

4. De Valck, *Film Festivals*, 15.

5. Jacob served as festival director between 1978 and 2001, when he assumed his current title.

6. "*Chacun son cinéma: To Each His Own Cinema*," Festival de Cannes, 2007, http://www.festival-cannes.com/en/archives/ficheFilm/id/4427023/year/2007.html.

7. The subtitle roughly translates as "the way the heart races when the lights go out and the film begins."

8. Kira Cochrane, "Where Are the Women Film-makers at Cannes?," *Guardian*, May 21, 2007, http://www.guardian.co.uk/film/filmblog/2007/may/22/wherearethe womenfilmmakers.

9. I take Cannes as my primary example because of its status and visibility and because French conceptualizations of auteurism and film art are so pervasive. Venice and Cannes are the oldest and most prestigious prize-granting festivals. Venice's top prize, the Golden Lion, has been awarded to four women directors: Margarethe Von Trotta, Agnès Varda, Mira Nair, and Sofia Coppola. A-list status, conferred by the regulating body FIAPF (Fédération Internationale des Associations de Producteurs de Films), was later attained by Berlin as well as nine additional festivals. Many other festivals have achieved regional significance, including those in Hong Kong, Pusan, and Buenos Aires. In the North American context, Toronto and Sundance, the two most important festivals for the industry, have somewhat more equitable gender statistics, reflecting their size and programming philosophies and feminist personnel. See chapter 2 for further discussion.

10. The fact that these selections can fit in a footnote, although a cumbersome one, is telling: Varda's *Cleo from 5 to 7* competed in 1962 (she's had other films in Un Certain

Regard but never again in competition); Zetterling in 1965 and 1968; Duras in 1971 with *Le Camion* (and in 1959, 1960, and 1961 as screenwriter); Wertmüller with *Seduction of Mimi* in 1972 and *Love and Anarchy* in 1973; Cavani in 1974, 1981, and 1989; Gillian Armstrong with *My Brilliant Career* in 1979; Mészáros in 1980 and 1984; von Trotta in 1986 and 1988; Denis's debut *Chocolat* competed in 1988, but other films went to Venice (although *Trouble Every Day* appeared out of competition and caused a scandal at Cannes). Catherine Breillat didn't compete until *Vieille maîtresse / The Last Mistress* in 2007. Campion had four films (three shorts and her first television feature) at the festival in 1986, three in Un Certain Regard, and *Peel* won the Palme d'Or for short film in competion. *Sweetie* competed in 1989; *The Piano* won in 1993; and *Bright Star* competed in 2009. In 2013 she headed the Cinéfondation jury and the Short Film section and in 2014 headed the main jury.

11. In 2011, four women's films were selected out of nineteen (21 percent), but in 2012 there were again none, prompting two-time Jury Prize winner and 2012 jury member Andrea Arnold to call it "a great pity and a great disappointment" on opening night. Vanessa Thorpe, "Cannes 2012: Why Have No Female Film Directors Been Nominated for the Palme d'Or at Cannes?," *Guardian*, May 19, 2012, http://www .guardian.co.uk/film/2012/may/20/cannes-women-andrea-arnold-row. The French feminist group La Barbe went further, publishing a letter of protest in *Le Monde*. Fanny Cottençon, Virginie Despentes, and Coline Serreau, "A Cannes, les femmes montrent leurs bobines, les hommes, leurs films," *Le Monde*, May 11, 2012, http://www.lemonde .fr/idees/article/2012/05/11/a-cannes-les-femmes-montrent-leurs-bobines-les-hommes -leurs-films_1699989_3232.html. The letter collected more than 2,000 signatories, http://labarbeacannes.blogspot.fr/p/liste-des-signataires.html.

As feminists became more outspoken, coverage of the issue grew. In 2014, festival director Thierry Frémaux acknowledged: "It is important to show the presence of women in the industry. It is increasingly important in terms of numbers, but also in quality." The fact that it was "a good year for women" was, in his view, "a coincidence." Brian Alexander, "Women Filmmakers Take the Spotlight in Cannes," *USA Today*, May 13, 2014, http://www.usatoday.com/story/life/movies/2014/05/13/women-filmmakers-cannes-2014/8988269/. Campion was appointed head of a majority female jury that year, but she wasn't going to sweep the problem under the rug: "Frémaux told us that only 7 per cent, out of the 1,800 films submitted . . . , were directed by women. . . . It seems very undemocratic. . . . Excuse me gentleman, but the guys seem to eat all the cake." Nigel M. Smith, "Cannes Jury President Jane Campion Calls Out the 'Inherent Sexism' of the Industry," *Indiewire*, May 15, 2014, http://www.indiewire.com/article /cannes-jury-president-jane-campion-calls-out-the-inherent-sexism-in-the-film-industry.

12. Review of *To Each His Own Cinema*, *Variety*, May 20, 2007.

13. Campion's career pathway contrasts with male Cannes favorites like the Coen brothers, who have had eight features in competition at the festival. Campion's next major project, *Top of the Lake* (2013), was a six-part television series coproduced by the Sundance Channel. Presented at the Sundance and Berlin Film Festivals, the miniseries is another example of women's work circulating outside the feature film format.

14. Tarr and Rollett, *Cinema and the Second Sex*. The head of UniFrance Films considers this relative equity a benefit of the French *exception culturelle* or cultural exception

principle in international trade agreements. In 2013, 23 percent of French feature films were directed by women. Kim Willsher, "Women Bridge Gender Gap as French Film Embraces a New Nouvelle Vague," *Observer*, April 19, 2014.

15. One of the best known—and arguably most French, given her particular attention to questions of female desire—Catherine Breillat, screened *The Last Mistress* in competition in the same 2007 edition of the festival and might not have been at liberty to make a short. Even if the weight of history on the anniversary project had raised the bar of auteurist connoisseurship (so that French directors Agnès Jaoui and Anne Fontaine were not considered "universally famous" enough despite previous invitations to the festival), a nod—however compensatory—to Agnès Varda or Claire Denis, two women directors at the top of most auteurist lists, would not have been amiss. Both released features in 2008 that premiered at Venice; perhaps they too were just too busy to celebrate the history of Cannes.

16. Recent permutations of the omnibus film have otherwise sought out gender diversity. This includes political projects like *11'09"01—September 11* (2002), with contributions by both Mira Nair and Samira Makhmalbaf, and cosmopolitan ones like *New York, I Love You* (2008), with Nair and Natalie Portman.

17. Sarris, *The American Cinema*, 216.

18. Catherine Grant writes, "Until quite recently . . . feminists' reluctance to move beyond the film text in their explorations of women's authorial agency left many of them ill equipped to answer convincingly at least one simple question: what exactly were the feminist objectives of studying *women's* cinema within the conceptual frameworks they inherited?" "Secret Agents," 115.

19. Elsaesser, "Leni Riefenstahl."

20. Blonski, Creed, and Freiberg, *Don't Shoot Darling!*; McHugh, *Jane Campion*; Polan, *Jane Campion*.

21. The costume recalls Isabella Rossellini's *Green Porno* series on insect reproduction produced for the Sundance Channel, a good example of short films made on the woman director's own terms: http://www.sundancechannel.com/greenporno/.

22. "Others can't resist being their squirrelly selves with surrealism (Raoul Ruiz), oddness (Jane Campion), pretension (Michael Cimino), artiness (Wong Kar Wai) and political grandstanding (Amos Gitai)." Kirk Honeycutt, review of *To Each His Own Cinema*, *Hollywood Reporter*, May 20, 2007.

23. Michael Sicinski, "To Each His Own Cinema," August 12, 2009, The Academic Hack (blog), http://www.academichack.net/chacun.htm.

24. Woolf, *A Room of One's Own*, 108.

25. McHugh, *Jane Campion*, 48–53.

26. Schwartz, *It's So French!*, 57.

27. See Schwartz, *It's So French!*, 92–93; and de Valck, *Film Festivals*, 85–122. Best Foreign Language Film Oscar nominees are determined by national nominations (one film per country, regardless of the size of the industry) to this day. In 2009 revisions to the selection and voting process helped ensure that films recognized on the festival circuit were at least in the running. Another significant change was that a film's foreign language need not be the dominant language of the submitting nation. See chapter 2 for a discussion of *Water* in this context.

28. English, *The Economy of Prestige*, 76.

29. Elsaesser, "Film Festival Networks," 91. Subsequent references to this work given in the text.

30. Rissient is credited with bringing Chinese cinema to Cannes with *A Touch of Zen* (King Hu, 1971). Interestingly, the first (and still the only) Palme d'Or for a Chinese film was in 1993, when *Farewell My Concubine* (Chen Kaige) shared the prize with *The Piano*.

31. Villiers, "We Are the World Cinema."

32. The epigraph to the account of the festival's history on the website for Cannes is this quote from Jean Cocteau: "The Festival is an apolitical no-man's-land, a microcosm of what the world would be like if people could make direct contact with one another and speak the same language." http://www.festival-cannes.com/en/about/aboutFestival History.html. Still, a number of the individual short films in *Chacun son cinéma* explored culturally specific scenes of exhibition that inevitably contrasted with those on the Croisette.

33. Elsaesser, "Film Festival Networks," 88.

34. The Film Festival Research Network's bibliography includes a robust section on LGBT festivals, as the formation has been an important source of arguments about festivals as counterpublic spheres and alternative distribution systems. There are only a handful of English-language resources on women's film festivals, a dissymmetry that prompts comment from the bibliographers. "9.1.2 Women's Film Festivals," *Film Festival Research*, July 27, 2012, http://www.filmfestivalresearch.org/index.php/ffrn -bibliography/9-specialized-film-festivals/9-1-identity-based-festivals/9-1-2-womens -film-festivals/. Chapter 4 discusses these networks further.

35. See Ramanathan, *Feminist Auteurs*, for a consideration of women filmmakers' reworking of the category of the aesthetic as the condition for a feminist film politics.

36. Catherine Shoard and Rachel Millward [director of the Birds Eye View film festival], "Does It Matter That There Are No Women Up for the Palme d'Or?," *Observer*, May 16, 2010, http://www.guardian.co.uk/theobserver/2010/may/16/cannesfilm festival-women.

37. The longtime (male) directors of Cannes, Venice, and Berlin clearly stamp the festivals with their preferences. Manfred Salzgeber of Berlin's Panorama had an explicitly gay agenda. Each festival's mix, and history, deserve individualized study. Chapter 5 discusses in more detail the role programs like Cinefondation play in cultivating directors, including women, from outside Europe. Brigitte Rollet's research reveals how institutions of French cinema bestow prestige on African women directors.

38. The 2000 award was shared with *Songs from the Second Floor*; *Persepolis* shared with *Silent Light*, and *Fish Tank* shared the award with *Thirst*.

39. Before the institution of the Palme d'Or, the Grand Prix was the festival's top prize. In Cannes's first year, Danish woman codirector Bodil Ipsen won a Grand Prix (these were distributed to various countries).

40. English, *The Economy of Prestige*, 78.

41. Cited in Rich, "The Confidence Game."

42. La Barbe, "Men of the Cannes Film Festival, Keep Defending Those Masculine Values," Open Letter, *Guardian*, May 15, 2012, http://www.theguardian.com/comment isfree/2012/may/15/cannes-film-festival-men-open-letter.

43. Falicov, *The Cinematic Tango*, 115; Leslie Moore, "Women in a Widening Frame," 10.

44. Andrew O'Hehir, "Why the Cannes Boo Birds Are Wrong (as Usual)," *Salon*, May 25, 2008, http://www.salon.com/2008/05/25/martel/. Martel notes, "Cinema, due to its characteristics, enables us to express a way of thinking through a story. But a story is a trick. It's something on top. It's artificial," and O'Hehir concludes, "Even in the world's leading showcase for cinema-as-art—or, to put it more accurately, for art-cinema-as-commodity—people don't necessarily want to confront that idea."

45. Armond White, known for provocative opinions, lambasted Martel's fans as well as the director in his review of *The Headless Woman*: "Martel is a very minor art-filmmaker. Not especially insightful, she exemplifies the second-rate aesthetics of underdeveloped cultures." "The Headless Woman," *New York Press*, August 9, 2009, http://nypress.com/the-headless-woman/.

46. Peter Brunette, "La Mujer sin Cabeza," *Hollywood Reporter*, May 20, 2008, http://www.hollywoodreporter.com/review/la-mujer-sin-cabeza-125596#.

47. See Falicov's extensive discussion of *La historia oficial* in *The Cinematic Tango*, 65–74. That this represents a literal generational change is underscored by the successful career of Lucía Puenzo, Luis Puenzo's daughter.

48. "Argentina's Flourishing Film Industry," *WIPO Magazine*, May 2005, http://www.wipo.int/wipo_magazine/en/2005/03/article_0011.html. Export revenue from the film sector increased 1,000 percent in 2004 over the 2003 figures, with some seventy films produced that year.

49. Franco's examples of "art romance" include best sellers like Isabel Allende's *La casa de los espíritus* (House of Spirits) and Laura Esquivel's *Como agua para chocolate* (Like Water for Chocolate), 226, both of which were made into popular transnational films.

50. Spoiler alert: we catch a glimpse of a dog's body in the rearview mirror at this point of the film, which nevertheless proceeds to make us doubt the conclusiveness of this image along with just about everything else we've seen.

51. In this blend of horror and domestic melodrama, the film resembles Todd Haynes's *Safe* (2005), which in turn pays homage to Chantal Akerman's *Jeanne Dielman* (1975).

52. "Sexist ideology is no less present in the European art film because stereotyping appears less obvious. . . . In fact, an argument could be made for the art film inviting a greater invasion of myth. . . . In fact, because iconography offers in some ways a greater resistance to realist characterizations, the mythic qualities of certain stereotypes become far more easily detachable and can be used as a shorthand for referring to an ideological tradition." Johnston, "Women's Cinema as Counter Cinema," 110.

53. Taubin, "Identification of a Woman," 23.

54. De Beauvoir, *The Second Sex*, 7, 667.

55. For this reading of *Vertigo*, see Modleski, *The Women Who Knew Too Much*. Richard Brody's expressive description of Antonioni's use of Vitti as muse resonates powerfully with Onetto in Martel's film: "The glossy idol of bourgeois abstraction, she dominates the film with a wide-eyed glare that seems bewildered by obscure guilt." Richard Brody, "Getting Wasted," *New Yorker*, June 14, 2010, http://www.newyorker.com/arts/events/revivals/2010/06/14/100614gomo_GOAT_movies_brody#ixzzotCQMKYdf.

56. An alternative release title for Martel's film in Spanish-speaking markets was *La mujer rubia* (The blonde woman). Women go missing in both Hitchcock's and Antonioni's films and part of these works' erotic fascination consists in the heroines' fixation on these missing women. Ella Shohat points out that Carlotta, the "cause" of Judy/ Madeleine's desire, is identified with California's history of Spanish conquest. The blonde Carlotta could be seen as doubled in Vero as well. Shohat and Stam, *Unthinking Eurocentrism*, 222.

Another intriguing dimension of the racialization of Martel's heroine is provided in the director's notes in the film's press book:

> Last night I dreamt again. I was coming out of my Grandma's house after a visit and, when looking for my car keys in my purse, I found a black hand. Dark skin. I realized I killed a black woman. The keys in my purse are not my car keys but the keys to an apartment where I am going and where I know the body is. I woke up crying and screaming.
>
> —Who did the hand belong to?
> —I guess the maid's. Poor thing.
> —And you never cry for the people you killed?
> —Well, I hardly know them.
>
> This movie was created in the vapor of this conversation.

57. John Waters's heartfelt shout-out to *The Headless Woman* on his 2009 top ten list mentions Candita as one of the film's central enigmas: "Bleached hair, hit-and-run accidents, in-laws with hepatitis? Huh? I didn't get it, but I sure did love it!" The character is richer in intertextual meaning because it is portrayed by Inés Efron, who debuted as the intersex protagonist of xxy and would go on to play a lesbian in Puenzo's second film, *El niño pez / The Fish Child* (2010).

58. In *Crisis and Capitalism in Contemporary Argentine Cinema*, Page describes a reflexive breakdown of the allegorical in Martel's first two features, and *The Headless Woman* supports this interpretation. For Page, what may seem apolitical in Martel's films is actually a refiguring of the opposition between public and private that instead opens up the political.

59. Brunette, "La Mujer sin Cabeza."

60. Teresa de Lauretis applauds women's film practices that "open up a space of contradiction in which to demonstrate the non-coincidence of woman and women." *Alice Doesn't*, 7. This distinction animates her work on representation (*Woman*) and experience (engendering and ungendering of women in relation to representation). I draw upon it to indicate the necessary difference of the female subject as filmmaker and the figure of Woman as constructed and deconstructed in her films.

61. The theme of landscaping in the film evokes the sharing of this territory. Vero and her relatives buy planters from the village where the drowned boy lived and worked, and in a different manifestation of such local displacements, get out of their car to examine trees that appear to have changed position, ostensibly a result of the flood.

62. One could persuasively read this as a strategy of deterritorialization in line with

Deleuze's conception of minor cinema. See Butler, *Women's Cinema*; White, "Lesbian Minor Cinema."

63. Martel is a canny player of the game of auteur celebrity—as she waited for financing for feature projects, she made a few short films, including one for Miu Miu. *Muta* (2011) features glamorous insect-like women in sunglasses who communicate in a secret language and undergo a mysterious transformation. The short, which premiered at Venice, extends Martel's auteurist preoccupations while making explicit the connection between commerce and aesthetics in the film festival circuit.

64. Examples of locations with metaphorical resonance in Samira's films include the enclosed yard of the family in *The Apple*, the mountainous border region in *Blackboards*, and the ruins the family occupies in *At Five in the Afternoon*, including a wrecked airplane. Perhaps the most vivid example of this practice in the work of the Makhmalbaf Film House is the location shooting in the rubble of Hana Makhmalbaf's *Buddha Collapsed out of Shame*.

65. Jonathan Romney, "It's a Family Affair," *Independent*, April 18, 2004.

66. Leslie Camhi, "Daughter of Iran, Shades of Her Father," *New York Times*, February 21, 1999.

67. The question of just how informed the actors' consent could really have been, given the girls' mental state and the father's limited perspective, is begged by the blind mother's peripheral, noncompliant presence in *The Apple*. Samira's disturbing *Two-Legged Horse* also raises questions about the ethics of directing nonprofessionals.

68. Farahmand, "Perspectives on Recent (Acclaim for) Iranian Cinema."

69. The significance of this date should not be overlooked. The events of 9/11 made the film and its view of the Afghan people's plight the object of what Hamid Dabashi describes as political abuse (used to justify the U.S. invasion in October of that year). Dabashi, *Makhmalbaf at Large*, 194–195. The chapter is called "Beauty of the Beast, from Cannes to *Kandahar*."

70. See Farahmand, "Disentangling the International Festival Circuit."

71. See Negar Mottahedeh's fascinating argument that postrevolutionary Iranian cinema used form and visual codes to constitute itself as a "women's cinema," in *Displaced Allegories*. Kiarostami's *10* and *Shirin* are almost entirely composed of close-ups of women (with headscarves, but otherwise challenging ideas of modesty), and he has continued to work with female protagonists in his films made in France. Jafar Panahi, who was imprisoned by the regime in 2010, is known for his feminist films *The Circle* (2000) and *Offside* (2006).

72. See Sheila Whitaker, "Inside the Revolution," *New Statesman*, April 3, 2008, 41; Langford, "Practical Melodrama." Milani was arrested for the content of her film about the Revolution, *The Hidden Half / Nimeh-ye penhan* in 2001. An international petition secured her release and she has made several subsequent features.

73. Makhmalbaf also participated in the French-commissioned omnibus film *11'09"01—September 11*. All of her films have received European funding, starting with Hubert Bals and MK2 financing of *The Apple*. *At Five in the Afternoon* and *Two-Legged Horse* are coproductions between Makhmalbaf and the French company Wild Bunch productions. Forced to leave Iran after the contested 2009 presidential elections, the family has relocated to France.

74. Dabashi, *Makhmalbaf at Large*, 219.

75. Hana filmed the protests and incorporated the footage into a story of a depressed young woman confronting the reality of contemporary Tehran. Eluding government attempts to confiscate her film, Hana premiered *Green Days* at the 2009 Venice Film Festival, where she had debuted with *Joy of Madness*. As Elsaesser notes, as public, calendar-driven events, festivals are positioned to incorporate events and topical references, which both actualizes their public role and enhances their publicity. A last-minute invitee, *Green Days*, alongside exilic Iranian artist Shirin Neshat's prize-winning debut *Women without Men* (see chapter 2), accented the red carpet pomp with the vivid green worn by supporters of the Iranian protesters. The women cineastes represented culture, politics, and sartorial power.

76. Suner, "Cinema without Frontiers," 68.

77. Flanagan, "Towards an Aesthetic of Slow in Contemporary Cinema."

78. García Lorca, "Lament for Ignacio Sánchez Mejías."

79. A much younger Afghan girl's desire to attend school is the premise of Hana's haunting *Buddha Collapsed out of Shame* (2007), written by Marzieh Meshkini.

80. Chaudhuri and Finn, "The Open Image." They cite the apple at the end of Samira's film of that name; the surreal scene of prosthetics being parachuted down to the Red Cross camp in *Kandahar* would be another example.

81. The photos were displayed at Cannes in 2001 and are featured on the Makhmalbaf Film House website, http://www.makhmalbaf.com.

82. De Lauretis, *Technologies of Gender*, 2.

83. See Hamid Dabashi, *Makhmalbaf at Large*, 199, for a fascinating discussion of the critical practice of opposing poetic images to political content and a passionate indictment of the wall of news images portraying Afghanistan. *Kandahar* was made before 9/11 and thus staked a claim on the images coming out of the country prior to the cable news onslaught. The family's subsequent films in Afghanistan, *Stray Dogs*, *Buddha Collapsed out of Shame*, and *Two-Legged Horse*, hew to this tactic of modernist minimalism, and are most effective when the location shots bear witness to the ravages of the war.

84. The film's original title was *My Mad Sister*. Hana Makhmalbaf also produced a making-of film for Samira's *Two-Legged Horse* (images and dialogue list on the Makhmalbaf Film House website, http://www.makhmalbaf.com).

2. Framing Feminisms

1. While the use of the term "middlebrow" to distinguish cultural from high art (cinema) on the one hand and mass culture on the other conjures Dwight Macdonald's excoriation of aspirational culture in "Masscult and Midcult," I do not intend the term pejoratively. Rather I want to explore the convergence of arthouse cinema and middle-class women's taste, in the sense used by Bourdieu as a means of social distinction. Bourdieu notes "the traditional division of labor assigns to women familiarity with the things of art and literature." *Distinction*, 63. See Rubin, *The Making of Middle-Brow Culture*, and Radway, *A Feeling for Books*.

2. In his discussion of independent cinema institutions, Michael Z. Newman claims that "the indie phenomenon has . . . replac[ed] the mid-century's dominant conception

of alternative cinema as serious, intellectually demanding, high modernist, and Continental with a new conception that was a product of the multicultural and postmodern currents within elite Western culture of the 1980s and 1990s." *Indie*, 76. I would note that during both periods the consumption of high modernist and elite forms may remain middlebrow. Newman's notion of the influence of multiculturalism on independent film is especially relevant to this analysis.

3. See Randal Johnson, "Editor's Introduction," in Bourdieu, *The Field of Cultural Production*, 7.

4. Peter Knegt's *Indiewire* Winners and Losers column for fall 2009 notes the trend: "Winners: Female Protagonists, Female Directors and Female Audiences. . . . Never have female-centered options dominated the indie landscape this way. . . . Of the top ten grossing limited released narrative films of 2009, four were directed by women ('Hurt Locker,' 'Coco,' 'An Education' and 'Bright Star')." His losers: "anyone that paid to see 'Amelia.'" Peter Knegt, "Box Office 2.0: Fall Winners and Losers," *Indiewire*, November 24, 2009, http://www.indiewire.com/article/box_office_2.0_fall_winners _and_losers#.UfWM9TqAvcM.

5. A number of "women's films" by women directors were among the Hollywood releases in 2009 as well, including *The Proposal, Julie and Julia, It's Complicated, Whip It*, and *Jennifer's Body*. According to the Motion Picture Association of America (MPAA), "in 2009, the number of tickets sold to females was unusually high" at 55 percent. "Theatrical Market Statistics 2012," http://www.mpaa.org/wp-content /uploads/2014/03/2012-Theatrical-Market-Statistics-Report.pdf, 15.

6. In 2008 Warner Bros. closed Warner Independent and Picturehouse, and Paramount Vantage was scaled back. The number of films released by specialty divisions peaked in 2007 at eighty-two, and was down precipitously to thirty-seven by 2010. MPAA, "Theatrical Market Statistics 2012," 20.

7. I have not been able to quantify an increase in the number of independent films by women released over the first decade of the 2000s. "Exploring the Barriers and Opportunities for Independent Women Filmmakers," the report commissioned by Sundance Institute and Women in Film Los Angeles, tracked how many films by women in both documentary and fiction categories were shown in the festival during 2002–2012. Overall, the study found 22 percent in fiction competition and 41 percent in documentary, but analysis did not show a sustained increase over the period studied. Martha M. Lauzen found a similar statistic in the first of her "Independent Women" studies of festival films: Women constituted 22 percent of the directors in this study, as opposed to the 9 percent of those employed on top-grossing films from the same period (June 2008–May 2009). The number of films released theatrically is much lower than the number shown in festivals. There is no data on whether independent films by women are acquired at slower rates than men's; stars, genre, subject matter, and buzz are more salient factors and might also be gendered discourses.

8. One hundred critics were polled on films either released theatrically or premiered in festivals in the first half of 2010. Peter Knegt, "Mid-Year Report: 'Everyone,' 'Delaware' and 'Weather' Top CriticWIRE," *Indiewire*, June 29, 2010, http://www .indiewire.com/article/mid-year_report_everyone_else_leads_criticwires_mid-year _analysis/?sms_ss=google.

9. Newman, *Indie*, 57.

10. Rickey was one of several top critics whose positions were eliminated during this period. Anne Thompson, "Carrie Rickey Follows Michael Sragow out Newspaper Critic Door: Farewell Post at Philly Inquirer," *Indiewire*, October 16, 2011, http://blogs .indiewire.com/thompsononhollywood/carrie_rickey_follows_michael_sragow_out _newspaper_critic_door_farewell_pos.

11. Fifty-seven percent of respondents to the 2013 Art House Convergence national survey of art house audiences were over fifty-five; 41 percent reported an annual income of $100,000 or more; and 46 percent held advanced degrees. The racial and gender composition of audiences was not studied. In the commercial realm, according to the MPAA's "Theatrical Market Statistics," "Caucasians now account for less than 50% of frequent moviegoers and are underrepresented relative to their portion of the population," and "the gender composition of moviegoers . . . in 2013 skewed slightly more towards women than the overall population." "Theatrical Market Statistics 2013," http://www.mpaa.org/wp-content/uploads/2014/03/MPAA-Theatrical-Market -Statistics-2013_032514-v2.pdf, 12–13.

The Ritz is now described under this umbrella language: "Landmark Theatres is a recognized leader in the industry for providing to its customers consistently diverse and entertaining film products in a sophisticated adult-oriented atmosphere. Our theaters showcase a wide variety of films—ranging from Independent and Foreign film to 3-D movies and smart films from Hollywood. Landmark Theatres is the nation's largest theater chain dedicated to exhibiting and marketing independent film." http://test .landmarktheatres.com/lmk/AboutUs.html.

12. Dennis Lim, "Oscars Try to Navigate through Babel," *New York Times*, January 29, 2010, http://www.nytimes.com/2010/01/31/movies/awardsseason/31oscar.html?_r=1.

13. *Amelia* reviews tabulated at Rotten Tomatoes, http://www.rottentomatoes.com /m/amelia_2009/. Nair's film had by far the biggest budget ($40 million) of these productions. Powerful distributor Fox Searchlight opened the film in 800 theaters, targeting older female audiences (with an opening-night party at Bloomingdale's), but the film was a box-office disappointment. Three films by women directors were strong box-office successes in 2009: Anne Fletcher's *The Proposal* (ranked number 16), Nancy Meyers's *It's Complicated* (28), and Nora Ephron's *Julie and Julia* (34). Bigelow's *The Hurt Locker* is the next highest grossing at 116; none of the specialty films appear in the top 100: *Amelia* (128), *An Education* (132), *Coco before Chanel* (157), *Bright Star* (163). "2009 Domestic Grosses," Box Office Mojo, http://boxofficemojo.com/yearly/chart/?page =2&view=releasedate&view2=domestic&yr=2009&p=.htm.

14. Brunsdon, *Screen Tastes*, 109–110.

15. For a historical analysis of the economics and ideologies of taste underlying the establishment of art house theaters in America, see Barbara Wilinsky, *Sure Seaters: The Emergence of Art House Cinema* (Minneapolis: University of Minnesota Press, 2001). For a discussion of the revival of art house cinemas around independent cinema since the late 1980s, see Newman, *Indie*, chapter 2.

16. Amireh and Majaj, *Going Global*, 13.

17. See McHugh, "The World and the Soup," for further consideration of this transnational movement.

18. Joe Satran, "Cameron Bailey, Toronto International Film Festival's Artistic Director, Picks Diversity over Oscars," *Huffington Post*, September 6, 2012, http://www.huffingtonpost.com/2012/09/06/cameron-bailey-toronto-international-film-festival_n_1858932.html.

19. Sundance began as the United States Film Festival, and while it introduced world dramatic and documentary competitions in 2007 (competing for premieres of such works with Toronto), it is still largely identified with U.S. independent film. However, several of the international filmmakers analyzed in this book have participated in the Sundance Institute, where producers', directors', and writers' labs and other programs have had a significant impact on women's filmmaking.

In 2012, the Sundance Institute and Women in Film Los Angeles announced an initiative to study the challenges facing women filmmakers in the United States. "Exploring the Barriers and Opportunities for Independent Women Filmmakers," the study of films screened at Sundance over a twelve-year period, showed the percentage of women directors of U.S. independent fiction films at a steady 18 percent, twice that of Hollywood box-office hits—while, not surprisingly, showing twice again as many women in documentary filmmaking. Analysis of projects admitted to and shepherded through the Sundance labs was much more encouraging, with women participating in numbers nearly equal to men's and finishing and exhibiting work in festivals at the same rate. The initiative was spearheaded by institute director Keri Putnam and is overseen by senior programmer Caroline Libresco, evidence of strong institutional structures supporting women's contributions at Sundance itself. Stacy L. Smith, Katherine Pieper, Marc Choueiti, and their students conducted the research as part of the Media, Diversity and Social Change Initiative at USC's Annenberg School for Communication and Journalism. The lab successes especially resemble the outcomes of state policy, funding initiatives, and festival talent campuses internationally. On signs of shifts in the festival's identity, see Rastegar, "Evolving Narrative Structures Forge New Cine-Love at the 2012 Sundance Film Festival."

20. Although restricting opening night at TIFF to Canadian films might be seen as increasing the chance for a woman director's film to grab the coveted slot, to date only *I've Heard the Mermaids Singing* (Patricia Rozema, 1987) has shared this honor. In 2005 *Water* was one of four films by women directors among the twenty featured in the high-profile Gala section of TIFF, or 20 percent (in contrast, in 2010, there were none). The same year's edition of the smaller and more staid New York Film Festival, a late-September audience-oriented event that is not attended by film professionals, included just one feature film by a woman (Dorota Kędzierzawska's *I Am* from Poland) among its twenty-five feature selections, 4 percent. Sundance's achievement of 25 percent women's films in feature programming that year was publicized as a breakthrough (as noted, in 2013 competition films reached 50 percent). As I argued in chapter 1, while the numbers game is not the most nuanced way to think about women's role in cinema, issues of basic equity are still so glaring that it seems a legitimate place to start.

21. On TIFF's role in Canadian national cinema, see Liz Czach, "Film Festivals, Programming, and the Building of National Cinema."

22. Levitin, "An Introduction to Deepa Mehta," 273. Levitin isolates many of the dimensions of Mehta's reception that I analyze here. Czach discusses debates over TIFF's

presentation of *Fire* in "Film Festivals," 86, and Sharon Tay devotes a chapter to Mehta in *Women on the Edge*.

23. Andrew Sarris, "*Water*," review, *New York Observer*, July 19, 2006.

24. Saltzman, *Shooting Water*.

25. Amireh and Majaj, "Introduction," in *Going Global*, 7.

26. The melodramatic mode—muteness, music, tears, the mechanisms "too late" and "just in time"—structures *Water's* affective resonance. If melodrama and art cinema converge around representations of female suffering, neither genre is barred from setting out the dimensions of this oppression in feminist terms. In chapter 3 I explore in more detail how women filmmakers use the women's picture genre to rewrite patriarchal narratives of national cinema and reach transnational audiences. And in chapter 5 I return to women directors' strategies for representing human rights issues in national and transnational frames that do not position women as victims.

27. For an insightful reading of the film's water imagery, see Mukherjee, "Deepa Mehta's Film *Water*."

28. Mohanty, *Feminism without Borders*, 23.

29. It was while working on the *Young Indiana Jones Chronicles* in Varanasi that she had the idea for *Water*. Press kit, *Water*.

30. For feminist scholarship on sati, see Mani, *Contentious Traditions*.

31. The tag line is "The scriptures say that widows have three options: marry your husband's younger brother, burn with your dead husband, or lead a life of self-denial."

32. See, for example, Prasad, "Surviving Bollywood," 48–49.

33. Sujata Moorti, "Inflamed Passions: *Fire*, the Woman Question, and the Policing of Cultural Boundaries," *Genders* 32 (2000): http://www.genders.org/g32/g32_moorti .html. Quoted in Butler, *Women's Cinema*, 121.

34. "Books and Arts: Deep Trouble; Asian Cinema," *Economist*, October 22, 2005, 99.

35. The films are readable in classic women's picture terms, an important dimension of reception and address whose articulation with the art house framework I explore further in chapter 3. See Herman, "Memory and Melodrama." Mehta's little-seen follow up to *Water*, *Heaven on Earth* (2007), is about a Punjabi bride who becomes the victim of domestic violence in Canada. Its principal coverage was online journalism tracking Bollywood goings-on, as Mehta cast the star Preity Zinta (who debuted opposite Shahrukh Shan in Mani Ratnam's *Dil Se*) as the immigrant bride. The film was released in India dubbed into Hindi under the title *Videsh* and poorly reviewed there as well.

36. Amarshi quote from press materials; Roger Ebert, review of *Water*, *Chicago Sun Times*, May 5, 2006, http://www.rogerebert.com/reviews/water-2006.

37. Saltzman, *Shooting Water*, 254–256.

38. Kavoori and Punathambekar, *Global Bollywood*.

39. A full discussion of the place of Indian women diasporan filmmakers is beyond the scope of this chapter. See Desai, *Beyond Bollywood*, and Mani, *Aspiring to Home*. In a ritual of citizenship and status, in 2012 Mehta received the Governor General's Performing Arts Awards for Lifetime Artistic Achievement, the highest civilian award for an artist in Canada. The release that year of *Midnight's Children*, cowritten with Salman Rushdie, sealed, through the link with the most famous work of Indian diasporan lit-

erature, Mehta's image as both daring and mainstream, outspoken and scripted, insider and outsider, citizen of the world.

40. Ghosh, "An Affair to Remember," 64.

41. Corrigan, "The Commerce of Auteurism," 96.

42. Richard Corliss and Mary Corliss, "*Persepolis* Finds Love in the Afternoon," *Time*, May 23, 2007, http://www.time.com/time/arts/article/0,8599,1624714,00.html #ixzz1Feuc6LZP.

43. Naficy speaks of "using the film's frame as a writing tablet." *An Accented Cinema*, 25.

44. Satrapi's second feature, *Chicken with Plums* (2012), though based on a graphic novel drawn in roughly the same style as *Persepolis* (and also using family material) is filmed in live action with some animated sequences. The film's magic realist style is, however, consistent with Satrapi's embrace of the antireferential to facilitate identification across cultures.

45. In *An Accented Cinema*, Naficy writes of these chronotopes, "[Representations] of the homeland tend . . . to emphasize boundlessness and timelessness. . . . The representation of life in exile and diaspora . . . is cathected to sites of confinement and control," 5. Arguably the garden functions as both; Neshat writes that the garden is "central to the mystical literature in Persian and Islamic traditions . . . as the space for 'spiritual transcendence.' In Iranian culture, the garden has also been regarded in political terms, suggesting ideas of 'exile,' 'independence' and 'freedom.'" Neshat explains what drew her to the novel: "I very much appreciated the way the story moved in between the space of an 'orchard' where one could delve into most universal, timeless and existential crisis of a few individuals; versus the city of Tehran where one was confronted by socio-political, and historical crisis of a specific country." Leila Darabi, "*Women without Men*: A Conversation with Shirin Neshat," TehranBureau, WGBH, May 5, 2010, http://www.pbs.org/wgbh/pages/frontline/tehranbureau/2010/05/women -without-men-a-conversation-with-shirin-neshat.html#ixzz1ylRZtjJM.

46. As mentioned in chapter 1, Hana Makhmalbaf's *Green Days* (2011), a fictional film that incorporated footage shot on the streets during the protests, was also screened at Venice amid displays of solidarity green. She had been detained leaving Iran with the film. Makhmalbaf and the rest of her family left their homeland later that year.

47. C. Roger Denson, "Shirin Neshat: Artist of the Decade," *Huffington Post*, December 30, 2010, http://www.huffingtonpost.com/g-roger-denson/sherin-neshat-artist-of -t_b_802050.html#s216201&title=Attributed_to_alWasiti.

48. Ali Jafaar, "Satrapi Blasts Iran's 'Persepolis' Protest," *Variety*, May 23, 2007, http://www.variety.com/article/VR1117965713.

49. Naficy traces the "evolution of the Iranian accented feature films . . . from an overcathected preoccupation with homeland and the culture of politics toward a concern with life in exile and the politics of culture." *An Accented Cinema*, 77.

50. Naficy, *The Making of Exile Cultures*, 76.

51. Lauren Collins, "A Moving Picture," News Desk, *New Yorker*, April 29, 2010, http://www.newyorker.com/online/blogs/newsdesk/2010/04.

52. Amireh and Majaj, *Going Global*, 13.

53. Although the emphasis of the chapter does not afford space to discuss the many

women directors working within Iran and India, a few names are crucial. Poet Forugh Farrokhzad's legendary documentary *The House Is Black* (1963) has had a profound influence on Iranian cinema and on artists like Neshat. I have already named Rakhshan Bani-Etemad and Tahmineh Milani, who maintain quite critical positions toward the theocracy while continuing to make films with popular appeal.

There is a significant tradition of women directors working in India's parallel cinema. Independent director Aparna Sen has produced a considerable corpus of films critical of communalism and women's role in traditional society. A number of films by younger women directors can be considered alongside Mehta's: Shonali Bose's *Amu* (2006) is about a young Indian American woman's discovery of a genocidal history. Nandita Das, who played Sita in *Fire*, directed a film about the riots in Gujarat, *Firaaq* (2008). Increasing numbers of women directors are also working in Bollywood film, including Farah Khan, who directed the Shahrukh Khan vehicle *Om Shanti Om* (2007), and Zoya Akhtar, *You Only Live Once* (2011).

3. The Age of the Chick Flick

1. Angela McRobbie's "Postfeminism and Popular Culture" is quoted on page 1 of, and reprinted in, Tasker and Negra, *Interrogating Postfeminism*.

2. Chick lit as a global publishing phenomenon is more developed and commented upon. Rachel Donadio, "The Chick-Lit Pandemic," *New York Times*, March 19, 2006. See also Ferriss and Young, *Chick Lit*. On chick flicks in relation to traditional women's pictures, see Radner, *Neo-feminist Cinema*.

3. Some examples of contemporary women directors whose films are both melodramas and auteur cinema include Yasmin Ahmad, *Talentime* (Malaysia, 2009); Tata Amaral, *Antonia* (Brazil, 2006); Susanne Bier, *Elsker dig for evigt / Open Hearts* (Denmark, 2002); Cristina Comencini, *La bestia nel cuore / The Beast in the Heart* (Italy, 2005); Julia Solomonoff, *Hermanas / Sisters* (Argentina/Brazil/Spain, 2005).

4. "A bittersweet treat," Colin Colvert, *Minneapolis Star Tribune*; "a sweeter and more believable version of *Steel Magnolias*, Middle Eastern style," Claudia Puig, *USA Today*; "sweet but not saccharine," Kenneth Turan, *Los Angeles Times*. Collected from "Caramel Reviews," Rotten Tomatoes, http://www.rottentomatoes.com/m/caramel/reviews/?type=top_critics.

5. Jeong made a second feature in 2005, another ensemble cast youth film set within in-line skating culture, *The Aggressives*; her next work was not released until 2012: the feature-length documentary *Talking Architect* and the short *Give Me Back My Cat*, a comic tale of contemporary youth in Seoul. Jeong's career pattern is not unlike that of many independent U.S. women directors who experience difficulties in maintaining work as directors after promising debuts. For example, Julie Dash did not find a suitable script or financing for her own projects after the landmark *Daughters of the Dust* (1991), and Kimberly Peirce followed up *Boys Don't Cry* (1999) with her second feature, *Stop-Loss*, only in 2008 after many projects fell apart. The sophomore slump is a matter of industry barriers, not of lack in creativity or talent. Women working in countries with state-subsidized industries and competitive arts funding mechanisms tend to have more steady career patterns.

6. Derek Elley, "*Take Care of My Cat (Goyangireul Butakhae),*" *Variety*, November 26, 2001, 28. The film was withdrawn after a week in distribution on nineteen screens. An effort to get the film back in release did not take off. Chi-Yun Shin cites Elley and contrasts this figure with the male buddy film *Friend*, with its 8.2 million admissions the same year. Shin, "Two of a Kind," 118.

7. An art house distributor known for its nontheatrical and DVD distribution of classic films, Kino has released a number of important women's films: *Ke tu qui hen / Song of the Exile* (Ann Hui, 1990), *Old Joy* (Kelly Reichardt, 2006), and *Treeless Mountain* (So Yong Kim, 2008).

8. Leslie Felperin, "*Take Care of My Cat,*" *Sight and Sound* 13.2 (2003): 62–64.

9. Shin, "Two of a Kind."

10. Of the "Whispering Corridors" series, *Memento Mori* (Kim Tae-Yong and Min Kyu-dong, 1999) has an overt lesbian premise.

11. Chris Berry quoted in Choi, *The South Korean Film Renaissance*, 5.

12. Kim, *The Remasculinization of Korean Cinema*, 6.

13. Within the independent / art cinema press and international cinephile blogosphere, some of the best-known Korean woman directors are transnational: Korean Canadian director Helen Lee, Korean American So Yong Kim, and Gina Kim, who has lived and worked in the United States since attending art school in the early 1990s.

14. As Ji-hye Ahn notes, however, this means that they do not come up through an apprenticeship system that fosters the contacts they will need to emerge as directors of top-budgeted films. I am indebted to her research into the gender determinants of the current industry in "The Status and Future of Female Directors in the Korean Film Industry."

15. Filmmaker Helen Lee (personal communication, July 3, 2012), who taught directing and film studies at KNUA at the end of the decade, writes:

> After Jeong Jae-eun's time and before my time there was a period of a decade when half the directing majors at the school were women! The Dean Park Kwangsu at the time told me this. . . . But [this was] obviously not reflected in the industry per se. . . . Most if not all those women [who released features in the early to mid-2000s] were film school grads. . . . Previously the only way you could make your feature debut was if you toiled for a decade as someone's assistant director. . . . So when film departments started to open up, things got a bit more equitable for women directors—they could train in film school, write commercially viable scripts, make a short to prove their directorial ability, and get funded by Chungmuro [the film industry].

16. Oh Jung-wan is a veteran producer. Myung Films' producers have brought several women's films to the screen.

17. On this point see McRobbie's discussion of Bridget Jones in "Post-feminism and Popular Culture."

18. Elley, "*Take Care of My Cat,*" 27–28.

19. Stephen Holden, "Take Care of My Cat (2001); Film Festival Review; Unlike Cats, Cellphone Dependent," *New York Times*, March 22, 2002.

20. Choi, *The South Korean Film Renaissance*, 123.

21. There are some striking resonances in Jia Zhang-ke's *Shijie / The World* (2004), in which texting is linked with air travel in whimsically animated sequences.

22. While several reviewers remark on the absence of a heterosexual romance plot, they do not then detect a lesbian subtext. Holden's pejorative description, worth quoting in full, seems almost willfully blind to this possibility: "The movie's portrait of post-adolescence in South Korea is strikingly different from depictions of the same age group in films from other countries. The five seem to be sexually uninitiated and are not especially boy crazy. They also seem somewhat younger than their years. When they are first seen in their high school uniforms, their hysterically giggly camaraderie is more the behavior of grade-school children." "Take Care of My Cat (2001)."

23. For the place of the city in Lebanese cinema, see, for example, Jocelyne Saab's *Once Upon a Time in Beirut* (1994).

24. Lebanese female stars are prominent in the Arabic pop recording industry. Labaki directed Ajram's breakthrough video "Akhasmak Ah" and several additional award-winning clips. Their collaboration "Fi Hagat" is at this writing the most-viewed Arabic video on the Internet. YouTube, http://www.youtube.com/watch?v=ovxMNY-mNXA. Ajram is Coca-Cola's Middle Eastern spokesperson and a UNICEF Goodwill ambassador. Labaki also directed the video for the Lebanese reality show *Star Academy*. For a discussion of the show, see Kraidy, *Reality Television and Arab Politics*.

25. Financing deals, filmmaker labs, and festival showcases have benefited Labaki and other young women filmmakers from North Africa and the Middle East, including Palestinians Annemarie Jacir (*Salt of This Sea*, 2008; *When I Saw You*, 2012) and Cherien Dabis (*Amreeka*, 2009; *May in the Summer*, 2013) and Moroccan Laïla Marrackhi (*Marock*, 2005; *Rock the Casbah*, 2013). Ali Jaafar, "Women Rock Mideast Film Scene," *Daily Variety*, July 28, 2006. Elsa Keslassy, "Femme Filmmakers Break Barriers in Morocco," *Variety*, December 1, 2013.

26. Nick Dawson, "Nadine Labaki: 'Caramel,'" *Filmmaker*, February 1, 2008, http://www.filmmakermagazine.com/news/2008/02/nadine-labaki-caramel/.

27. "'Caramel' Director Nadine Labaki on Remaking the Chick Flick," *New York*, January 30, 2008, http://nymag.com/daily/entertainment/2008/01/caramel_director_nadine_labaki.html.

28. "'Caramel' Director Nadine Labaki on Remaking the Chick Flick."

29. See Gayatri Gopinath's discussion of this theme in *Fire in Impossible Desires*.

30. Karin Albou's *Le chant des mariées / Wedding Song* (2008), about the close relationship between two friends, Jewish and Muslim, during World War II in Tunis, includes an especially intense scene of pubic shaving in the hamam on the evening of one girl's wedding.

31. Iranian American director Maryam Keshavarz's *Circumstance* (2011) provides an interesting counterpoint. Much more explicit in its depiction of the erotic entanglements between the two sixteen-year-old schoolgirls at its center, the film appeals directly to LGBT Western and global gay audiences as well as Iranian diasporan audiences. See White, "Circumstantial Lesbianism."

32. Khatib, *Lebanese Cinema*, 288.

33. Press release, *Caramel* (Roadside Attractions, 2007).

34. Dawson, "Nadine Labaki."

35. Press release, *Caramel*.

36. Labaki was dramatically unveiled in January 2012 as the new spokesperson for Johnnie Walker's social media campaign Keep Walking Lebanon, which invites users to select one of three projects to benefit the country. Caroline Labaki's promotional video, "Walk with Nadine Labaki," was featured on the campaign's home page and YouTube channel as well as on the official Nadine Labaki YouTube channel: http://www.youtube .com/user/labakinadine?feature=results_main. "Nadine Labaki—Keep Walking Lebanon," also directed by her sister, includes the following introduction: "Listen to Nadine Labaki's words of inspiration as she adopts the mantle of mother, citizen, and director to deliver a powerful message to the Lebanese." According to the ad agency responsible for the campaign, Leo Burnett Beirut, "The percentage of female interaction with the brand doubled to 49% versus just 24% last year." "2012 Winners and Shortlists— Media," Dubai Lynx, http://www.dubailynx.com/winners/2012/media/entry.cfm ?entryid=107&award=99&order=2&direction=1.

37. Marks, "What Is That *and* between Arab Women and Video?" See the curated programs and online cinema database of Arte East: Arts and Culture of the Middle East, directed by Livia Alexander, http://www.arteeast.org/, in particular the multipart exhibition *Mapping Subjectivity: Experimentation in Arab Cinema, 1960–Now*, curated by Rasha Salti, and *The Calm after the Storm: Making Sense of Lebanon's Civil War*.

4. Network Narratives

1. I refer to East and Southeast Asian cinema. For an excellent discussion of the concept of the transnational in film studies that draws on its use within scholarship on Chinese and East Asian cinemas, see Higbee and Lim, "Concepts of Transnational Cinema."

2. See, for example, Wong, "The Hong Kong International Film Festival as Cultural Event," in her *Film Festivals*, 190–222.

3. Wang, *Chinese Women's Cinema*, 39.

4. Bordwell, *The Way Hollywood Tells It*, 100.

5. The Network of Asian Women's Film Festival had its first meeting in Seoul in 2011. "The First 3 Years of NAWFF—an Interview of Ms. Lee Hyae-Kyoung, Chairperson of NAWFF," NAWFF, February 6, 2013, http://nawff.org/wordpress/?p=543.

6. There are direct models for these open narratives in television anthology formats, serials, and in Asian art films by Wong Kar Wai and Apichatpong Weerasethukal (I address the latter's work briefly below).

7. For a richly textured and culturally contextualized reading of the film, see Imanjaya, "The Curious Cases of Salma, Siti, and Ming."

8. Indeed, a question about the role of these references in the film provoked visible emotion in the filmmaker, as she spoke of her decision not to visit Aceh and attract attention to herself, questioning both the motives of those who did and her own ability to bear witness. Interview with the author, New York, May 2006.

9. "While the full human impact of the Asian tsunami in Aceh Province, in terms of lives lost or damaged, may never be fully measured, the resulting female deficit will

likely be the tsunami's most deeply felt and prolonged impact." Shannon Doocy, Abdur Rofi, Claire Moodie, Eric Spring, Scott Bradley, Gilbert Burnham, and Courtland Robinson, "Tsunami Mortality in Aceh Province, Indonesia," *Bulletin of the World Health Organization* 85.4 (2007): 273–278, http://www.ncbi.nlm.nih.gov/pmc/articles /PMC2636329/.

10. See Imanjaya's summary of the debates and controversies in "The Curious Cases of Salma, Siti, and Ming."

11. Rony, "Transforming Documentary."

12. In addition to *Perempuan punya cerita / Chants of Lotus* (2007) and *Pertaruhan / At Stake* (2008), Dinata produced *Working Girls* (2011), a documentary on women and work featuring segments by both male and female directors.

13. Khoo, "The Minor Transnationalism of Queer Asian Cinema."

14. See Grossman, *Queer Asian Cinema*; Berry, "Asian Values, Family Values."

15. See Lim, *Celluloid Comrades*, for chapters on Kwan and Tsai.

16. Kawase Naomi from Japan, Guo Xiaolu and Li Yu from China, and the Thai director Anocha Suwichakornpong are recent examples of women acclaimed in global art cinema and enabled by its festival and funding networks. Several Asian women directors of Hui's generation were key figures in national film industries, including Malaysian feature film and advertising director Yasmin Ahmad and Filipina filmmaker and film school founder Marilou Diaz-Abaya, both prematurely deceased.

17. See Martin, "Appendix: Interview with Shi Tou," in *Backward Glances*.

18. Grant, "www.auteur.com," 106. Very few lesbian directors anywhere in the world have made multiple queer features, again in contrast to queer male auteurs. A favorable subsidy system or a healthy independent sector and market circumstances are required as well as credible distribution opportunities through and beyond the LGBT festival network. Monika Treut tapped German TV funding sources to make multiple feature films starting in the 1980s, and she has continued to work in and out of features and documentaries. Interestingly, she has worked in Taipei, including directing a film that includes a profile of young Taiwan filmmaker DJ Chen Yin-jun (*Formula 17*) and a feature film, *Ghosted*, in which a German artist's dead Taiwanese girlfriend is reincarnated. Another German director, Angelina Maccarone, has made several queer-themed features, short of Fassbinder's thirty-plus film oeuvre, but impressive nonetheless. The New Queer Cinema was notorious for the late blooming of lesbian features, and the careers of its star lesbian directors Kim Peirce (*Boys Don't Cry*) and Rose Troche (*Go Fish*) evince the long gap between feature film work typical of independent U.S. women directors. Jamie Babbit targeted lesbian audiences in modestly budgeted features like *But I'm a Cheerleader*, *The Quiet*, *Itty Bitty Titty Committee*, and *Breaking the Girls*, often produced by Babbit's partner, Andrea Sperling. Indeed lesbian producers have longer filmographies than most directors; Christine Vachon is by far the most important lesbian auteur of New Queer Cinema. Even Lisa Cholodenko—who, somewhat like Chou, is an out lesbian filmmaker with an auteurist mark who has crossed into a wider market with lesbian-themed films—has had considerable time between projects. Chantal Akerman and Ulrike Ottinger, key art cinema auteurs of an earlier generation (though Akerman's work is not overtly lesbian), have greater affinity with art film tradition than the narrative filmmakers I've just named, but they accessed feature-length production

and international circulation through arts subsidies, thus providing a model for more conventional storytellers. Barbara Hammer, indisputably the most prolific lesbian filmmaker, enjoys a central, global reputation in the lesbian community perhaps because of, rather than despite, her eschewal of the feature format. The phenomenon of the iconic community filmmaker that Hammer embodied in the 1970s confirms that authorship plays an important role in the grassroots circulation of lesbian films. It is no accident that she was an invited guest of the precarious Beijing Gay and Lesbian Film Festival.

19. Two groundbreaking English-language studies—Helen Hok-Sze Leung's *Undercurrents: Queer Culture and Postcolonial Hong Kong*, and Fran Martin's *Backward Glances*, on the female homoerotic imaginary in contemporary Chinese popular culture—address and theorize this juncture in transnational Chinese lesbian culture and have been invaluable sources for me as a nonspecialist.

20. A statistic that gives a sense of this crisis: Taiwan features numbered seventy-six in 1990; only twelve were produced in 1998. Zhang, *Chinese National Cinema*, 274.

21. Yeh, "Taiwan," 156–168.

22. Martin, Jackson, McLelland, and Yue, *Asiapacifiqueer*, 2.

23. Martin, "Situating Sexualities," 5.

24. Lim, "How to Be Queer in Taiwan."

25. Berry, "Wedding Banquet."

26. Hu, "*Formula 17*."

27. See "Profile: Michelle Yeh, Producer of 'Formula 17,' 'Heirloom,' and 'The Shoe Fairy,'" Taiwan Cinema, March 6, 2007, http://www.taiwancinema.com/ct.asp?xItem =52908&ctNode=125&mp=2.

28. Huang and Wang, "Post-Taiwan New Cinema Women Directors and Their Films," 136.

29. Chiu, "The Vision of Taiwan New Documentary," 17–32. The film is narrated in French, not by an omniscient character but by a wanderer of the night streets of Taipei. As the voiceover says, "Sometimes it is easier to express myself in a strange language. Especially if things are difficult to say." These noir-style reflections are intertwined with interviews with the bar's patrons and owners. Chiu writes, "The alienation effect brought by the French language points to the otherness of gay language and culture, and thus denies the audience the possibility of fully mastering what it sees and hears in the film." It also very concretely represents the idea of self-exile, of strangeness. Although the rainbow flag beckons at the bar's entrance, the film is not a global gay coming-out, visibility narrative. The story of the bar's closing is one of homophobia and loss. Indeed, the movie is haunted by absence; the bar has been ghosted. In one scene an impresario retraces the steps of drag queens performing at a long-ago party in front of a mute projection of the footage.

And of course French is also a language of eroticism—we see the two lovers learning the tongue. Elsewhere, we see what we presume to be the same women making love, first in a hot tub, later in a bedroom while being photographed. These scenes contrast with those in the bar, but they are not mapped strictly onto gender bifurcation, with lesbians in private, gay men in (semi)public. The lesbian personal narrative fits obliquely into the public history, serving as a forceful authorial inscription in the wider history the film traces and the spaces it maps.

30. Both *Formula 17* and Nia Dinata's *Arisan!*, the first Indonesian gay film, have in common the fact that they were directed by young women with professional roots in television or music video production. The youth audience and aesthetic also establishes viewing networks.

31. Martin, "Taiwan (Trans)national Cinema," 131–145. A France/Taiwan coproduction, *Blue Gate Crossing* was produced by Peggy Chiao, a Taiwan film scholar at the center of nurturing Chinese-language filmmaking. *Blue Gate Crossing* is part of her company Arc Light's Tales of Three Cities project of films by Hong Kong, Taiwanese, and mainland directors.

32. See, for example, the discussion forum at the Korean pop chat site Soompi: "Spider Lilies / Tattoo / Mandala," Soompi, March 2007, http://www.soompi.com/forums /index.php?showtopic=119718.

33. Martin, *Backward Glances*, 254n7. *Spider Lilies* appeared too late to be fully incorporated into Martin's argument in this book. She develops her reading in Fran Martin, "Love and Remembrance: Women's Same-Sex Love in Trans-national Chinese Media and Popular Cultures," unpublished manuscript.

34. That Chou is deliberate in her queer associations is recognized by a Taiwan reviewer: "The lesbian director strategically links gay culture with a localized identity." Ho Yi, "A Sassy Melodrama on Lesbian Love," *Taipei Times*, March 30, 2007.

35. Takeko's ethnic difference is narratively motivated by the ancient art of tattoo but extratextually useful as an excuse for Leong's accented Mandarin.

36. Disappointment in the casting was expressed by Taiwan lesbians, Huang and Wang, "Post-Taiwan New Cinema Women Directors and Their Films," 150.

37. Martin, *Backward Glances*, 251–252n25.

38. Martin, *Backward Glances*, 164.

39. Silverman, *The Acoustic Mirror*, 218.

40. Huang and Wang analyze Chou's three queer-themed features as her tongzhi trilogy ("Post-Taiwan New Cinema Women Directors and Their Films," 144); perhaps the other rainbow stripes have been deferred. Her project after *Drifting Flowers*, for public television, *Wavebreaker* (2009), was a fiction feature about brothers with a hereditary condition causing brain damage, showing a recurrent authorial interest in disability and trauma. Her subsequent projects were high profile: the television drama *Gloomy Salad Days* and the costume drama *Ripples of Desire*. The mixed reception of *Ripples of Desire* in Taiwan may have betrayed some trepidation with Chou's role in narrating the nation: costume dramas had been long out of favor and her use of pop idols in a beloved story sacrificed some credibility. Deborah Young in the *Hollywood Reporter* (March 23, 2013) characterized the film as "more feminist romance than bodice ripper" but missed the eroticism in the portrayal of the twin courtesan sisters' bond: "A break from her lesbian-themed films . . . and with hetero erotic touches, it could earn Taiwanese filmmaker Chou Zero a broader fan base among festival goers and Asian film lovers." Curiously, the idea of a break from lesbian material appears across the coverage of the film, suggesting it was described as such in the press materials. The effect is to instill a binarism between Chou's hetero and LGBT films but also to signal that she has not aban-

doned her core constituency. Derek Elley is particularly judgmental about the film and the director: "It could have been a big step up for the Taiwan film-maker, taking her out of the lesbian film-making ghetto through which she made her name at festivals . . . and into a wider arena—sexually, thematically and geographically." "Ripples of Desire," *Film Business Asia*, July 17, 2013, http://www.filmbiz.asia/reviews/ripples-of-desire.

41. The phrase comes from Dennis Altman's key essay about his work as a queer anthropologist, "Global Gaze / Global Gays," although I use it somewhat differently to suggest that a Western global gaze powerfully constructs non-Western subjects in its own image. See Lisa Rofel's thoughtful critique of Altman in "Qualities of Desire."

42. Berlin's prominence among the major festivals in promoting queer cinema is attributable to the key role of gay activist Manfred Salzgeber, who founded and pro-grammed the festival's alternative section, Panorama, until 1992. Salzgeber died of AIDS in 1994 and was succeeded by Speck, who had already worked with Panorama for a decade and is an equally important figure in the promotion of international queer cinema.

43. See, for example, the online press release of the Government Information Office of Taiwan: "GIO-assisted films 'Spider Lilies' and 'Mei' in competition at 57th Berlin Film Festival," February 8, 2007, E-government Entry Point of Taiwan, http://www.taiwan.gov.tw/, which promotes *Spider Lilies* as a youth subculture film with stars.

44. See Loist, "Precarious Cultural Work," and Zielinski, "On the Production of Het-erotopia." For a historical account, see Loist, "The Queer Film Festival Phenomenon." The growing field of scholarship on queer film festivals is documented in the bibliog-raphy compiled by Loist and Marijke de Valck, "9.1.1 LGBT/Queer Film Festivals," Film Festival Research, January 20, 2014, http://www.filmfestivalresearch.org/index.php /ffrn-bibliography/9-specialized-film-festivals/9-1-identity-based-festivals/9-1-1-LGBT -queer-film-festivals/. The Big Queer Film Festival List, http://www.queerfilmfestivals .org/, maintained by Mel Pritchard, lists about 230 active festivals in June 2014. It is very difficult to be precise about the extent of the network, but it clearly remains a significant force in local and global queer cultures.

45. See Rich, *New Queer Cinema*, on the phenomenon in general and on the festivals in particular.

46. Jenni Olson, "Film Festivals," *glbtq*, 2002, http://www.glbtq.com/arts/film _festivals.html.

47. In fact, Tsai's films are not regularly shown in gay festivals, although they do stage scenes of queer spectatorship. On Tsai's temporalities see Ma, *Melancholy Drift*. Gayatri Gopinath writes on the dynamics of queer diasporan spectatorship in the South Asian context in *Impossible Desires*, ch. 4. Gopinath's essay "Queer Regions: Locating Lesbians in *Sancharram*" opens with an anecdote about watching this film from Kerala at the Frameline festival.

48. See Egoyan and Balfour, *Subtitles*.

49. Merck, "Dessert Hearts." Women directors increasingly use lesbian characters or homoerotic subtexts to signify (the need for) feminism. See Jigna Desai's reading of Deepa Mehta's *Fire* and my discussion of *Caramel* in chapter 3.

50. See King, "There Are No Lesbians Here."

51. Rhyne, "The Global Economy of Gay and Lesbian Film Festivals," 618.

52. Olson, "Film Festivals."

53. Ching, "'Bridges and Battles' Queer Film and Video Festival Forum, Take Two," 606. For an equally enlightening perspective on the specificities of queer programming in Asia, see Joel David's contribution to the roundtable, "Queer Shuttling."

54. Huang, "'Creating and Distributing Films Openly.'" Huang and Wang discuss the founding and mission of the festival in "Post-Taiwan New Cinema Women Directors and Their Films," 134–135.

55. Perspex, "The First Asian Lesbian Film and Video Festival in Taipei."

56. Lisa Rofel, "Desiring China: Experiments in Neoliberalism, Sexuality, and Public Culture." See also David Eng's reading of Stanley Kwan's *Lan Yu* (2001), "The Queer Space of China."

57. See http://www.queercomrades.com. The clip "Top 10 Asian Chinese-Language Lesbian Films" can be viewed at Queer Comrades, YouTube, September 28, 2009, http://www.youtube.com/watch?v=tlgj7UZjP6Y.

58. For the role of new technology in the larger Asian queer context, see the groundbreaking anthology by Berry, Martin, and Yue, *Mobile Cultures*.

59. Ann Cvetkovich's *An Archive of Feelings* helps conceptualize the diverse formations of lesbian public cultures.

60. Neither a genealogical saga nor a soap opera, the film uses its three segments in a way that can almost be described as superimposition. Interestingly, *Let's Love Hong Kong* is also about three intertwined lesbian stories. But rather than plotting a critique of the disjunctures and frustrations of globalization as Yau's (at once more cerebral and more carnal) film does with this strategy, Chou's seems interested in the opportunity the multiple structure offers of compiling a variety of lesbian stories in one film. Another successful 2008 Taiwan lesbian film, Chen Hung-i's *Hua chi le na nv hai* / *Candy Rain*, tells four stories. The historical dimension, however fuzzy, of *Drifting Flowers* comes closer to the conceit of *If These Walls Could Talk 2* (Jane Anderson, Martha Coolidge, Ann Heche, 2000), in which one Los Angeles household shelters three sapphic tales over time.

61. I use female pronouns here following the English subtitles, but the question of Diego's gender identification is an interesting one that I lack the linguistic skills and contextual knowledge to address. See Helen Hok-Sze Leung's "Thoughts on Lesbian Genders in Contemporary Chinese Cultures" and her chapter on trans politics and culture in *Undercurrents* for the complexity of the translation of activist discourses around transgender to Chinese-speaking contexts.

62. Derek Elley, "Review: 'Drifting Flowers,'" *Variety*, February 21, 2008, http://variety.com/2008/film/reviews/drifting-flowers-1200547844/.

63. Yu-Shan Huang and Chun-Chi Wang read the use of "femme" in the review as a literal reference to feminine lesbians and criticize the lack of sub- and cultural awareness in "Post Taiwan New Cinema Women Directors," 150.

64. Leung, *Undercurrents*, 8.

65. The image on the diegetic poster is not the same as the promotional image that circulated for *Spider Lilies*. Mystifyingly, two men, rather than two women, are featured in the lovers' poses. This may be intended as an image more appropriate to appeal to

Yen's longing as a gay man. My fanciful reading is that *Spider Lilies* has become such a beloved text of Asian camp that the poster is a transformative work.

66. Brian Hu, "Outfest 2008: Capsule Reviews," Asian Pacific Arts, August 8, 2008, http://asiapacificarts.usc.edu/w_apa/showarticle.aspx?articleID=8816. Hu ranks the film as best Taiwan drama of 2008 in an unusually strong field and notes that his top ten includes two other lesbian films and a second woman director.

5. Is the Whole World Watching?

1. Grewal, *Transnational America*, chapter 3.

2. Hesford, *Spectacular Rhetorics*, ix.

3. The PBS documentary *Half the Sky* (Maro Chermayeff, 2012), based on Nicholas Kristof and Sheryl WuDunn's best seller on global activism on behalf of women and girls, is an example of the "women's human rights" genre. Films in the long tradition of independent feminist documentary on such key issues of transnational feminist activism as sexual trafficking, rape as a tactic of war, "honor" crimes, and femicide include: Mimi Chakarova's *The Price of Sex* (2011), Laura F. Jackson's *The Greatest Silence: Rape in the Congo* (2007), Daniel Junge and Sharmeen Obaid-Chinoy's *Saving Face* (2011), and Lourdes Portillo's *Señorita Extraviada* (2001). These four titles are distributed in the U.S. by Women Make Movies. For a discussion of films on African women's rights distributed by Women Make Movies, see White, "Documentary Practice and Transnational Feminist Theory."

4. In 2013, *Zinda Bhaag*, directed by Meenu Gaur and Farjad Nabi, and produced by Gaur's husband Mazhar Zaidi, was submitted by Pakistan for Academy Award consideration, its first submission.

5. Shohat, "Post-Third-Worldist Culture," 292.

6. Small-nation cinema, according to Hjort and Petrie, *The Cinema of Small Nations*, functions between the mandate to preserve language and mediate the nation to its citizens and the need to sustain itself through address to audiences outside its borders. Although Pakistan is the world's sixth most populous nation, and its industry, exemplified in the flourishing of "Lollywood"—Lahore-produced popular musical films—was robust before Islamicization and piracy brought it to a near standstill, Sabiha Sumar's film practice is illuminated by Hjort and Petrie's category.

7. Hjort and Petrie, *The Cinema of Small Nations*.

8. The only other women who have won the award at the Berlinale are Márta Mészáros and Larisa Shepitko, back in 1975 and 1977. The fact that three of the four directors are Eastern European is testament to the festival's historical role in mediating East-West relations (see de Valck, *Film Festivals*) and to the relative prominence of women directors under socialism.

9. Jaikumar, "Translating Silences," 220. Subsequent references to this work given in the text.

10. Iordanova, *Cinema of Flames*, 210.

11. In the Global North, celebrities are used to bring humanitarian attention to women's rights violations. *Half the Sky* features a multicultural group of U.S. "celebrity

activists." Angelina Jolie's directorial debut, *In the Land of Blood and Honey* (2011), is about sexual violence during the Bosnian war.

12. "World Cinema Fund Frequently Asked Questions," Internationale Filmfestspiele Berlin, http://www.berlinale.de/en/branche/world_cinema_fund/06_faqs/wcf_faqs .html.

13. Maheem Bashir Adamjee, "The Dream Merchant: Sabiha Sumar Talks about 'Rafina,'" *Newsline*, September 23, 2011, http://www.newslinemagazine.com/2011/09 /the-dream-merchant-sabiha-sumar-talks-about-rafina/. Sher Khan, "The End of the Road for Lollywood?," *Express Tribune*, July 12, 2012, notes that 2012 looked likely to be Lahore's year of fewest film releases.

14. "We had to create mobile theatre halls for *Khamosh Pani* and those theatre halls used to travel from village to village, town to town to set up screenings for people. To our surprise, as many as 1,000 people showed up at certain screenings and the questions that were asked afterwards were far more mature than what you expect from a rural audience." Rafay Mamood, "Sabiha's Cinderella," *Express Tribune*, February 24, 2011, http://tribune.com.pk/story/123393/sabihas-cinderella/.

15. Dorit Naaman reads the protagonist's decision to keep her unborn child and name it after her mother at the end of *Silences of the Palace* as "an attempt to redefine gender and class relations in the newly emerged Tunisian nation." "Woman/Nation," 341.

16. Ensler, *Necessary Targets*. Testifying to the connections formed within the transnational feminist response to Bosnia, a path leads from this play to a later film by Žbanić. *For Those Who Can Tell No Tales* (2013) is a collaboration with Australian actress Kym Vercoe, who appeared in a production of Ensler's play.

17. Grewal, "Transnational America," 123.

18. Brian Brooks, "Indiewire Interview: Jasmila Žbanić, Director of 'Grbavica: The Land of My Dreams,'" *Indiewire*, February 17, 2007, http://www.indiewire.com/article /indiewire_interview_jasmila_zbanic_director_of_grbavica_the_land_of_my_drea.

19. Mazaj, "Marking the Trail." Žbanić is explicitly interpellated by an international humanitarian gaze through her participation in the omnibus film *Stories of Human Rights* (2008). The fact that she is one of the best-known Bosnian filmmakers internationally does not align her with the national film establishment. She was denied funding by the Bosnian Culture Ministry's Cinema Fund for her film *Love Island* (2013), shot in Croatia. "The story at the time was that the film was rejected for funding because of homosexual and pedophilic content. But that wasn't the reason. It was because of corruption." Andreas Wiseman, "Jasmila Žbanić, for Those Who Can Tell No Tales," *Screendaily*, September 7, 2013, http://www.screendaily.com/features/interviews /jasmila-zbanic-for-those-who-can-tell-no-tales/5060158.article.

20. Meta Mazaj, review of *Grbavica*, *Cineaste* 32.3 (2007): 61.

21. Mazaj, review of *Grbavica*; this discussion is reprised and expanded in "Marking the Trail."

22. See B. Ruby Rich's reading of this scene in *Chick Flicks*, 318–325.

23. Zimmermann, *States of Emergency*, 75. The film is also Iordanova's central example of feminist media response to the rapes in chapter 10 of *Cinema of Flames*,

206–209. In a wider analysis of visual rhetorics of human suffering that call upon Western viewers to recognize "others" as human rights subjects to govern, Wendy Hesford also sees the documentary's emphasis on testimony as exemplary. *Spectacular Rhetorics*.

24. Mazaj, "Marking the Trail."

25. See Stiglmayer, *The War against Women in Bosnia-Herzegovina*.

26. Match Factory, founded in 2006, represents a number of coproductions by women directors, including the work of Turkish director Yeşim Ustaoğlu (*Araf / Somewhere in Between*, 2012) and a film directly addressing women's human rights: the screen adaptation of Somali-born model Walis Dirie's memoir *Desert Flower* (Sherry Hormann, 2009), which deals with female genital cutting. The company describes its "passion to work with films of signature and vision from around the globe." "About Us," Match Factory, http://www.the-match-factory.com/about-us.html. See Randal Halle's "Offering Tales They Want to Hear" on the ideological effects of European, specifically German, coproduction arrangements.

27. In France the Centre National du Cinema's Fonds Sud, founded in 1984, supports filmmakers from developing countries. International Film Festival Rotterdam's Hubert Bals Fund has done the same since 1989; adding to the means of support, Oslo's Films from the South festival established the Norwegian South Film Fund in 2012.

28. Boyd van Hoeij, "Review: *The Milk of Sorrow*," *Variety*, February 14, 2009, http://variety.com/2009/film/reviews/the-milk-of-sorrow-1200473657/.

29. Quoted in Barrow, "Images of Peru."

30. In "Hegemony Conditions in the Coproduction Cinema of Latin America," Villazana notes that by 2008, 201 films had been funded by Ibermedia. Ratified in 1997, Ibermedia is funded primarily by Spain, with mandatory contributions from Latin American member nations. See also Alvaray, "The National, Regional, and Global."

31. Vargas Llosa's report for the government-appointed commission to investigate the massacre of eight journalists in the Andean village of Uchuraccay in the Ayacucho region in 1983, at the height of government forces' war against the Maoist Senderistas, was widely criticized for its presentation of the peasantry as backward and violent. He wrote about the massacre in "Inquest in the Andes," *New York Times Magazine*, July 31, 1983. Advocating neoliberal reforms, Vargas Llosa lost a 1990 presidential bid to Alberto Fujimori in Peru. He now resides mostly in Spain.

32. Pilar Roca, "Madeinusa o el insulto hecho cine" [Madeinusa or an Insult Made into Film], Servindi, http://www.servindi.org/actualidad/1134/1134. Quoted in and translated by John McGowan, "Madeinusa," Posthegemony, November 8, 2007, http://posthegemony.blogspot.com/2007/11/madeinusa.html.

33. McGowan, "Madeinusa."

34. Again, auteurist discourses of exceptionality as individual achievement and/or national representativeness remain prevalent in positioning internationally circulating women's films. But it is important to note that Llosa is not alone in her accomplishments, even if she does demand to be taken on her own terms, not least for having put Peruvian cinema back on the map. She is part of a cohort of women directors, including in Peru. For example, Rosario García-Montero trained in the United States and Peru; her *Las malas intenciones / The Bad Intentions* (2011) screened at international

film festivals. Besides the young Argentine and Mexican directors mentioned in chapter 1, several young women from Chile have had U.S. exposure: Marialy Rivas's *Joven y alocada / Young and Wild* (2012) won the best international screenwriting award at Sundance 2012, and Alicia Scherson's third feature, the Rolando Bolanas adaptation *Il Futuro* (2013), was released by Strand.

35. D'Lugo, "Authorship, Globalization, and the New Identity of Latin American Cinema," 103, 104.

36. Latin America is one of the target eras of the World Cinema Fund, a joint venture of the festival and German government partners whose guidelines specify that "the support is focused on the following regions: Latin America, Central America, the Caribbean, Africa, the Middle East, Central Asia, Southeast Asia and the Caucasus." While funded projects must have a German partner, "the WCF is interested in supporting local stories. It wants to support subjects strongly linked to the cultural reality/identity of the country. The 'voice' of a local director is essential for the WCF. Therefore, the director must have the nationality of one of the WCF regions." See https://www.berlinale .de/en/.

37. Truth and Reconciliation Commission, *Final Report*, http://www.cverdad.org.pe /ingles/ifinal/index.php.

38. Theidon, *Entre Prójimos*.

39. Brandon Harris, "Interview with Claudia Llosa, Milk of Sorrow," *Filmmaker*, August 25, 2010, http://www.filmmakermagazine.com/news/2010/08/claudia-llosa -the-milk-of-sorrow/.

40. Halle, "Offering Tales They Want to Hear."

41. In 2012 the Peruvian women's group DEMUS succeeded in extending the class of people entitled to reparations for sexual violence—not rape alone but other crimes; Mattia Cabitza, "Peru Widens Civil War Compensation for Victims of Sexual Violence," *Guardian*, June 28, 2012, http://www.guardian.co.uk/global-development/2012/jun/28 /peru-civil-war-victims-sexual-violence.

42. Iordanova, Martin-Jones, and Vidal, "Introduction," in *Cinema at the Periphery*, 5.

43. Jaikumar, "Translating Silences," 223.

Bibliography

Ahn, Ji-hye. "The Status and Future of Female Directors in the Korean Film Industry." In International Women's Film Festival in Seoul, *The Global Cartographies of Cine-Feminisms*, conference proceedings, April 14, 2008, Seoul, South Korea, 101–114.

Altman, Dennis. "Global Gaze / Global Gays." *GLQ* 3.4 (1997): 417–436.

Alvaray, Luisela. "The National, Regional, and Global: New Waves of Latin American Cinema." *Cinema Journal* 47.3 (spring 2008): 48–65.

Amireh, Amal, and Lisa Suhair Majaj, eds. *Going Global: The Transnational Reception of Third World Women Writers*. New York: Garland, 2000.

Andrew, Dudley. "An Atlas of World Cinema." In *Remapping World Cinema*, edited by Stephanie Dennison and Song Hwee Lim, 19–29. London: Wallflower, 2006.

Appadurai, Arjun. "Disjuncture and Difference in the Global Cultural Economy." In *Modernity at Large: Cultural Dimensions of Globalization*. Minneapolis: University of Minnesota Press, 1996.

Armatage, Kay. "Toronto Women and Film International 1973." In *Film Festival Yearbook 1: The Festival Circuit*, edited by Dina Iordanova with Ragan Rhyne. St. Andrews: St. Andrews Film Studies, 2009.

Art House Convergence, Bryn Mawr Film Institute and Avenue ISR. "Art House Convergence National Audience Study 2013." January 15, 2014.

Austin-Smith, Brenda, and George Melnyk, eds. *The Gendered Screen: Canadian Women Filmmakers*. Waterloo, ON: Wilfrid Laurier University Press, 2010.

Barrow, Sarah. "Images of Peru: A National Cinema in Crisis." In *Latin American Cinema: Essays on Modernity, Gender and National Identity*, edited by Lisa Shaw and Stephanie Dennison, 39–58. Jefferson, NC: McFarland, 2005.

Berry, Chris. "Asian Values, Family Values." *Journal of Homosexuality* 40.3 (2001): 211–231.

Berry, Chris. "Wedding Banquet: A Family (Melodrama) Affair." In *Chinese Films in Focus: 25 New Takes*, edited by Chris Berry, 183–190. London: BFI, 2003.

Berry, Chris, Fran Martin, and Audrey Yue, eds. *Mobile Cultures: New Media in Queer Asia*. Durham, NC: Duke University Press, 2003.

Betz, Mark. *Beyond the Subtitle: Remapping European Art Cinema*. Minneapolis: University of Minnesota Press, 2009.

Blonski, Annette, Barbara Creed, and Freda Freiberg. *Don't Shoot Darling! Women's Independent Filmmaking in Australia*. Richmond, Australia: Greenhouse, 1987.

Bobo, Jacqueline. *Black Women Film and Video Artists*. New York: Routledge, 1998.

Bordwell, David. *The Way Hollywood Tells It: Story and Style in Modern Movies*. Berkeley: University of California Press, 2006.

Bourdieu, Pierre. *Distinction: A Social Critique of the Judgement of Taste*. Cambridge, MA: Harvard University Press, 1984.

Bourdieu, Pierre. *The Field of Cultural Production*. Edited by Randal Johnson. New York: Columbia University Press, 1993.

Brunsdon, Charlotte. *Screen Tastes: Soap Opera to Satellite Dishes*. London: Routledge, 1997.

Butalia, Urvashi. *The Other Side of Silence: Voices from the Partition of India*. Durham, NC: Duke University Press, 2000.

Butler, Alison. *Women's Cinema: The Contested Screen*. London: Wallflower, 2002.

Camera Obscura Collective. "*Camera Obscura* at Thirty: Archiving the Past, Imagining the Future." *Camera Obscura* 61 (2006): 1–2.

Camera Obscura Collective. "*Camera Obscura* Questionnaire on Alternative Film Distribution." *Camera Obscura* 1–2 (1979): 157–175.

Casanova, Pascale. *The World Republic of Letters*. Cambridge, MA: Harvard University Press, 2004.

Chaudhuri, Shohini. *Contemporary World Cinema: Europe, the Middle East, East Asia and South Asia*. Edinburgh: Edinburgh University Press, 2005.

Chaudhuri, Shohini, and Howard Finn. "The Open Image: Poetic Realism and the New Iranian Cinema." *Screen* 44.1 (2003): 38–57.

Ching, Yau. "'Bridges and Battles,' Queer Film and Video Festival Forum, Take Two: Critics Speak Out." *GLQ* 12.4 (2006): 606.

Chiu, Kuei-fen. "The Vision of Taiwan New Documentary." In *Cinema Taiwan: Politics, Popularity and the State of the Arts*, edited by Darrell William Davis and Ru-Shou Robert Chen, 17–32. London: Routledge, 1997.

Choi, Jinhee. *The South Korean Film Renaissance: Local Hitmakers, Global Provocateurs*. Middletown, CT: Wesleyan University Press, 2010.

Chow, Rey. *The Age of the World Target: Self-Referentiality in War, Theory, and Comparative Work*. Durham, NC: Duke University Press, 2006.

Chow, Rey. *Primitive Passions: Visuality, Sexuality, Ethnography, and Contemporary Chinese Cinema*. New York: Columbia University Press, 1995.

Chow, Rey. *Sentimental Fabulations, Contemporary Chinese Films: Attachment in the Age of Global Visibility*. New York: Columbia University Press, 2007.

Collins, Jim. *Bring on the Books for Everybody: How Literary Culture Became Popular Culture*. Durham, NC: Duke University Press, 2010.

Columpar, Corinn, and Sophie Mayer, eds. *There She Goes: Feminist Filmmaking and Beyond*. Detroit: Wayne State University Press, 2009.

Corrigan, Timothy. "The Commerce of Auteurism." In *Film and Authorship*, edited by

Virginia Wright Wexman, 96–110. New Brunswick, NJ: Rutgers University Press, 2003.

Crofts, Stephen. "Reconceptualizing National Cinema/s." In *Film and Nationalism*, edited by Alan Williams, 25–51. New Brunswick, NJ: Rutgers University Press, 2002.

Cvetkovich, Ann. *An Archive of Feelings: Trauma, Sexuality, and Lesbian Public Cultures.* Durham, NC: Duke University Press, 2003.

Czach, Liz. "Film Festivals, Programming, and the Building of National Cinema." *Moving Image* 4.1 (spring 2004): 76–88.

Dabashi, Hamid. *Makhmalbaf at Large.* London: I. B. Tauris, 2008.

David, Joel. "Queer Shuttling: Korea–Manila–New York." *GLQ* 12.4 (2006): 614–617.

de Beauvoir, Simone. *The Second Sex.* Translated by Constance Borde and Sheila Malovany-Chevalier. New York: Knopf, 2010.

de Lauretis, Teresa. *Alice Doesn't: Feminism, Semiotics, Cinema.* Bloomington: Indiana University Press, 1984.

de Lauretis, Teresa. "Rethinking Women's Cinema: Aesthetics and Feminist Theory." In *Technologies of Gender: Essays on Theory, Film, and Fiction*, 127–148. Bloomington: Indiana University Press, 1987.

de Lauretis, Teresa. *Technologies of Gender: Essays on Theory, Film, and Fiction.* Bloomington: Indiana University Press, 1987.

Deleuze, Gilles. *Cinema 2.* Minneapolis: University of Minnesota Press, 1986.

Dennison, Stephanie, and Song Hwee Lim, eds. *Remapping World Cinema.* London: Wallflower, 2006.

Desai, Jigna. *Bollywood: The Cultural Politics of South Asian Diasporic Film.* New York: Routledge, 2004.

de Valck, Marijke. *Film Festivals: From European Geopolitics to Global Cinephilia.* Amsterdam: Amsterdam University Press, 2007.

D'Lugo, Marvin. "Authorship, Globalization, and the New Identity of Latin American Cinema: From the Mexican 'Ranchera' to Argentinian 'Exile.'" In *Rethinking Third Cinema*, edited by Anthony R. Guneratne and Wimal Dissanayake, 103–125. New York: Routledge, 2003.

Doane, Mary Ann. "The 'Woman's Film': Possession and Address." In *Re-vision: Essays, in Feminist Film Criticism*, edited by Mary Ann Doane, Patricia Mellencamp, and Linda Williams. Frederick, MD: University Publications of America, 1984.

Dönmez-Colin, Gönül. *Women, Cinema, and Islam.* London: Reaktion, 2004.

Dove, Lindiwe. "New Looks: The Rise of Black African Female Filmmakers." *Feminist Africa* 16 (2012): 18–36.

Ďurovičová, Nataša, and Kathleen Newman, eds. *World Cinemas / Transnational Perspectives.* London: Routledge, 2009.

Egoyan, Atom, and Ian Balfour, eds. *Subtitles: On the Foreignness of Film.* Cambridge, MA: MIT Press and Alphabet City Books, 2004.

Elsaesser, Thomas. "Film Festival Networks: The New Topographies of Cinema in Europe." In *European Cinema: Face to Face with Hollywood.* Amsterdam: Amsterdam University Press, 2005.

Elsaesser, Thomas. "Leni Riefenstahl: The Body Beautiful, Art Cinema and Fascist

Aesthetics." In *Women and Film: A Sight and Sound Reader*, edited by Pam Cook and Philip Dodd, 186–197. Philadelphia: Temple University Press, 1993.

Eng, David. "The Queer Space of China: Expressive Desire in Stanley Kwan's *Lan Yu*." *positions: east asia cultures critique* 18.2 (fall 2010): 459–487.

English, James F. *The Economy of Prestige: Prizes, Awards, and the Circulation of Cultural Value*. Cambridge, MA: Harvard University Press, 2005.

Ensler, Eve. *Necessary Targets: A Story of Women and War*. New York: Villard, 2001.

Ezra, Elizabeth, and Terry Rowden, eds. *Transnational Cinema: The Film Reader*. London: Routledge, 2006.

Falicov, Tamara. *The Cinematic Tango: Contemporary Argentine Cinema*. London: Wallflower, 2007.

Farahmand, Azadeh. "Disentangling the International Festival Circuit: Genre and Iranian Cinema." In *Global Art Cinema*, edited by Rosalind Gault and Karl Schoonover, 263–281. Oxford: Oxford University Press, 2010.

Farahmand, Azadeh. "Perspectives on Recent (Acclaim for) Iranian Cinema." In *The New Iranian Cinema: Politics, Representation, Ideology*, edited by Richard Tapper, 86–108. London: I. B. Tauris, 2002.

Feng, Peter X. *Identities in Motion: Asian American Film and Video*. Durham, NC: Duke University Press, 2002.

Ferriss, Suzanne, and Mallory Young. *Chick Lit: The New Women's Fiction*. New York: Routledge, 2006.

Fischer, Lucy. *Shot / Counter Shot: Film Tradition and Women's Cinema*. Princeton, NJ: Princeton University Press, 1989.

Flanagan, Michael. "Towards an Aesthetic of Slow in Contemporary Cinema." *16:9* (November 2008).

Foster, Gwendolyn Audrey. *Women Filmmakers of the African and Asian Diaspora: Decolonizing the Gaze, Locating Subjectivity*. Carbondale: Southern Illinois University Press, 1997.

Franco, Jean. "Afterword: From Romance to Refractory Aesthetic." In *Latin American Women's Writing: Feminist Readings in Theory and Crisis*, edited by Anny Brooksbank Jones and Catherine Davies, 226–237. Oxford: Clarendon, 1996.

García Lorca, Federico. "Lament for Ignacio Sánchez Mejías." In *The Selected Poems of Federico García Lorca*, 137. New York: New Directions, 2005.

Gault, Rosalind, and Karl Schoonover, eds. *Global Art Cinema: New Theories and Histories*. Oxford: Oxford University Press, 2010.

Ghosh, Bisnupriya. "An Affair to Remember. Scripted Performances in the 'Nasreen Affair.'" In *Going Global: The Transnational Reception of Third World Women Writers*, edited by Amal Amireh and Lisa Suhair Majaj, 39–83. New York: Garland, 2000.

Giorgi, Liana, Monica Sassatelli, and Gerard Delanty, eds. *Festivals and the Cultural Public Sphere*. New York: Routledge, 2011.

Gopinath, Gayatri. *Impossible Desires: Queer Diasporas and South Asian Public Cultures*. Durham, NC: Duke University Press, 2005.

Gopinath, Gayatri. "Queer Regions: Locating Lesbians in *Sancharram*." In *A Companion to Lesbian, Gay, Bisexual, Transgender, and Queer Studies*, edited by George E. Haggerty and Molly McGarry, 341–354. Malden, MA: Blackwell, 2007.

Grant, Barry Keith, ed. *Auteurs and Authorship: A Film Reader*. Malden, MA: Blackwell, 2008.

Grant, Catherine. "Secret Agents: Feminist Theories of Women's Film Authorship." *Feminist Theory* 2 (April 2001): 113–130.

Grant, Catherine. "www.auteur.com?" *Screen* 41 (spring 2000): 101–108.

Grant, Catherine, and Annette Kuhn, eds. *Screening World Cinema: A Screen Reader*. London: Routledge, 2006.

Grewal, Inderpal. *Transnational America*. Durham, NC: Duke University Press, 2005.

Grewal, Inderpal, and Caren Kaplan, eds. *Scattered Hegemonies: Postmodernity and Transnational Feminist Practices*. Minneapolis: University of Minnesota Press, 1994.

Grewal, Inderpal, and Caren Kaplan. "*Warrior Marks*: Global Womanism's Neo-colonial Discourse in a Multicultural Context." *Camera Obscura* 13 (September 1996): 4–33.

Grossman, Andrew, ed. *Queer Asian Cinema: Shadows in the Shade*. Binghamton, NY: Harrington Park Press, 2000.

Guneratne, Anthony R., and Wimal Dissanayake, eds. *Rethinking Third Cinema*. New York: Routledge, 2003.

Halberstam, Judith. *In a Queer Time and Place: Transgender Bodies, Subcultural Lives*. Durham, NC: Duke University Press, 2005.

Halle, Randall. "Offering Tales They Want to Hear: Transnational European Film Funding as Neo-Orientalism." In *Global Art Cinema*, edited by Rosalind Gault and Karl Schoonover, 303–319. Oxford: Oxford University Press, 2010.

Hansen, Miriam. *Babel and Babylon: Spectatorship in American Silent Cinema*. Cambridge, MA: Harvard University Press, 1991.

Haraway, Donna. "A Manifesto for Cyborgs: Science, Technology and Socialist Feminism in the 1980s." *Socialist Review* 15.2 (1985): 65–107.

Herman, Jeannette. "Memory and Melodrama: The Transnational Politics of Deepa Mehta's *Earth*." *Camera Obscura* 20 (2005): 107–147.

Hesford, Wendy. *Spectacular Rhetorics: Human Rights Visions, Recognitions, Feminisms*. Durham, NC: Duke University Press, 2011.

Higbee, Will, and Song Hwee Lim. "Concepts of Transnational Cinema: Towards a Critical Transnationalism in Film Studies." *Transnational Cinemas* 1.1 (2010): 7–21.

Higson, Andrew. "The Concept of National Cinema." In *Film and Nationalism*, edited by Alan Williams, 52–67. New Brunswick, NJ: Rutgers University Press, 2002.

Hillauer, Rebecca. *Encyclopedia of Arab Women Filmmakers*. Rev. and updated ed. Cairo: American University in Cairo Press, 2005.

Hjort, Mette, and Duncan Petrie. *The Cinema of Small Nations*. Edinburgh: Edinburgh University Press, 2007.

Hu, Brian. "*Formula 17*: Testing a Formula for Mainstream Cinema in Taiwan." *Senses of Cinema*, no. 34 (2005): http://sensesofcinema.com/2005/feature-articles /formula_17/.

Huang, Yu-Shan. "'Creating and Distributing Films Openly': On the Relationship between Women's Film Festivals and the Women's Rights Movement in Taiwan." *Inter-Asia Cultural Studies* 4.1 (2003). doi: 10.1080/1464937032000060302.

Huang, Yu-Shan, and Chun-Chi Wang. "Post-Taiwan New Cinema Women Directors and Their Films: Auteurs, Images, Languages." Translated by Robin Visser and

Thomas Moran. In *Chinese Women's Cinema: Transnational Contexts*, edited by Ling-zhen Wang, 132–253. New York: Columbia University Press, 2011.

Imanjaya, Ekky. "The Curious Cases of Salma, Siti, and Ming: Representations of Indonesia's Polygamous Life in *Love for Share*." *Jump Cut*, no. 51 (spring 2009).

Iordanova, Dina. *Cinema of Flames: Balkan Film, Culture and the Media*. London: BFI, 2001.

Iordanova, Dina. "The Film Festival Circuit." In *Film Festival Yearbook 1: The Festival Circuit*, edited by Dina Iordanova with Ragan Rhyne, 23–39. St. Andrews: St. Andrews Film Studies, 2009.

Iordanova, Dina, David Martin-Jones, and Belén Vidal, eds. *Cinema at the Periphery*. Detroit: Wayne State University Press, 2010.

Jaikumar, Priya. "Translating Silences: A Cinematic Encounter with Incommensurable Difference." In *Transnational Feminism in Film and Media*, edited by Katarzyna Marciniak, Anikó Imre, and Áine O'Healy, 207–226. New York: Palgrave Macmillan, 2008.

Jameson, Fredric. "Remapping Taipei." In *The Geopolitical Aesthetic: Cinema and Space in the World System*, 114–158. Bloomington: Indiana University Press, 1995.

Jermyn, Deborah, and Sean Redmond, eds. *The Cinema of Kathryn Bigelow: Hollywood Transgressor*. London: Wallflower, 2003.

Johnston, Claire. "Women's Cinema as Counter Cinema." In *Notes on Women's Cinema*, edited by Claire Johnston. London: Society for Education in Film and Television, 1973. Reprinted in Bill Nichols, ed. *Movies and Methods*. Berkeley: University of California Press, 1979.

Kaplan, Caren. "The Politics of Location as Transnational Feminist Cultural Practice." In *Scattered Hegemonies: Postmodernity and Transnational Feminist Practices*, edited by Inderpal Grewal and Caren Kaplan, 137–152. Minneapolis: University of Minnesota Press, 1994.

Kaplan, Caren, Norma Alarcón, and Minoo Moallem, eds. *Between Woman and Nation: Nationalisms, Transnational Feminisms, and the State*. Durham, NC: Duke University Press, 1999.

Kaplan, Caren, and Inderpal Grewal. "Transnational Feminist Cultural Studies: Beyond the Marxism/Poststructuralism/Feminism Divides." In *Between Woman and Nation: Nationalisms, Transnational Feminisms, and the State*, edited by Caren Kaplan, Norma Alarcón, and Minoo Moallem, 349–361. Durham, NC: Duke University Press, 1999.

Kaplan, E. Ann, ed. *Feminism and Film*. London: Oxford University Press, 2000.

Kaplan, E. Ann. "Interview with British Cine-Feminists." In *Women and the Cinema: A Critical Anthology*, edited by Karyn Kay and Gerald Peary. New York: Dutton, 1977.

Kaplan, E. Ann. *Looking for the Other: Feminism, Film, and the Imperial Gaze*. New York: Routledge, 2012.

Kavoori, Anandam P., and Aswin Punathambekar. *Global Bollywood*. New York: New York University Press, 2008.

Khatib, Lina. *Lebanese Cinema: Imagining the Civil War and Beyond*. London: I. B. Tauris, 2008.

Khoo, Olivia. "The Minor Transnationalism of Queer Asian Cinema: Female Authorship and the Short Film Format." *Camera Obscura* 84 (2014): 33–57.

Kim, Kyung Hyun. *The Remasculinization of Korean Cinema.* Durham, NC: Duke University Press, 2004.

Kim, So-young. "From Cine-mania to Blockbusters and Transcinema: Reflections on Recent South Korean Cinema." In *Theorising National Cinemas*, edited by Valentina Vitali and Paul Willemen, 186–201. London: BFI, 2006.

King, Geoff. *American Independent Cinema.* Bloomington: Indiana University Press, 2005.

King, Katie. "There Are No Lesbians Here." In *Queer Globalizations: Citizenship and the Afterlife of Colonialism*, edited by Arnaldo Cruz-Malavé and Martin F. Manalansan IV. New York: New York University Press, 2002.

Kraidy, Marwan. *Reality Television and Arab Politics: Contention in Public Life.* New York: Cambridge University Press, 2009.

Langford, Michelle. "Practical Melodrama: From Recognition to Action in Tahmineh Milani's Fereshteh Trilogy." *Screen* 51 (2010): 341–364.

Lauzen, Martha M. "The Celluloid Ceiling: Behind-the-Scenes Employment of Women on the Top 250 Films of 2008." San Diego: Center for the Study of Women in Television and Film, 2009. Updated annually.

Lauzen, Martha M. "Independent Women: Behind-the-Scenes Representation on Festival Films in 2008–2009." San Diego: Center for the Study of Women in Television and Film, 2009. Updated in 2012 and 2014.

Lauzen, Martha M. "Kathryn Bigelow: On Her Own in No-(Wo)Man's-Land." *Camera Obscura* 78 (2011): 146–153.

Laviosa, Flavia, ed. *Visions of Struggle in Women's Filmmaking in the Mediterranean.* Basingstoke, U.K.: Palgrave Macmillan, 2010.

Leung, Helen Hok-Sze. "Thoughts on Lesbian Genders in Contemporary Chinese Cultures." *Journal of Lesbian Studies* 6.2 (2002): 122–132.

Leung, Helen Hok-Sze. *Undercurrents: Queer Culture and Postcolonial Hong Kong.* Vancouver: University of British Columbia Press, 2008.

Levitin, Jacquelin. "An Introduction to Deepa Mehta: Making Films in Canada and India (with Extracts from an Interview Conducted by Kass Banning)." In *Women Filmmakers: Refocusing*, edited by Jacqueline Levitin, Judith Plessis, and Valerie Raoul, 273–283. New York: Routledge, 2003.

Lim, Song Hwee. *Celluloid Comrades: Representations of Male Homosexuality in Contemporary Chinese Cinemas.* Honolulu: University of Hawai'i Press, 2006.

Lim, Song Hwee. "How to Be Queer in Taiwan: Translation, Appropriation, and the Construction of a Queer Identity in Taiwan." In *Asiapacifiqueer*, edited by Fran Martin, Peter A. Jackson, Mark McLelland, and Audrey Yue, 235–250. Urbana: University of Illinois Press, 2008.

Lionnet, Françoise, and Shumei Shi, eds. *Minor Transnationalisms.* Durham, NC: Duke University Press, 2005.

Loist, Skadi. "Precarious Cultural Work: About the Organization of (Queer) Film Festivals." *Screen* 52.2 (2011): 268–273.

Loist, Skadi. "The Queer Film Festival Phenomenon in a Global Historical Perspective (the 1970s–2000s)." In *Une histoire des festivals: XXe–XXIe siècle*, edited by Anaïs Fléchet, Pascale Gœtschel, Patricia Hidiroglou, Sophie Jacotot, Caroline Moine, and Julie Verlaine, 109–121. Paris: Publications de la Sorbonne, 2013.

Loist, Skadi, and Marijke de Valck. "Film Festivals / Film Festival Research: Thematic, Annotated Bibliography, Second Edition." Hamburg, Germany: Media Studies / Hamburg: Reports and Papers 91, 2010. http://www1.uni-hamburg.de/Medien //berichte/arbeiten/0091_08.html.

Ma, Jean. *Melancholy Drift: Marking Time in Chinese Cinema*. Hong Kong: Hong Kong University Press, 2010.

Macdonald, Dwight. "Masscult and Midcult." *Partisan Review* (spring 1960).

Mani, Bakirathi. *Aspiring to Home: South Asians in America*. Stanford, CA: Stanford University Press, 2011.

Mani, Lata. *Contentious Traditions: The Debate on Sati in Colonial India*. Berkeley: University of California Press, 1998.

Marciniak, Katarzyna, Aniko Imre, and Aine O'Healy, eds. *Transnational Feminism in Film and Media*. London: Palgrave Macmillan, 2008.

Marks, Laura. "What Is That *and* between Arab Women and Video? The Case of Beirut." *Camera Obscura* 54 (2003): 41–69.

Martin, Fran. *Backward Glances: Contemporary Chinese Cultures and the Female Homoerotic Imaginary*. Durham, NC: Duke University Press, 2010.

Martin, Fran. "Love and Remembrance: Women's Same-Sex Love in Transnational Chinese Media and Popular Cultures." Invited presentation at "International Conference on Queer Diaspora," National Taiwan University, June 11–12, 2010.

Martin, Fran. *Situating Sexualities: Queer Representation in Taiwan Fiction, Film and Public Culture*. Hong Kong: Hong Kong University Press, 2003.

Martin, Fran. "Taiwan (Trans)national Cinema: The Far-Flung Adventures of a Taiwanese Tomboy." In *Cinema Taiwan: Politics, Popularity and the State of the Arts*, edited by Darrell William Davis and Ru-Shou Robert Chen, 131–145. London: Routledge, 1997.

Martin, Fran, Peter A. Jackson, Mark McLelland, and Audrey Yue, eds. *Asiapacifiqueer*. Urbana: University of Illinois Press, 2008.

Mayne, Judith. *Claire Denis*. Urbana: University of Illinois Press, 2005.

Mayne, Judith. *Directed by Dorothy Arzner*. Bloomington: Indiana University Press, 1994.

Mayne, Judith. *The Woman at the Keyhole: Feminism and Women's Cinema*. Bloomington: Indiana University Press, 1990.

Mazaj, Meta. "Marking the Trail: Balkan Women Filmmakers and the Transnational Imaginary." In *After Yugoslavia: The Cultural Spaces of a Vanished Land*, edited by Radmila Gorup, 200–218. Stanford, CA: Stanford University Press, 2013.

McHugh, Kathleen. *Jane Campion*. Urbana: University of Illinois Press, 2007.

McHugh, Kathleen. "The World and the Soup: Historicizing Media Feminisms in Transnational Contexts." *Camera Obscura* 72 (2009): 110–151.

McRobbie, Angela. "Post-feminism and Popular Culture." *Feminist Media Studies* 4.3 (2004): 255–264.

Mellencamp, Patricia. *A Fine Romance: Five Ages of Film Feminism*. Philadelphia: Temple University Press, 1995.

Merck, Mandy. "Dessert Hearts." In *Queer Looks: Perspectives on Lesbian and Gay Film and Video*, edited by Martha Gever, Pratibha Parmar, and John Greyson, 377–382. New York: Routledge, 1993.

Modleski, Tania. *The Women Who Knew Too Much*. London: Routledge, 1988.

Mohanty, Chandra. *Feminism without Borders*. Durham, NC: Duke University Press, 2003.

Moore, Lesley. "Women in a Widening Frame: (Cross-)Cultural Projection, Spectatorship, and Iranian Cinema." *Camera Obscura* 59 (2005): 1–33.

Morris, Meaghan. *Too Soon Too Late: History in Popular Culture*. Bloomington: Indiana University Press, 1998.

Mottahedeh, Negar. *Displaced Allegories: Post-revolutionary Iranian Cinema*. Durham, NC: Duke University Press, 2008.

Mukherjee, Tutun. "Deepa Mehta's Film *Water*: The Power of the Dialectical Image." *Canadian Journal of Film Studies* 17.2 (autumn 2008): 35–47.

Mulvey, Laura. "Visual Pleasure and Narrative Cinema." *Screen* 16 (1975): 6–18.

Naaman, Dorit. "Woman/Nation: A Postcolonial Look at Female Subjectivity." *Quarterly Review of Film and Video* 17.4 (2000): 333–342.

Naficy, Hamid. *An Accented Cinema: Exilic and Diasporic Filmmaking*. Princeton, NJ: Princeton University Press, 2001.

Naficy, Hamid. *The Making of Exile Cultures: Iranian Television in Los Angeles*. Minneapolis: University of Minnesota Press, 1993.

Nagib, Lúcia. "Towards a Positive Definition of World Cinema." In *Remapping World Cinema*, edited by Stephanie Dennison and Song Hwee Lim. London: Wallflower, 2006.

Nagib, Lúcia. *World Cinema and the Ethics of Realism*. New York: Continuum, 2011.

Nagib, Lúcia, Chris Perriam, and Rajinder Dudrah, eds. *Theorizing World Cinema*. London: I. B. Tauris, 2012.

Neale, Steve. "Art Cinema as Institution." *Screen* 22.1 (1981): 11–40.

Newman, Michael Z. *Indie: An American Film Culture*. New York: Columbia University Press, 2013.

Ortner, Sherry B. *Not Hollywood: Independent Film at the Twilight of the American Dream*. Durham, NC: Duke University Press, 2013.

Pagán-Teitelbaum, Iliana. "Glamour in the Andes: Indigenous Women in Peruvian Cinema." *Latin American and Caribbean Ethnic Studies* 7.1 (2012): 71–93.

Page, Joanna. *Crisis and Capitalism in Contemporary Argentine Cinema*. Durham, NC: Duke University Press, 2009.

Perspex. "The First Asian Lesbian Film and Video Festival in Taipei Celebrates a New Form of Social Activism." *Inter-Asia Cultural Studies* 7.3 (2006): n.p.

Polan, Dana. *Jane Campion*. London: BFI, 2001.

Porton, Richard, ed. *Dekalog 3: On Film Festivals*. London: Wallflower, 2009.

Prasad, A. Mahvad. "Surviving Bollywood." In *Global Bollywood*, edited by Anandam P. Kavori and Aswin Punatambekar, 41–52. New York: New York University Press, 2008.

Radner, Hilary. *Neo-feminist Cinema: Girly Films, Chick Flicks and Consumer Culture*. New York: Routledge, 2011.

Radway, Janice. *A Feeling for Books: The Book-of-the-Month Club, Literary Taste, and Middle-Class Desire*. Chapel Hill: University of North Carolina Press, 1997.

Ramanathan, Geetha. *Feminist Auteurs: Reading Women's Films*. London: Wallflower, 2006.

Rashkin, Elissa J. *Women Filmmakers in Mexico: The Country of Which We Dream*. Austin: University of Texas Press, 2001.

Rastegar, Roya. "Evolving Narrative Structures Forge New Cine-Love at the 2012 Sundance Film Festival." *Camera Obscura* 81 (2012): 146–156.

Rhyne, Ragan. "The Global Economy of Gay and Lesbian Film Festivals." *GLQ* 12.4 (2006): 618.

Rich, Adrienne. "Notes towards a Politics of Location" (1984). In *Blood, Bread, and Poetry: Selected Prose, 1979–1985*, 210–231. London: Little, Brown, 1986.

Rich, B. Ruby. *Chick Flicks: Theories and Histories of the Women's Film Movement*. Durham, NC: Duke University Press, 1998.

Rich, B. Ruby. "The Confidence Game." *Camera Obscura* 82 (2013): 157–165.

Rich, B. Ruby. *New Queer Cinema: The Director's Cut*. Durham, NC: Duke University Press, 2013.

Rofel, Lisa. "Qualities of Desire: Imagining Gay Identities in China." *GLQ* 5.4 (1999): 454–456.

Rony, Fatimah Tobing. "Transforming Documentary: Indonesian Women and Sexuality in the Film *Pertaruhan [At Stake]*." In *Women and the Media in Asia: The Precarious Self*, edited by Youna Kim, 159–178. Basingstoke, U.K.: Palgrave Macmillan, 2012.

Rubin, Joan Shelley. *The Making of Middle-Brow Culture*. Chapel Hill: University of North Carolina Press, 1992.

Saltzman, Devyani. *Shooting Water: A Memoir of Second Chances, Family, and Filmmaking*. New York: Newmarket, 2006.

Sarris, Andrew. *The American Cinema: Directors and Directions, 1929–1968*. New York: Da Capo, 1996.

Schwartz, Vanessa. *It's So French! Hollywood, Paris, and the Making of Cosmopolitan Film Culture*. Chicago: University of Chicago Press, 2007.

Sedgwick, Eve. *The Epistemology of the Closet*. Berkeley: University of California Press, 1990.

Shapiro, Michael J. *Cinematic Geopolitics*. London: Routledge, 2009.

Shin, Chi-Yun. "Two of a Kind: Gender and Friendship in *Friend* and *Take Care of My Cat*." In *New Korean Cinema*, edited by Julian Stringer and Chi-Yun Shin, 117–131. Edinburgh: Edinburgh University Press, 2005.

Shohat, Ella. "Gendered Cartographies of Knowledge: Area Studies, Ethnic Studies, and Postcolonial Studies." In *Taboo Memories, Diasporic Voices*, 1–16. Durham, NC: Duke University Press, 2006.

Shohat, Ella. "Post-Third-Worldist Culture: Gender, Nation, and the Cinema." In *Feminist Genealogies, Colonial Legacies, Democratic Futures*, edited by Jacqui Alexander and Chandra Mohanty, 183–212. New York: Routledge, 1997.

Shohat, Ella. *Taboo Memories, Diasporic Voices*. Durham, NC: Duke University Press, 2006.

Shohat, Ella, and Robert Stam, eds. *Multiculturalism, Postcoloniality, and Transnational Media*. New Brunswick, NJ: Rutgers University Press, 2003.

Shohat, Ella, and Robert Stam. *Unthinking Eurocentrism: Multiculturalism and the Media*. New York: Routledge, 1994.

Silverman, Kaja. *The Acoustic Mirror*. Bloomington: Indiana University Press, 1988.

Silverstein, Melissa. *In Her Voice; Women Directors Talk Directing*. Vol. 1. New York: Women and Hollywood, 2013.

Smaill, Belinda. "The Male Sojourner, the Female Director and Popular European Cinema: The Worlds of Susanne Bier." *Camera Obscura* 85 (2014): 5–31.

Smaill, Belinda. "Sofia Coppola." *Feminist Media Studies* 13.1 (2013): 148–162. doi:10.1080/14680777.2011.595425.

Smith, Valerie. *Not Just Race, Not Just Gender: Black Feminist Readings*. New York: Routledge, 1998.

Spivak, Gayatri Chakravorty, and Rosalind C. Morris. *Can the Subaltern Speak? Reflections on the History of an Idea*. New York: Columbia University Press, 2010.

Stiglmayer, Alexandra. *The War against Women in Bosnia-Herzegovina*. Translations by Marion Faber. Lincoln: University of Nebraska Press, 1994.

Sundance Institute and Women in Film Los Angeles. "Exploring the Barriers and Opportunities for Independent Women Filmmakers." Los Angeles: University of Southern California, 2013.

Suner, Asumen. "Cinema without Frontiers: Transnational Women's Filmmaking in Iran and Turkey." In *Transnational Feminism in Film and Media*, edited by Katarzyna Marciniak, Anikó Imre, and Áine O'Healy. London: Palgrave Macmillan, 2008.

Tarr, Carrie, and Brigitte Rollet. *Cinema and the Second Sex: French Women's Filmmaking in the 1980s and 1990s*. New York: Continuum, 2001.

Tasker, Yvonne, and Eylem Atakav. "*The Hurt Locker*: Male Intimacy, Violence and the Iraq War Movie." *Sine/Cine: Journal of Film Studies* 1.2 (2010).

Tasker, Yvonne, and Diane Negra, eds. *Interrogating Postfeminism: Gender and the Politics of Popular Culture*. Durham, NC: Duke University Press, 2007.

Taubin, Amy. "Identification of a Woman." *Film Comment* 45 (July/August 2009).

Tay, Sharon Lin. *Women on the Edge: Twelve Political Film Practices*. New York: Palgrave Macmillan, 2009.

Theidon, Kimberly. *Entre Prójimos: El conflicto armado interno y la política de la reconciliación en el Perú*. Lima: Instituto de Estudios Peruanos, 2004.

Trinh T. Minh-ha. *When the Moon Waxes Red*. Bloomington: Indiana University Press, 1991.

Trinh T. Minh-ha. *Woman, Native, Other: Writing Postcoloniality and Feminism*. Bloomington: Indiana University Press, 1989.

Vargas Llosa, Mario. *Making Waves: Essays*. New York: Macmillan, 1990.

Villazana, Libia. "Hegemony Conditions in the Coproduction Cinema of Latin America: The Role of Spain." *Framework* 49.2 (fall 2008): 65–85.

Villiers, Nicolas de. "We Are the World Cinema." *Senses of Cinema*, no. 45 (2007): http://sensesofcinema.com/2007/feature-articles/chacun-son-cinema/.

Vitali, Valentina, and Paul Willeman, eds. *Theorising National Cinema*. London: BFI, 2006.

Wang, Lingzhen, ed. *Chinese Women's Cinema: Transnational Contexts*. New York: Columbia University Press, 2011.

White, Patricia. "Circumstantial Lesbianism." In *World Cinemas / Global Networks*, edited by Elena Gorfinkel and Tami Williams. New Brunswick, NJ: Rutgers University Press, forthcoming.

White, Patricia. "Documentary Practice and Transnational Feminist Theory: The Visibility of FGC." In *Blackwell Companion to Documentary*, edited by Alisa Lebow and Alexandra Juhasz, 217–237. Malden, MA: Blackwell, 2014.

White, Patricia. "The Last Days of Women's Cinema." *Camera Obscura* 63 (2006): 145–151.

White, Patricia. "Lesbian Minor Cinema." *Screen* 49.4 (winter 2008): 410–425.

Williams, Raymond. *Keywords: A Vocabulary of Culture and Society*. New York: Oxford University Press, 1985.

Wong, Cindy Hing-Yuk. *Film Festivals: Culture, People, and Power on the Global Screen*. New Brunswick, NJ: Rutgers University Press, 2011.

Woolf, Virginia. *A Room of One's Own* (1929). New York: Harcourt Brace, 1991.

Yeh, Emilie Yueh-yu. "Taiwan: Popular Cinema's Disappearing Act." In *Contemporary Asian Cinemas: Popular Culture in a Global Frame*, edited by Anne Tereska Ciecko, 156–168. Oxford: Berg, 2006.

Zhang, Yingjin. *Chinese National Cinema*. London: Routledge, 2004.

Zielinski, Ger. "On the Production of Heterotopia, and Other Spaces, in and around Lesbian and Gay Film Festivals." *Jump Cut: A Review of Contemporary Media* 54 (2012).

Zimmermann, Patricia R. *States of Emergency: Documentaries, Wars, Democracies*. Minneapolis: University of Minnesota Press, 2000.

Filmography

Afghan Star. Havana Marking, 2009, U.S.

After the Wedding. Susanne Bier, 2006, Denmark.

All about Love / Duk haan chau faan. Ann Hui, 2011, Hong Kong.

Amelia. Mira Nair, 2009, U.S.

Amreeka. Cherien Dabis, 2009, U.S.

Amu. Shonali Bose, 2005, India/U.S.

Antonia. Tata Amaral, 2006, Brazil.

Apple, The / Sib. Samira Makhmalbaf, 1999, Iran.

Arisan! Nia Dinata, 2003, Indonesia.

At Five in the Afternoon / Panj é asr. Samira Makhmalbaf, 2003, Iran/France.

Beast in the Heart, The / La bestia nel cuore. Cristina Comencini, 2005, Italy.

Beauty Academy of Kabul, The. Liz Mermin, 2004, U.S.

Blackboards / Takhté siah. Samira Makhmalbaf, 2000, Iran/France.

Bright Star. Jane Campion, 2009, U.K./Australia.

Brothers / Brødre. Susanne Bier, 2004, Denmark.

Buddha Collapsed out of Shame. Hana Makhmalbaf, 2007, Iran.

Butterfly / Hu die. Yan Yan Mak, 2004, Hong Kong.

Calling the Ghosts: A Story of Rape, War, and Women. Mandy Jacobsen and Karmen Jelincic, 1996, U.S.

Camila. Maria Luisa Bemberg, 1984, Argentina/Spain.

Caramel / Sukkar banat. Nadine Labaki, 2007, France/Lebanon.

Chants of Lotus / Perempuan punya cerita. Upi Avianto, Nia Dinata, Lasja F. Susatyo, Fatimah Rony, 2007, Indonesia.

Circumstance. Maryam Keshavarz, 2011, U.S.

Coco before Chanel. Anne Fontaine, 2009, France.

Corners / Si jiao luo. Zero Chou, 2001, Taiwan.

Crush and Blush / Missue Hongdangmu. Lee Kyoung-mi, 2008, South Korea.

Danzón. María Novaro, 1991, Mexico.

Day I Became a Woman, The / Roozi ke zan shodam. Marzieh Meshkini, 2000, Iran.

Dead King / Rey Muerto. Lucrecia Martel, 1995, Argentina.

Desert Flower. Sherry Hormann, 2009, U.K.

Diary for My Children / Napló gyermekeimnek. Márta Mészáros, 1984, Hungary.

Dinner with the President. S. Sathananthan and Sabiha Sumar, 2007, Pakistan/Germany.

Drifting Flowers / Piao lang qingchun. Zero Chou, 2008, Taiwan.

Education, An. Lone Scherfig, 2009, U.K.

11'09"01—September 11. Youssef Chahine et al., 2002, France.

Fill the Void / Lemale et ha'halal. Rama Burshtein, 2012, Israel.

Firaaq. Nandita Das, 2008, India.

Fire. Deepa Mehta, 1996, Canada/India.

Fish and Elephant / Jīn nián xià tiān. Yu Li, 2001, China.

Fish Child, The / El niño pez. Lucía Puenzo, 2009, Argentina.

Fish Tank. Andrea Arnold, 2009, U.K.

For a Place under the Heavens. Sabiha Sumar, 2003, Pakistan/Germany/France.

Forever the Moment / Uri saengae choego-ui sungan. Yim Soonrye, 2008, South Korea.

Formula 17, The / 17 sui de tian kong. D. J. Chen, 2004, Taiwan.

For Those Who Can Tell No Tales. Jasmila Žbanić, Bosnia and Herzegovina, 2013.

Gina Kim's Video Diary. Gina Kim, 2002, U.S./Korea.

Give Me Back My Cat / Goyang-ileul Dollyeojwo. Jeong Jae-eun, 2012, South Korea.

Grbavica: The Land of My Dreams. Jasmila Žbanić, 2006, Bosnia and Herzegovina/
    Croatia/Austria/Germany.

Greatest Silence: Rape in the Congo, The. Laura F. Jackson, 2007, U.S.

Green Days. Hana Makhmalbaf, 2009, Iran.

Half the Sky. Maro Chermayeff, 2012, U.S.

Headless Woman, The / La mujer sin cabeza. Lucrecia Martel, 2008, Argentina.

Heaven on Earth. Deepa Mehta, 2008, Canada.

Hidden Half, The / Nimeh-ye penhan. Tahmineh Milani, 2001, Iran.

Holy Girl, The / La Niña Santa. Lucrecia Martel, 2004, Argentina.

Hurt Locker, The. Kathryn Bigelow, 2009, U.S.

In a Better World / Haevnen. Susanne Bier, 2010, Denmark.

Inch' Allah Dimanche. Yamina Benguigui, 2001, France.

Jeanne Dielman: 23 Quai du Commerce, 1080 Bruxelles. Chantal Akerman, 1975, Belgium.

Joy of Madness / Lezate divanegi. Hana Makhmalbaf, 2003, Iran.

Kandahar. Mohsen Makhmalbaf, 2011, Iran/France.

Kiss Me Not on the Eyes / Dunia. Jocelyne Saab, 2005, Egypt/Lebanon/France.

Kite, The / Le cerf volant. Randa Chahal Sabbag, 2003, Lebanon/France.

La Ciénaga. Lucrecia Martel, 2001, Argentina.

Lady Bug, The. Jane Campion, 2007, Australia.

La nouba des femmes de Mount Chenoa. Assia Djebar, 1977, Algeria.

Let's Love Hong Kong / Ho Yuk. Yau Ching, 2002, Hong Kong.

Look at Me / Comme une image. Agnès Jaoui, 2004, France.

Love for Share / Berbagi Suami. Nia Dinata, Indonesia, 2006.

Madeinusa. Claudia Llosa, 2006, Spain/Peru.

Madres de la Plaza de Mayo, Las. Susana Blaustein Muñoz and Lourdes Portillo, 1985,
    U.S.

Marock. Laïla Marrakchi, 2005, France/Morocco.

Me and You and Everyone We Know. Miranda July, 2005, U.S.

Milk of Sorrow, The / La teta asustada. Claudia Llosa, 2009, Spain/Peru.

Monsoon Wedding. Mira Nair, 2001, India/U.S./France/Italy/Germany.

Mourning Forest, The / Mogari no mori. Kawase Naomi, 2007, Japan/France.

One Way or Another / De cierta manera. Sara Gomez, 1964, Cuba.

Open Hearts / Elsker dig for evigt. Susanne Bier, 2002, Denmark.

Persepolis. Marjane Satrapi and Vincent Paronnaud, 2007, France.

Piano, The. Jane Campion, 1993, Australia.

Polisse. Maïwenn, 2011, France.

Pomegranates and Myrrh / Al-mor wa al rumman. Najwa Najjar, 2008, Palestine.

Price of Sex, The. Mimi Chakarova, 2011, U.S.

Question of Silence, A / Die stilte rond. Christine M., Marleen Gorris, 1982, the Netherlands.

Rafina / Good Morning Karachi. Sabiha Sumar, 2011, Pakistan.

Red Road. Andrea Arnold, 2006, U.K./Denmark.

Return. Liza Johnson, 2011, U.S.

Ripples of Desire / Hua yang. Zero Chou, 2012, Taiwan.

Salt of This Sea. Annemarie Jacir, 2008, Palestine.

Sambizanga. Sarah Maldoror, 1972, Angola.

Saving Face. Daniel Junge and Sharmeen Obaid-Chinoy, 2011, U.S.

Saving Face. Alice Wu, 2004, U.S.

Señorita Extraviada. Lourdes Portillo, 2001, U.S.

She, a Chinese. Xiaolu Guo, 2009, China.

Silences of the Palace / Samt el qusur. Moufida Tlatli, 1994, Tunisia.

Silent Waters / Khamosh Pani. Sabiha Sumar, 2004, Pakistan.

Sisters / Hermanas. Julia Solomonoff, 2005, Argentina/Brazil/Spain.

Snow / Snejig. Aida Begić, 2008, Bosnia and Herzegovina.

Somewhere in Between / Araf. Yeşim Ustaoğlu, 2012, Turkey/France/Germany.

Song of the Exile / Ke tu qiu hen. Ann Hui, 1990, Hong Kong/Taiwan.

Spider Lilies / Ci qing. Zero Chou, 2007, Taiwan.

Splendid Float / Yan guang si she ge wu tuan. Zero Chou, 2005, Taiwan.

Take Care of My Cat / Goyangileul butaghae. Jeong Jae-eun, 2001, South Korea.

Talentime. Yasmin Ahmad, Malaysia, 2009.

35 Shots of Rum / 35 Rhums. Claire Denis, 2008, France.

Treeless Mountain. So Yong Kim, 2008. U.S./South Korea.

UFO in Her Eyes. Guo Xiaolin, 2011, Germany.

Under the Skin of the City / Zir-e poost-e shahr. Rakshan Bani-Etemed, 2005, Iran.

Wadjda. Haifaa Al-Mansour, 2012, Saudi Arabia.

Wakolda / The German Doctor. Lucia Puenzo, 2013, Argentina/Spain/Norway/France.

Water. Deepa Mehta, 2005, Canada/India.

Way Home, The / Jibeuro. Lee Jeong-hyang, 2002, Taiwan.

Wedding Song / Le chant des mariées. Karin Albou, 2009, France/Tunisia.

Wendy and Lucy. Kelly Reichardt, 2008, U.S.

Where Do We Go Now? / Et maintenant on va où? Nadine Labaki, 2011, Lebanon/France.

White Material. Claire Denis, 2009, France.

Who Will Cast the First Stone? Sabiha Sumar, 1988, U.K.

Winter's Bone. Debra Granik, 2010, U.S.

Women without Men / Zanan-e bedun-e mardan. Shirin Neshat, 2009, Germany/France/U.S./Austria/Italy/Ukraine/Morocco.

xxy. Lucía Puenzo, 2007, Argentina/Spain/France.

Yes. Sally Potter, 2004, U.K.

Index

Note: Page numbers in *italics* refer to images.

Asian Lesbian Film and Video Festival (ALFF), 160

Asiapacifqueer, 147

At Five in the Afternoon / Panj é asr, 22–23, 40, 55, 60–67, 62, 214n64, 214n73

At Stake / Pertaruhan, 141, 225n12

audiences, 2, 27, 30, 53, 133, 145, 153, 161, 177, 179–180, 198; Arab, 131; Argentinian, 47, 195; art cinema, 54, 70–73, 75, 80, 82, 194; Asian diasporan, 143–144, 156, 168; Balkan, 182; Chinese diasporan, 25, 148, 157; class and, 46, 217n11; domestic, 4, 7, 21, 23, 26, 45; female, 44, 74, 104, 132, 141, 152, 164, 216n4, 217n13; feminist, 68, 119–120; film festival, 39, 77, 130, 200–201, 218n20; French, 92; global gay, 149, 154–158, 168, 223n31; Hong Kong, 158–159; Indian, 176; Indian diasporan, 87; Indonesian, 135, 139, 141; international, 21, 23, 26, 45, 96, 107, 170, 172–173, 175, 186, 189, 219n26, 230n6; Iranian, 58; Iranian diasporan, 92, 101–102, 223n31; Lebanese, 131; North American, 79, 89, 144; Pakistani, 176, 180, 231n14; queer, 25, 85, 141, 143–144, 157, 225n18; South Asian diasporan, 102; Taiwanese, 135, 146, 148–149; youth, 108, 112, 149, 148–151, 164, 168, 227n30, 228n43. *See also* address; cineastes

Australia, 44, 231n16

Australian cinema, 34–35, 42. *See also* individual directors, festivals, and films

Austria, 96

Austrian cinema, 181. *See also* individual directors and films

auteurs, 110–111; exceptionality discourse of, 22, 56, 232n34; female, 2–3, 52, 56, 78, 108, 132–133, 142, 187, 221n3; feminism and, 2–3, 9, 17; film festivals and, 18–20, 29–39, 60, 146, 214n63; French definitions of, 208n9, 210n15; lesbian, 143–145, 168, 225n18; male, 6, 51, 58, 78, 108, 132–133, 142; nationalism and, 21, 24, 41–48, 58, 188, 197; tensions with women's cinema, 7, 33, 120–122, 131, 200. *See also* authorship; public personas; *individual directors*

authorship, 21, 24, 43, 55–56, 74, 79, 88, 105, 131, 174, 227n40; aesthetics of, 93, 96, 166; class and, 51–53; economics of, 91; ethics and, 30; feminism and, 2, 8, 15–16, 19, 33, 44–48, 203n5; 210n18; film festivals and, 22, 36, 38–39, 68, 102; genre and, 108–109;

121; limits of concept, 10, 13–14, 26; nationalism and, 51–53, 56–67, 89–90, 122, 128–129, 187–190, 195–197, 200; sexuality and, 142–145, 151, 153–154, 157, 162–164, 225n18, 226n29. *See also* auteurs; public personas

autobiography, 27, 88, 91, 96–97, 102

avant-garde cinema, 24, 72, 76, 190

Avatar, 98, 130

Babbit, Jamie: films, 225n18

Babel, 134

Bad Intentions, The / Las malas intenciones, 232n34

Bae Doona, 113, 117

Bailey, Cameron, 77

Balkans cinema, 184, 186. *See also* individual countries, directors, festivals, and films

Bandit Queen, 80

Bangkok Alternative Love Film Festival, 158

Bani-Etemad, Rakhshan, 58, 220n53

Barcelona International Gay and Lesbian Film Festival, 157

Barendretch, Wouter, 158

Bart, Peter S., 203n4

Battleship Potemkin, The, 85

Beaches of Agnès, The, 72

Beast in the Heart, The / La bestia nel cuore, 221n3

Beauty Academy of Kabul, The, 63

Bedoya, Ricardo, 188

Begić, Aida, 6; *Children of Sarajevo*, 174; *Snow*, 174, 182

Beijing Lesbian and Gay Film Festival, 160–161, 225n18

Bemberg, María Luisa, 76; *Camila*, 47; *La Ciénaga* (producer), 45

Benguigui, Yamina: *Inch' Allah Dimanche*, 5

Berlin International Film Festival (Berlinale), 29, 31, 44, 144, 162, 166, 190, 209n13; Golden Bear award, 151, 173, 181, 187–188, 230n8; role in festival circuit, 154–155, 228n42; staff, 207n48; Teddy Award, 151, 154. *See also* World Cinema Fund

Berry, Chris, 110

Bhutto, Benazir, 61, 176

Bier, Susanne, 20; *After the Wedding*, 204n15; *Brothers*, 72, 204n15; *In a Better World*, 6, 204n15; *Open Hearts*, 221n3

Bigelow, Kathryn, 32, 203n4; *The Hurt Locker*, 1–4, 71, 216n4, 217n13; *Zero Dark Thirty*, 204n11

class, 10, 70, 72, 89, 106, 187, 190, 215n1, 217n11; in *At Stake*, 141; in *Fire*, 79; in *Formula 17*, 148; in *The Headless Woman*, 22, 45–46, 48–49, 53–54; in *Love for Share*, 136; in *Madeinusa*, 189; middlebrow cinema, 23, 68–69, 73–75, 86, 102, 215n2; in *Milk of Sorrow*, 192–193, 195; in *Persepolis*, 92, 96; in *A Question of Silence*, 185; in *Silences of the Palace*, 231n15; in *Women without Men*, 97

Cleo from 5 to 7, 208n10

Cochrane, Kira, 31

Coco before Chanel, 70, 73–74, 210n15, 217n13

Cocteau, Jean, 211n32

Coen brothers, 38, 66, 209n13

Cold War, 154, 174

colonialism, 26, 76, 83, 87, 123, 158, 175; neocolonialism, 16, 20, 23, 39, 89, 204n11. *See also* imperialism; postcolonialism

Comencini, Cristina: *The Beast in the Heart*, 221n3

comics, 89, 92, 96, 102, 108; anime, 132; graphic novels, 76, 88, 91, 220n44; manga, 132

Console-ing Passions conference, 206n26

consumption (of media), 97, 172–173, 187, 215n2; gender and, 9, 106, 154; sexuality and, 149, 158, 161; world cinema, 4, 6–7, 17, 23, 55, 76, 86, 101–102, 139, 156. *See also* audiences

Contemporary Women's Cinema Forum, 206n26

Convention on the Elimination of All Forms of Discrimination against Women, 170

convergence media, 97, 110, 131

Coolidge, Martha: *If These Walls Could Talk 2*, 229n60

Coppola, Francis Ford, 91

Coppola, Sofia, 22, 58–59, 208n9; *Marie Antoinette*, 40, 74

coproduction arrangements, 7, 47, 90, 132, 146, 149, 171, 181, 208n3; role in women's cinema, 26, 42–43, 59, 123, 144, 187–188, 194, 214n73, 232n26. *See also individual production companies*

Corners / Si jiao luo, 145, 148, 160

Corrigan, Timothy, 90–91

Cortázar, Julio, 53

countercinema, 8–9, 23

Crash, 134

critics, 4, 13, 45–46, 199, 204n8, 206n29, 216n8; on Argentinian cinema, 7; on

Asian cinema, 132–133, 146; *Cahiers du cinema* critics, 3; on Campion, 74; on chick flicks, 106; feminist critics, 27, 50, 72, 85, 203n5, 217n10; on Iranian cinema, 7; LGBT film festivals and, 155, 157–158; on Samira Makhmalbaf, 56; on Neshat, 100; on women's cinema, 6, 9, 200; on world cinema, 15, 71

Croatian cinema, 181, 184, 231n19. *See also individual directors and films*

Cronenberg, David, 78

Crush and Blush / Missue Hongdangmu, 111

Cuban cinema, 172; Havana Film Festival, 44

Cui Zi'en, 160

cultural capital, 22, 37, 40–41, 68, 70, 74, 79, 88, 102, 190

Czach, Liz, 218n22

Czech cinema, Karlovy Vary International Film Festival, 41

Dabashi, Hamid, 59, 214n69, 215n83

Dabis, Cherien: *Amreeka*, 72, 206n28, 223n25; *May in the Summer*, 223n25

Danish cinema, 6, 20, 72, 74, 204n15, 211n39, 221n3. *See also individual directors and films*

Danzón, 47

Dardenne brothers, 66

Dargis, Manohla, 27

Darrieux, Danielle, 92

Das, Nandita: *Firaaq*, 220n53

Dash, Julie: *Daughters of the Dust*, 221n5

Dayan, Daniel, 39

Day I Became a Woman, The / Roozi ke zan shodam, 61

Dead King / Rey Muerto, 47

de Beauvoir, Simone, 51

Deblokada, 182

De Lauretis, Teresa, 10–11, 14, 63, 205n19, 213n60

Deleuze, Gilles, 12, 165, 213n62

DEMUS, 233

Deneuve, Catherine, 92

Denis, Claire, 22, 210n15; *Chocolat*, 208n10; *35 Shots of Rum*, 72; *Trouble Every Day*, 208n10

Denson, G. Roger, 100

Desai, Jigna, 84, 88

Desert Flower, 232n26

Despentes, Virginie, 41

deterritorialization, 13, 54, 93, 96, 98, 171, 213n62

Made in the USA
Lexington, KY
08 June 2018